MW01002560

The Epic Battles
for Ticonderoga, 1758

III

THE EPIC BATTLES FOR TICONDEROGA, 1758

WILLIAM R. NESTER

STATE UNIVERSITY OF NEW YORK PRESS

𝒯𝒟

Published by
STATE UNIVERSITY OF NEW YORK PRESS, ALBANY

© 2008 State University of New York   ·

All rights reserved

Printed in the United States of America

No part of this book may be used or reproduced in any manner whatsoever
without written permission. No part of this book may be stored in a retrieval
system or transmitted in any form or by any means including electronic,
electrostatic, magnetic tape, mechanical, photocopying, recording, or
otherwise without the prior permission in writing of the publisher.

For information, contact State University of New York Press,
www.sunypress.edu

Production by Marilyn P. Semerad
Marketing by Susan M. Petrie

Library of Congress Cataloging-in-Publication Data

Nester, William R., 1956–
The epic battles for Ticonderoga, 1758 / William R. Nester.
   p. cm.
Includes bibliographical references and index.
ISBN 978-0-7914-7321-4 (hardcover : alk. paper) —
ISBN 978-0-7914-7322-1 (pbk. : alk. paper) 1.
Ticonderoga, Battle of, N.Y., 1758. I. Title.
E199.N468 2007
973.2′6—dc22   2007102979

10 9 8 7 6 5 4 3 2 1

For Angela,
with the deepest love

CONTENTS

Illustrations

ACKNOWLEDGMENTS

I was extremely fortunate to have had such an outstanding acquisitions editor as Michael Rinella of SUNY Press for *The Epic Battles for Ticonderoga, 1758*. Michael spent an enormous amount of time carefully going over every line of my manuscript and offered excellent advice for its improvement. He also found or drafted all the maps and illustrations. Lisa Metzger, the freelance professional copyeditor, also made wonderful and meticulous suggestions for improving my manuscript.

I am also grateful to Marilyn Semerad, the Director of Production, for her strategic guidance. Finally I would like to extend my deep gratitude to the two anonymous readers for all their suggestions and encouragement.

XLII

INTRODUCTION

"Like Chaff before the Wind"

O my God, make them like whirling dust and like chaff before the wind. . . .
Drive them with your tempest and terrify them with your storm. . . . Fill their
faces with shame . . . let them perish in disgrace.
—Psalm 83

Ticonderoga is among North America's most visually and historically haunting places. Named after a corrupted Mohawk word that may mean "great carrying place" or "land between the two great waters," Ti-conderoga is a small peninsula and the surrounding area where the La Chute River joins the southern tip of Lake Champlain in northern New York.[1] A fort has dominated those narrows since 1755. The vista from Fort Ticonderoga's stone ramparts is stunning, with the lake running north and south, forested hills on either flank, and mountain ranges looming in the distance.

Yet while viewing that sweeping beauty, one is haunted by the knowledge that one is standing on hallowed ground. Thousands of men died trying to take or defend that patch of land. It was so strategic that it was widely believed to be the "key to a continent" during both the conflict known as the French and Indian War and then during the American Revolution.

On August 21, 1758, the fort, then called Carillon, was the scene of an especially poignant ceremony. Massed in silent contemplation within a horseshoe-shaped breastwork on a low plateau a half mile in-land from the fort were 3,528 French regulars, 2,671 Canadian marines and militia, and 470 Indians of numerous tribes. Standing before them were their commander, General Louis Joseph, Marquis de Montcalm Gozon de Saint Veran and Father Francois Picquet. A large wooden

Map 1: Overview Map

cross towered behind the barricade. A Te Deum or Catholic hymn of thanksgiving was about to begin.[2]

Seven weeks earlier most of those men had lined the hastily constructed breastworks and for hours steadily loaded, leveled, and fired their muskets at charge after desperate charge of British regular and provincial infantry. That battle's stakes could not have been higher. The French army had its back to Lake Champlain. The British outnumbered the French four to one. If the British broke through they would have bagged three of every five defenders of New France between Fort Carillon and Montreal, one hundred and fifty miles north. If vigorously led, that British army could then have overwhelmed any French forces in its way to Canada. Within a month that army would have marched into Montreal and not long after into Quebec. Canada's eventual conquest would have been spared two years of vicious fighting and heaps of dead and maimed. The battle of Fort Carillon would have been the decisive turning point in the French and Indian War.

But that was not to be. When the gunsmoke finally cleared on July 8, nearly two thousand British troops lay dead or wounded before the French breastworks. The British commander, Major General James Abercromby, who had ordered those attacks, now ordered his army to retreat. The survivors streamed to safety along the two-and-a-half-mile road from Fort Carillon to Lake George. The retreat did not end there. The following day they packed into over one thousand boats and rowed thirty-two miles up Lake George to its narrow southern shore.[3] Upon disembarking, the general dispersed his regiments in camps from there to Albany. Though it was midsummer, Abercromby's campaign against Canada was over. The end of his military career in North America would follow, after Prime Minister William Pitt learned of his blood-soaked wilderness debacle.

During Father Picquet's mass for the victorious French forces, he cited the 83rd Psalm, which invokes God's help to sweep away the enemy in future battles: "O my God, make them like whirling dust and like chaff before the wind. Drive them with your tempest and terrify them with your storm . . . Fill their faces with shame . . . let them perish in disgrace." He profusely thanked God for His divine aid when the French had "conquered and put to flight" the British army in the battle before Fort Carillon.[4]

Setting aside the issue of God's presence, Father Picquet was only half right. Fort Carillon's valiant defenders may have routed the British army, but they had hardly conquered their enemy. France was incapable of doing that in North America. With New France's settlers outnumbered twenty to one by their restless and aggressive British neighbors, at best French forces could merely stave off a likely inevitable defeat. Significant as it was, that is all the battle of Fort Carillon accomplished.

By inflicting such a bloody disaster on the British, the French threatened to stalemate this latest frontier war in North America, just as they had stalemated four previous conflicts. This most recent war had erupted four years earlier, on May 28, 1754. On that date, troops led by Lieutenant Colonel George Washington opened fire on those led by Ensign Joseph Coulon de Villiers de Jumonville in disputed territory in the upper Ohio river valley. Though what exactly happened that day remains hazy, the source of their conflict is clear.

Over the previous century and a half, France and Britain had carved ever-larger empires from North America's wilderness. Those empires now ground against each other at numerous strategic flash points. A long frontier stretched between them, from the Chignecto Isthmus of Acadia to the Creek villages of Georgia. In 1754, the most hotly contested region was that surrounding the forks of the Ohio River, where the British and French each raced to build a fort that would bar the other and cow the local Indian tribes into allegiance and trade. A small British force won that race, but within weeks it surrendered to a superior French and Indian army. Four years of bloody warfare would pass before the British retook that fort.

Although two campaigns would subsequently be launched for the Ohio forks, the most sustained fighting, as in previous wars, would blaze along the shortest corridor through the mountains between the two empires—that linking Albany and Montreal. It was little more than a couple of hundred miles as the crow flies from Montreal dead south to Albany; it was a little longer if that proverbial bird perched upon a canoe paddled by one of the many smugglers that plied the route between the two towns. The Richelieu River flows into the St. Lawrence River below Montreal. A skilled canoeist could paddle up the Richelieu, portage around the rapids at Fort Chambly, and continue south upstream until the river flows out of Lake Champlain. He could then follow Lake Champlain for roughly a hundred miles until he reached the narrows at the La Chute River mouth—the area the Indians called Ticonderoga.

From there the voyageur could choose between two routes. The less difficult route led south on Lake Champlain and then along Wood Creek until it shallowed near Fort Anne. There the canoeist would face a ten-mile portage to the Hudson River and then a forty-five-mile paddle south to Albany. But if the canoeist really wanted a challenge, he could head up the two-and-a-half-mile-long La Chute River (portaging around its five falls), and then dig his paddle deep until he emerged into Lake George, called Lac Sacrament by the French. It took two days to paddle to Lake George's south end, with the magnificent lake flanked by mountains on both sides and dotted with scores of wooded islands. Fourteen miles of tangled forest then lay ahead for the traveler, between Lake George's southern shoreline and the Hudson River.

In 1755, Colonel William Johnson chose the tougher route for his two-thousand-man army, composed solely of American provincials, to move toward Montreal. A flotilla launched on Lake George was usually well beyond musket shot of either shore. In contrast, a traveler on Wood Creek must constantly peer into the thick forest to avoid ambush.

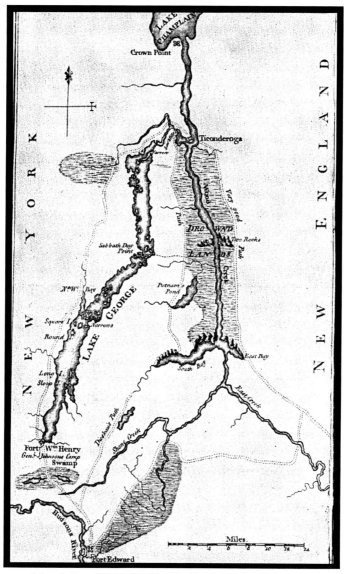

Map 2: Fort Edward to Fort St. Frederic (Crown Point)

Johnson ordered his troops to build what became known as Fort Edward a mile below where the Hudson, flowing from the west, angles south. There he had his men hack a road along an Indian trail leading to Lake George. At the shore, the troops would begin massing supplies and building boats for the campaign north.

When he got word of Johnson's advance, New France's Governor-
General Pierre-François de Rigaud de Vaudreuil de Cavagnal, ordered his
field commander, Major General Jean-Armand, Baron de Dieskau, to
move swiftly and attack the enemy. Dieskau led his 3,500 men to Fort St.
Frederic, paused briefly, and then continued a dozen miles to Ticonderoga, where he encamped two-thirds of them, and continued on with 216
grenadiers, 684 Canadians, and 600 Indians. On September 7, Dieskau
and his men had reached the road linking Fort Edward and Johnson's
camp (later called Fort William Henry), on Lake George. Dieskau reluctantly went along with his Indians, who were insistent on attacking the
1,300 troops at the Lake George camp, rather than the 500 at Fort Edward
on the Hudson. The result was a disaster. In three distinct battles on September 8, the American provincial army defeated the French; Dieskau was
wounded and captured.

After debating whether or not to follow up their victory, Johnson and
his officers agreed that the season was too late to advance against Fort St.
Frederic. Word of Dieskau's defeat prompted Governor Vaudreuil to
dispatch Lieutenant Michel Chartier de Lotbiniere, Marquis de Lotbiniere, to Ticonderogá with orders to construct what became known as
Fort Carillon.

From 1755 until the summer of 1757, neither side launched an offensive on the Lake George front. Instead, large raiding parties would slip
by water or forest between Forts William Henry and Carillon to attack
the other's supply convoys, patrols, or woodcutters. But in July 1757,
Dieskau's successor, General Montcalm, led 2,570 soldiers, 542 marines, 2,946 Canadians, and 1,799 Indians down Lake George against
Fort William Henry. After a nine-day siege—popularized by James
Fenimore Cooper's nineteenth-century novel *The Last of the Mohicans*—
the fort's commander reluctantly surrendered. Lieutenant Colonel
George Monro accepted Montcalm's terms that he give up the fort and
march away with the pledge that his 1,500 troops would not fight
again for the war's duration. Rather than push on to attack Fort Edward, Montcalm ordered Fort William Henry destroyed and its supplies hauled back to Fort Carillon.

Fort William Henry's destruction hardly ended the fighting around
Lake George. British and French forces continued to launch raids
against each other along both the Wood Creek and Lake George corridors between Forts Carillon and Edward. Then in the spring of 1758,
the latest British commander of His Majesty's forces in North America,
Major General James Abercromby, received orders to lead an army

against Forts Carillon and St. Frederic, and ideally on to Montreal. Abercromby's campaign was one of three planned for that year. Other British armies would attack Forts Louisbourg and Duquesne. It was hoped that 1758 would provide the war's turning point.

It did. The other British campaigns succeeded in capturing Forts Louisbourg and Duquesne, as well as destroying Fort Frontenac. After four years of stalemate the British could take heart that victory was within their grasp. In what had become the world's first global war, the fighting that had erupted at the forks of the Ohio river region had spread beyond North America to much of Europe, the Caribbean, parts of West Africa, Argentina, India, and the Philippines, and across the adjoining seas. Though it would take two more years of hard fighting for the British to conquer Canada, from 1758 the initiative was completely theirs and victory only a matter of time.

The victories of 1758, however, were marred by a single catastrophic failure: the British attempt to capture Fort Carillon. With nearly 2,500 combined casualties, the battle of Fort Carillon was the French and Indian War's bloodiest.[5] Surprisingly, although excellent books have been written about most of the war's major and even some of its minor battles, no book has yet provided an in-depth account of the ill-fated campaign in the New York wilderness that reached its climax in the battle before Fort Carillon.[6]

The Epic Battles for Ticonderoga, 1758 will address that gap in the literature. While technologies, tactics, ideologies, and personalities may change, the essence of battle—violence, terror, chaos, choices, misperceptions, and ambitions—remain constant throughout history. Although the events occurred nearly two and a half centuries ago, an exploration of the 1758 battles for Ticonderoga can provide a "distant mirror" that will help us better understand war at any time.

Every battle provides a unique setting in which commanders make decisions that not only determine the fate of the soldiers below them, but sometimes that of empires and the course of history. For that reason, the 1758 campaign cannot be understood without exploring the broader political, strategic, and logistical context in which the commanders and their subordinates made crucial decisions. In addition, it is sometimes as important to explore what did not happen as what did. Throughout *The Epic Battles for Ticonderoga, 1758*, the commanders' decisions will be weighed against the various options as they understood them, and the most likely scenarios had they chosen to follow a different path.

There is an additional category of challenges for those who explore that campaign and the period in which it was embedded. Researchers are rewarded with a goldmine of primary sources. Unfortunately, many of those sources must be handled with care. How the participants made sense of what was going on could be, unwittingly or not, as distorted or false as those of anyone else participating in and writing about the extraordinary events of any time and place, including, of course, here and now. Figures often do not add up even by those who should know better. Quartermasters sometimes did not get the math right in their accounts. Battle casualties are the most inconsistent. Commanders on both sides tended to downplay their own losses and exaggerate those of the enemy. And then there is spelling and grammar.

So what is an analyst to do? All along, I have tried my best to sort out fact from fancy, and explain the discrepancy. Most gaps between what people perceived and what was true are explained not as an attempt to commit fraud, but by the natural constraints on our ability as humans to understand complex, shifting realities and our tendency to engage in wishful thinking. So mostly I give the participants the benefit of the doubt, unless there is substantial evidence for a different conclusion. Varying versions of battle casualties are noted and, if possible, interpreted. I am grateful to my eagle-eyed editors for noting and correcting several columns of statistics whose inaccurate totals evaded me. As for spelling and grammar, unless a reader might be completely puzzled, most quotes are left with all the color and spice of the original.

The slaughter before Fort Carillon climaxed a year of raids and skirmishes in the surrounding forests. But while the sounds and smoke of battle drifted through the trees only intermittently, the struggle against nature was incessant. Just staying alive during a fierce northern New York winter was no easy task. Once spring weather broke and the ice melted, thousands of teamsters, laborers, and rowers filled rutted roads, waded surging rivers, and endured punishing portages to keep the troops and themselves supplied at distant forts and camps. Even more than the elements, politics determined the fate of Fort Carillon. Constant bitter political battles entangled both the French and British commands. The decisions or stalemates in those councils of war affected the grand strategy and tactics alike. Finally, there are the inner battles that each man constantly wrestles with that mold his outlook, choices, and relations with others. All these things would shape the epic battles for Ticonderoga in 1758.

CHAPTER 1

Opening Shots

I now thought it most prudent to retreat.
—Robert Rogers

Captain Rogers . . . quizzed him on the fresh meat they let him eat at Carillon.
M.Wolff answered him to be careful of himself when he comes again.
—Captain Malartic

WINTER RAIDS

By the time Robert Rogers and his troops got within a half dozen miles of Fort Carillon on March 13, 1758, they had endured three agonizing days and nights of cold and snow. By light and through hours of dark they had trudged on snowshoes up Lake George's ice toward Fort Carillon. The frigid air constantly seeped through the layers of wool capotes, blankets, caps, hunting shirts, and leggings that each man wore. Even the sun could be an enemy. Cloudless skies were usually colder and the sun's rays glaring off the snow-buried landscape was blinding. The nights were worse. Fires were forbidden. At best the men could chop down fir saplings, spread them across the snow, and shiver the dark away atop them. In addition to battling the elements, they were haunted by the constant fear that at any time musket shots and war screams would split the air—followed by a rush of hideously painted Indians brandishing tomahawks and scalping knives. Winter campaigns could rapidly break down most men physically and emotionally. Yet, when successful, they bloodied and demoralized the enemy while bringing back word of his numbers and intentions.

To minimize the chance of ambush, Rogers deployed his men in three parallel columns that marched fifty yards apart, each with advance, rear, and flank guards. Scouts ranged further ahead, from a quarter mile to several miles, depending on how well they knew the forest and the probable danger of colliding with an enemy war party. Rogers ensured that his men were equipped for the challenges ahead. In addition to adequate clothing, each man carried a musket, sixty rounds of ammunition, a hatchet, ice-creepers, snowshoes, and a haversack stuffed with rations; each dragged a sled with extra blankets and equipment. Nearly every one of his 181 troops were rangers, which comprised 11 officers, 11 sergeants, and 150 men among four companies. Joining the expedition from the 27th Inniskilling Regiment were 8 volunteers—3 officers, 3 cadets, a sergeant, and a private.[1]

The American rangers, mostly born on the frontier and veterans of many a winter march, were hardened to the icy hell. All were experts at wilderness survival and combat. This was not true of the volunteers who accompanied them. No English winter could match those of upper New York in cold or snow. Many of those regulars most likely cursed themselves for embarking on what they thought would be a grand adventure to prove their virility and to boast of for years to come.

The normally intrepid Rogers was unusually cautious the closer his troops got to Fort Carillon. He was aware that word of his expedition had already reached the French. Just two weeks earlier, Fort Edward's commander, Lieutenant Colonel William Haviland of the 27th Regiment, had ordered Captain Israel Putnam to lead his Connecticut company and some ranger volunteers on a reconnaissance near Fort Carillon. Putnam received the order on February 28 and departed the following day. He and his men got within eight miles of Fort Carillon without encountering any French patrols. Learning that 600 Indians were camped near Fort Carillon, Putnam decided to return. While he and his men were heading north, a French and Indian raiding party captured the rangers' sutler, a Mr. Best, and a deserter near Fort Edward. From them they learned of Putnam's sortie and another one soon to be led by Rogers and 400 troops.

If the French and Indians were now lying in wait, they would encounter less than half the number they expected. The rangers might well be blundering into a death trap. Haunted by that grim possibility, Rogers "viewed this small detachment of brave men . . . with no little concern and uneasiness of mind."[2]

To lift his spirits Rogers may well have recalled his previous raid of that winter. On December 17, 1757, he led 150 rangers out of Fort Edward for the brutal trek north toward Fort Carillon. Frostbite afflicted 8 men so badly that they had to turn back. The rest pushed on. By Christmas Eve, he and his men were huddled in the snow several hundred yards from Fort Carillon. Rogers hoped to ambush a French woodcutting party and hurry prisoners back to Fort Edward for prolonged interrogation. Late that morning they nabbed a lone sergeant who was out stretching his legs. As the day wore on, Rogers grew impatient. Around noon when a hunter headed their way, Rogers ordered a few of his men to chase him in hopes of drawing a rescue party from the fort into their ambush.

But the French stayed put. Rogers and his men could do nothing against an alerted garrison that refused to come out and fight. Instead, Fort Carillon's commander, Captain Louis-Philippe Le Dossu d'Hebecourt of La Reine battalion, ordered his gunners to fire grapeshot at the woods where the rangers had crept to snipe at the French soldiers lining the parapet. The rangers scrambled back out of range. All Rogers could do was order the fort's woodpiles torched and the cattle slaughtered. While the rangers were busy burning and butchering, the sergeant escaped. Two other Frenchmen, however, deserted to the rangers. As a parting touch, Rogers scribbled a note and tied it with a leather thong to the horn of one of the eighteen slain cattle. The note read: "I am obliged, Sir, for the repose you have allowed me to take; I thank you for the fresh meat you have sent me; I shall take care of my prisoners; I request you to present my compliments to the Marquis de Montcalm. Rogers, Commandant of the Independent Companies."[3] By December 27, Rogers and his men were safely back at Fort Edward.

Upon receiving the "compliments," General Montcalm remarked with wry annoyance that Rogers was a "rogue" who "exudes maybe a bit more spirit than is necessary." The raid, and especially that message, stung French pride. It was later reported that "Rogers, a great partisan, came roving in the neighborhood of Carillon . . . He caused to be attached to one of the oxen a letter addressed to the Commandant of the fort, the contents whereof were an ill-timed and very low piece of braggadocio."[4]

Having savored that fond memory, Rogers might well have recalled another. In early 1758, French lieutenant Wolff was dispatched under a truce flag to Fort Edward with letters from New France's Governor Vaudreuil and General Montcalm to their English counterparts concerning prisoner exchanges. Wolff enjoyed the civilities he received at Fort Edward, especially the banter with his respected opponent Rogers over his latest raid: "Captain Rogers . . . quizzed him on the fresh meat they let him eat at Carillon; M. Wolff answered him to be careful of himself when he comes again."[5] That warning was prescient.

FORT CARILLON

Rogers's raid worsened a miserable winter for Fort Carillon's garrison. With the right leaders, troops can endure and sometimes revel in the most wretched conditions. Fort Carillon's isolated snowbound defenders lacked that vital spark of leadership. Diminishing supplies, equipment, and pursuits gnawed at the soldiers' morale. Their swelling frustration burst into protests in November 1757, and threatened to do so again throughout that long winter. The officers not only were incapable of alleviating those complaints but may have aggravated them with their own mutterings of dissatisfaction, lethargy, and disdain.

What could be done to rejuvenate enthusiasm at that strategic post? Noncommissioned officers are any army's backbone. They, more than anyone else, determine whether the troops' morale will slouch or stiffen—on or off the battlefield. The army's second in command, General François Gaston, duc de Levis, grasped that simple truth. Montcalm and Vaudreuil eagerly approved his proposal to send among the troops tough but understanding veteran noncommissioned officers. Under the pretext of escorting a munitions convoy of sledges, eight sergeants and eight corporals arrived at Fort Carillon in February and were dispersed to each company. That infusion of vigorous leaders raised the garrison's morale on the eve of that winter's greatest military challenge.[6]

But noncommissioned officers are not enough to wring victories from battle. In this area, too, the garrison received a boost in early 1758. A master of wilderness warfare, marine Ensign Jean-Baptiste Levrault de Langis Montegron, arrived at Fort Carillon in mid-January. Then thirty-five years old, Levrault (better known today as Langy), had led numerous raids since the war began four years earlier and had proven to be every bit as audacious and skilled a leader as Rogers.

Within days Langy led a raiding party through forty-five miles of deep snows south to the trail near Fort Edward. There he ambushed a fifty-man American patrol on February 8. They killed twenty-three, and brought back five prisoners. Langy led another party out later that month which failed to find any prey. Three or four of his Indians lingered, and "fell in with a convoy of 30 sleighs loaded with provisions, which they plundered and dispersed, taking 4 scalps. They would have had greater success had one of them not been dangerously wounded."[7] With the infusion of dynamic leaders like Langy and the noncommissioned officers, the garrison would be ready the next time Rogers appeared at its doorstep.

THE BATTLE ON SNOWSHOES

Rogers and his troops were exhausted when they reached Lake George's north end on the morning of March 13, having trudged out of Fort Edward three days earlier. They had spent the first night at Halfway Brook, roughly six miles from Fort Edward. They hiked nearly twenty miles the second day and shivered away the night at Lake George's first narrows on the east shore. Rogers sent a scouting party three miles up the lake. The scouts returned to report no sign of the enemy. Nonetheless Rogers had scouts patrolling up the lake all night and ringed his camp with sentries. Shortly before sunrise on March 12, Rogers crossed his troops to the west shore and led them north. After three miles, they spotted a dog dashing across the lake toward an island. Rogers sent a patrol to scout the island where the dog had disappeared. They found nothing. He then led his troops to Sabbath Day Point where they rested until dark; scouts carrying spyglasses pushed further up the lake. After the scouts returned with the report of all clear, Rogers roused his weary men. He sent Lieutenant William Phillips and fifteen troops on ice skates up ahead, while Ensign Andrew Ross and a detachment plowed through the snow on shore. Rogers and the main body then followed along the lake's edge.

About eight miles from Fort Carillon, one of Phillips's men skated back with word to halt; the lieutenant thought he had spotted a fire on the east shore. Still cautious, Rogers sent Ensign James White to join Phillips and determine whether it was indeed a camp. An hour later, Phillips and White returned with word that the enemy was there. Rogers called in the rest of the advanced and flanking guards and moved into a thicket on the west shore. They were near the base of the five-hundred-foot eminence then called Bald (Pelee) Mountain and later Rogers' Rock. There they hid their sleds and packs. Leaving a small guard, Rogers led his men across the ice to attack the enemy camp. But when they crept close all they discovered were some patches of rotten wood that appeared to glow in the dark. They returned to their cache where they spent the remainder of the night.

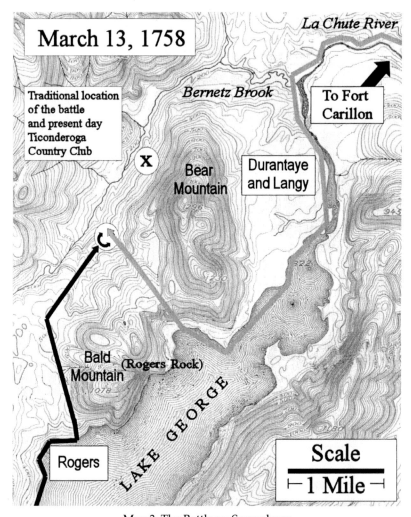

Map 3: The Battle on Snowshoes

Actual site of the battle roughly a mile southwest of traditional location, marked "X"

On the morning of March 13, Rogers and his officers decided to head inland through the rugged forests around Bald Mountain into the Bernetz Brook valley. The brook flows north for several miles before angling east to join the La Chute River where it bends toward Fort Carillon. That route was much more laborious but far safer than following the lake shore, where they could be easily spotted. But that route could also be a death trap if the enemy learned of their presence and dashed south along the lake to cut off their retreat.

The rangers shuffled atop the four-foot-deep snowdrifts until noon, when Rogers called a three-hour halt and explained his plan. They would advance toward Fort Carillon around three o'clock, after the French patrols had withdrawn for the day. The troops would be split into two groups. Captain Charles Buckley would command the first and Rogers the second; they would be followed by a small rear guard led by Ensigns James White and Joseph Waite. Should they encounter enemy troops, the first division would provoke a French attack then withdraw into an ambush set by the second. It was a good plan, provided Rogers had reliable knowledge of the enemy's whereabouts and a good bit of luck.

For the most part, Rogers's luck that day could not have been worse. The previous day marine Ensign Durantaye had led two hundred Nipissing Indians from the Sault St. Louis and Two Mountain missions, along with twenty Canadians, through Fort Carillon's gates. Those Indians were itching for the glory of combat, scalps, and loot. Yet it appears to have been divination by an Indian clairvoyant rather than scouts that unveiled Rogers and his rangers. A few days earlier, in the Indian camp near Fort Carillon, "an old sorcerer had assured them they would see the English before long." Then on March 12 that clairvoyant suddenly "began to prophesy. He said that the English were very close to Fort Carillon and that they should go out immediately and attack them. The other Indians were so convinced by this example of inspiration & went to the commandant's quarters to inform him that they wanted to set out the next day as they were sure they would come across an English raiding party." Canadians with long exposure to Indian ways did not take such visions lightly. In their mind, such prophesies may well have been the Devil's voice but nonetheless they were often prescient. Fort Carillon's commander, Captain d'Hebecourt, "although astounded by their idea, was very pleased with it as a means of getting rid of them."[8] For most frontier commanders, Indians were at best a nuisance, devouring supplies and making incessant demands while conducting few raids or even scouting missions.

Cutting loose the Indians became urgent when two Abenaki scouts hurried in around noon on March 13 with word they had discovered the tracks of an enemy force. D'Hebecourt gave permission for Langy and Durantaye to lead the Indians and half the garrison on a patrol down Lake George. Within minutes around a hundred Indians and Canadians, led by Durantaye, grabbed their muskets and surged from the fort. Not long after, a second force of nearly two hundred Indians and

French commanded by Langy set forth. The two forces followed the trail along the La Chute River from Fort Carillon to Lake George and then down the ice to Bald Mountain's north end where Langy caught up to Durantaye. Scouts dashed back with word of "numerous human footprints on the ice" at Bald Mountain's south end. Durantaye and Langy "immediately decided to go back into the woods through which the English had to pass."[9]

The French leaders correctly surmised that the enemy was following the Bernetz Brook route north.[10] With Durantaye's force leading and Langy's several hundred yards behind, they hurried west over the trail that cut from Lake George to the Bernetz valley, between Bald Mountain and Bear Mountain. Once in the Bernetz valley Durantaye and Langy expected to pick up the enemy trail heading toward Fort Carillon or Fort St. Frederic. What they could not know was that Rogers had called a three-hour halt and thus was just on the other side of the mountain. Tired from their own strenuous hike and not expecting to reach the enemy's rear for hours—if at all that day—the Indians and French probably paid little attention to the surrounding forest. They advanced straight into a trap.

Ranger scouts spotted Durantaye and his men as they wearily filed across a broad meadow on the east branch of the upper Bernetz Brook. The scouts hurried back to Buckley, who ordered his men to take cover and sent a runner back to Rogers. Rogers and his men closed with Buckley's. Shedding their packs and snowshoes, the rangers sprawled in a thin crescent facing northeast. It was a good position. Bald Mountain guarded their right flank and the small stream their left.

Rogers recalled that they tensely "waited till their front was nearly opposite to our left wing, when I fired a gun, as a signal for a general discharge . . . whereupon we gave them the first fire, which killed above forty Indians; the rest retreated, and were pursued by about one half of our people. I now imagined the enemy totally defeated, and ordered Ensign [Gregory] McDonald to head the flying remains of them that none might escape." Unfortunately, the rangers committed a grievous error. Determined to rip scalps and run down any survivors, they dashed after the enemy without reloading. "We soon found our mistake," Rogers admitted. He continued,

> The party we attacked were only their advanced guard, their main body coming up, consisting of 600 or more Canadians and Indians; upon which I ordered our people to retreat to their own ground, which we

gained at the expense of fifty killed, the remainder I rallied, and drew up in pretty good order, where they fought with such intrepidity and bravery as obliged the enemy (tho' seven to one in number) to retreat a second time; but we, not being in a condition to pursue them, they rallied again and recovered their ground, and warmly pushed us in front and both wings, while the mountain defended our rear; but they were so warmly received that their flanking parties soon retreated to their main body with considerable loss. This threw the whole again into disorder, and they retreated a third time; but our number being now too far reduced to take advantage of their disorder, they rallied again, and made a fresh attack upon us. About this time we discovered 200 Indians going up the mountain on our right . . . to attack our rear, to prevent which I sent Lieutenant Phillips with eighteen men to gain the first possession and beat them back; which he did, and being suspicious that the enemy would go round on our left and take possession of the other part of the hill, I sent Lieutenant [Edward] Crafton, with fifteen men, to prevent them there.[11]

A half dozen other troops, including two volunteer gentlemen, joined Crafton's party.

With the repulse, Langy ordered some of his men to fire on the enemy front while he dashed through the snow around their right flank with most of the others. The French and Indians pressed their attack, slipping through the trees and firing. The sheer weight of attackers finally broke the rangers. Rogers and twenty men retreated to a hill where the remnants of the parties led by Phillips and Crafton tried to join them. Crafton succeeded. Phillips called out to Rogers that he was going to surrender; his troops were exhausted, outgunned, and cut off, and a French officer offered him quarter. It proved to be a fatal mistake, because the Indians, "having discovered a chief's scalp in the breast of an officer's jacket, refused all quarter."[12] Those men who surrendered "were inhumanely tied to trees and hewn to pieces, in a most shocking and barbarous manner."[13]

The slaughter of Phillips and his men gave the remaining rangers a chance to escape. Rogers admitted that "I now thought it most prudent to retreat."[14] Nearly every one of his men was either killed or captured—144 scalps and 7 prisoners, while the French suffered 2 marine cadets, 1 Canadian, 15 Iroquois and an Abenaki wounded, and 5 Iroquois and 1 Nipissing killed; many of the Indian wounded would later die.

Some of Rogers's troops escaped the battle only to surrender later. Captain Henry Pringle of the 27th wrote of the hellish days he spent wandering the forests with two others: "we marched all night and on the morning of the 14th found ourselves entirely unacquainted with the ice . . . After struggling thro' the snow some hours, we were obliged to halt to make snowshoes . . . Here we remained all night without any blankets, no coat, and but a single waistcoat [sleeveless coat] each." The following morning they became lost in the snowbound forest west of the battlefield and for the next four days they plodded on in what they prayed was the direction of Fort Edward. On the fifth day "the wind pierced us like a sword; but instead of abating it increased together with a freezing rain, that incrusted [sic] us entirely with ice . . . We made a path round a tree and there exercised all night, though scarcely able to stand, or prevent each other from sleeping. Our guide notwithstanding repeated cautions, straggled from us where he sat down and died immediately." On their seventh day of wandering they finally emerged from the forest. But to their horror they discovered that for days they had plodded in a circle. It was not Fort Edward but Fort Carillon before them. At death's brink, there was no choice but to give up. They "approached with a white flag; the officers [from Fort Carillon] ran violently towards us and saved us from a danger we did not then apprehend; for we were informed that if the Indians, who were close after them, had seized us first, it would not have been in the power of the French to have prevented [us from being killed or carried away]." Captain d'Hebecourt "and all his officers treated us with humanity and politeness, and are solicitous in our recovery."[15]

What was Rogers's fate? The French initially thought that he was among the dead. Vaudreuil later wrote that Rogers "left on the field of battle his coat, and even the order he received from his General, which gave me every reason to believe that he had been killed, [more so] as an Indian assured me he had himself killed him."[16]

Rogers remained very much alive. It took four days for him and two score other frostbitten survivors to reach Fort Edward: "Our snowshoes breaking and scrambling up mountains, and across fallen timber, our nights without sleep or covering, and but little fire, gathered with great fatigue, our sustenance mostly water, and the bark and berries of trees . . . a freezing rain . . . encrusted us with ice."[17]

Upon his return, Rogers was greeted with both condemnation and accolades. Rogers admitted only to 131 dead while claiming his troops "killed 150 of them, and wounded as many more."[18] Most likely to downplay the decisiveness and humiliation of his defeat, Rogers exaggerated the enemy's losses as grossly as the number arrayed against him. Throughout the war he had stirred controversy with his personal daring and brilliant leadership, offset by an abrasive personality, the jealousy of his lessers, and rumors of financial corruption. Critics were primed and loaded to fire at any of his setbacks. The Battle on Snowshoes gave them their elusive target.

But Rogers had his supporters. An admirer described that "gallant & bloody" battle as rendering "considerable proof of his bravery and conduct. But envy that arch fiend will not allow him much merit."[19] After nearly four years of defeats, the British army was in desperate need of heroes and daring leaders. Brigadier General Howe was one such leader who recognized those qualities in others. Long inspired by Rogers's tireless bravery and exertions, Howe celebrated the Battle on Snowshoes as an example of British valor. He invited Rogers to his cozy headquarters at Albany, asked him to raise five new ranger companies, and, on April 6, 1758, promoted him to major.

Rogers returned to Fort Edward to command six ranger companies, of which four were composed of provincial volunteers, one of Stockbridge Indians, and the other of Mohican Indians. The provincial rangers now received a standard uniform of forest green regimental coat, waistcoat, and knee breeches, and dark blue bonnet. They would be ready for General Abercromby's campaign up Lake George that summer.

FOLLOW-UP RAIDS AND THWARTED PLANS

After spending a freezing night on the battlefield, the French and Indians returned triumphantly to Fort Carillon. Following native etiquette, Captain d'Hebecourt gathered the Indians and covered their dead with presents. He then promised them that Governor Vaudreuil would generously reward their great victory once they reached Montreal. The seven rangers captured at the Battle on Snowshoes yielded diverse and at times conflicting information. But the most important information was of a planned winter expedition by several thousand troops pulling mortars on sledges across Lake George's thick ice against Fort Carillon's understrength garrison. They also shared the rumor that the summer's most powerful British offensive would be against Louisbourg, although Abercromby had also targeted campaigns against Fort Carillon—if the winter expedition faltered—and Fort Duquesne. Other prisoners nabbed that winter and into the spring corroborated these reports.[20]

Durantaye and his troops escorted the rangers back to Montreal, bringing them before Vaudreuil and Montcalm on March 27. Upon interrogating them, the governor and general viewed with fatalism the word of a pending attack on Fort Carillon. Very little could be done to assist the fort in the short term. There were simply not enough sledges to convey all the supplies necessary to sustain enough troops to defend the fort successfully. Only a fraction of the number of necessary troops could be sent to counter the enemy. If the British expedition was as large as the prisoners claimed, any handful of reinforcements that reached Fort Carillon would most likely end up captured. Under the circumstances it was best to do nothing and hope that some mix of the harsh weather, British bumbling, and French élan would defeat the enemy expedition. Montcalm was confident that "the good guard and vigilance of d'Hebecourt, who commands there, will prevent" the fort's capture.[21]

The intelligence and hope were both correct. While few relished a winter campaign, the British were planning a winter thrust against Carillon. The plan's genesis was in a November 1757 reconnaissance of Fort Carillon by two intrepid regular British officers, Captains Matthew Clerk and James Abercrombie, escorted by Captain John Stark and a ranger company. They nabbed several French prisoners and deserters who revealed that the winter garrisons of Fort Carillon and Fort St. Frederic were only 350 and 150 troops, respectively. The harsh supply shortage would prevent the French from reinforcing either fort until May at the earliest and possibly June.

Upon their return to Fort Edward, Clerk and Abercrombie mulled what they had learned. They excitedly concluded that a winter expedition of 3,000 picked troops, the rangers, and a small battery of mortars and howitzers against those forts could capture them both. In December they submitted their proposal to His Majesty's commander in chief for North America, Major General John Campbell, Earl of Loudoun. Loudoun enthusiastically embraced the proposal, recognizing that the capture of those two forts would "forward matters greatly the next campaign."[22] He ordered the officers to work out its details. Major General James Abercromby inherited the strategy in March after he received Pitt's order to replace Loudoun. Rogers and his rangers would play a key role as the advance guard for that campaign, atop their raiding missions to harass Fort Carillon and gather intelligence.

Had the plan for a lightning strike been implemented the war might well have been significantly shortened. That year's summer campaign could have begun by around mid-July from Fort St. Frederic, fifty miles north of the actual jump off at Lake George's south end. Abercromby would have faced the combined armies of Montcalm and Levis at Fort

Isle aux Noix at Lake Champlain's north end. Whether Abercromby would have handled that campaign any differently than the historic one is, of course, impossible to say.[23]

Too much work, nature, and lethargy combined to abort the plan's execution. An essential element of that winter campaign was making enough snowshoes to supply more than 3,000 troops. That job was assigned to the rangers. But they had little time to make snowshoes in between raids up Lake George. A thaw on January 3 flooded Rogers Island, where they were encamped across from Fort Edward, and washed away their supplies and what snowshoes they had made. They resumed the tedious work. Then late-winter heavy snows made it impossible for that force to advance even on snowshoes. But by early April, the thaw of snow and ice rendered the snowshoe issue moot.

The troops, supplies, and bateaux were available at Fort Edward and nearby posts. Why did General Abercromby not transport them over to Lake George and lead them north as soon as the ice melted? Nothing in the existing records explains the lapse. A fleeting opportunity was lost.

Valor was not confined to Rogers and his rangers. While nearly all British and many French officers passed the winter huddled over cards, rum, and bawdy talk in their barracks, there were exceptions. Snow and bitter cold no more inhibited French, Canadian, and Indian war parties than they did American rangers.[24] All winter, blanket-clad war parties plowed south through the drifts to attack settlements and outposts along the American frontier. In doing so they obeyed Montcalm's order for "Canadian officers to go out nearly all winter with parties of thirty or forty savages."[25]

In New York, the Mohawk River valley was the prime target for raids from the French fort and mission at La Presentation on the St. Lawrence River. In November 1757, Lieutenant François-Marie Picote de Bellestre's party destroyed German Flats, a rich village fattened by trade with the Iroquois and just across the river from Fort Herkimer. The men were all butchered and the women and children dragged into captivity, with around a hundred and fifty settlers lost altogether. Later expeditions wiped out other hamlets in the region. Near Fort Herkimer, Captain Claude Nicolas Guillaume Lorimier de La Riviere's war party wiped out a patrol of forty troops and took three prisoners. Lieutenant Wolff led an Abenaki raid on the Massachusetts frontier. Colonial Lieutenant Charles Deschamps de Boishebert et de Raffetot commanded nearly seven hundred Acadians, Canadians, and Micmacs on the St. John's River to harass the British in Nova Scotia.[26]

But, as always, the most fiercely contested region was that from the southern end of Lake Champlain to the upper Hudson River. All winter long and into the spring Captain d'Hebecourt sent out expeditions. At one point eight bands of French, Canadian, and Indian troops prowled the forests around Fort Edward.[27] May was an especially active month. The thick green foliage made ambushes especially effective and tracking difficult. Langy was the most active of all the raiding leaders. Early that month he and sixteen Abenakis brought back four scalps and thirteen prisoners from near Fort Edward. Instead of resting on his laurels, Langy led another war party out of Fort Carillon on May 17. This time he returned empty-handed.[28] In early May, Lieutenant Dufay of La Reine battalion led a party that brought back three scalps taken in an attack on a supply convoy to Fort Edward. On May 30, Lord Outelas and Chief Kisensi led forty Nipissings in an attack on five British and eighteen Iroquois prowling along the La Chute River; they took two Indian and two British scalps and captured two British and seven Indians. When the Nipissings arrived at Montreal on June 4, their Iroquois allies greeted them with the demand that they immediately torture and kill the prisoners. Those Iroquois undoubtedly sought vengeance for their own losses in earlier raids. Vaudreuil immediately held a council with the Iroquois and Nipissings, rewarded them all generously, and then dispatched them on yet another raid. He warned them to return within twenty-five days. The governor hinted that he had an even bigger raid in mind that would require not only these loyal warriors but many more from other tribes.[29]

Apparently not all who lusted to sally forth against the British got their chance. Lieutenant Pean wintered at Fort Carillon, where he studied an Iroquois dialect. Upon returning to Montreal, he angrily wrote to War Minister Belle Isle that "it was out of my power, My Lord, to obtain permission from M. de Vaudreuil to organize during the winter any detachment against the enemy, although that was the sole motive which induced me to ask for leave to winter near the English. I have even been refused permission to march at the head of some Indians, whose confidence I acquired and who asked me to lead their war party." Why would a governor who was otherwise so enthusiastic about dispatching war parties to attack the British block the efforts of a skilled officer? Pean attributed it to jealousy: "there is no anxiety in Canada to employ the French in such a manner as to furnish them occasions for distinguishing themselves, these favors being reserved for the children of the soil."[30] His enforced inactivity, however, did not prevent the French lieutenant from requesting a promotion from the Canadian governor.

As for British raids, other than Rogers and his rangers, Mohawk allies were most frequently sent against Fort Carillon. At least one of those raids scored a bloody victory. In early May, Captain "d'Hebecourt having need of timber to cover the storehouses, had caused the banks of [lower Lake Champlain] . . . to be reconnoitered where the timber was to be cut; that he . . . sent a detachment thither of 45 men in 3 bateaux, one of which, containing 17 men, was fired upon on approaching land by 40 hostile Indians, who took or killed [all]. . .the other two bateaux prepared to fire and to return to the fort." That same Mohawk war party took "a gunner and a soldier of the Colony who had gone to hunt, notwithstanding the prohibition of the officers."[31] In separate raids, rangers killed a Canadian and captured three Germans near Fort Frederic, and captured a gunner and two soldiers near Fort Carillon.[32]

Raids when successful not only bloodied, disrupted, and discouraged the enemy. More importantly, they brought back word of the other's power and plans. What Governor Vaudreuil and General Montcalm learned would force them to abandon their own plan and concentrate their forces to defend against what seemed impossible odds.

CHAPTER 2

The Struggle for North America

What kind of a country is this then, unknown to the rest of the world, and
where nature is of a sort so different from ours?
—Voltaire, *Candide*

ADAPTING TO THE CHALLENGES
OF WARFARE IN NORTH AMERICA

What led men to stalk each other in the forests embracing Ticonderoga?
The 1758 struggle for Ticonderoga cannot be understood apart from the
one-hundred-fifty-year rivalry between France and Britain for the conquest of the eastern third of North America and, to a lesser extent, other
lands around the world.[1] While the fighting in North America and Europe was the most intensive, the battles between England and France for
trade and colonies extended to the Caribbean, West Africa, Argentina,
India, and the Philippines, and the seas linking those far flung regions.
What had begun as a dispute over control of the upper Ohio River in
1754 had, in the space of two years, expanded into a global struggle
between two empires over trade routes, peoples, and vast swaths of territory. This struggle had, in turn, drawn in all the great powers.

That global conflict was fought with eighteenth-century technologies, which constrained strategy and tactics, especially in the American
wilderness. Newly arrived French and British officers soon learned that
warfare on this continent differed starkly from that in Europe. The wilderness imposed tactical problems largely unknown among Europe's
large fields, which were broken by hamlets and patches of woods, or
strategic challenges removed from a continent with an extensive net-
work of cities, roads, canals, ports, warehouses, and manufacturers.

Problems of gathering enough supplies and sending them to the front was difficult enough in Europe, with armies dependent on tens of thousands of draft animals dragging thousands of wagons along muddy rutted roads. It was a Herculean task in a wilderness broken only by trails, along which roads had to be laboriously hacked out, and with all forage for the draft animals packed along.

Perhaps the most difficult aspect of warfare in the North American wilds was mastering the intricacies of Indian diplomacy and warfare. Indian allies were at once a curse and a blessing. It took a fortune in gifts, seemingly endless diplomacy, and battlefield victories just to entice a tribe from the enemy's side into neutrality, let alone to rally its warriors into allies. In camp, the incessant demands by Indians for provisions and councils irritated even the most sensitive of commanders. In the field, Indians could be either energetic or lethargic warriors. Many a British or French commander concluded that the only advantage of having Indians for allies was not having them for enemies.

Nonetheless, schooled by their Canadian counterparts, most French officers adapted quickly to the challenge of North American warfare. Only a handful of British officers did. The wilderness invigorated some, like General George Howe, but bewildered and frightened most others. They were haunted by General Edward Braddock's defeat in 1755, when a smaller French and Indian force routed his army and inflicted nearly a thousand dead and wounded. Like Braddock, General James Abercromby would cling all the more tightly to his concepts of "proper" warfare as the wilderness loomed ever more claustrophobically around him. And the bloodbath he would inflict on his troops would be even harsher than that inflicted by Braddock on his troops.

A TALE OF TWO EMPIRES

The armies that clashed around Ticonderoga in 1758 came from societies with distinct social values, systems of government, modes of production, and military traditions. These sharply affected the decisions and performance of the leaders and their followers in the field. The discovery of the "New World" in 1492 aroused the commercial, scientific, and imperial interests of prominent men in England and France. As Spain expanded and consolidated its toeholds in the Caribbean, Central America, and South America into one vast empire, the French and English governments, along with their counterparts in Portugal, Holland,

and other countries, fell under pressure to sponsor their own expeditions to the New World.

When the first French and English exploring expeditions were launched in the early sixteenth century, North America remained largely open for conquest. The Spanish had established tiny enclaves of missions and settlements in New Mexico and northern Florida. Elsewhere, the only obstacles to French and English imperialism were the native peoples, limited funds and volunteers, and each other. As various expeditions set foot and flag on beaches along North America's east coast, each made extravagant claims for their kingdom's ownership that were then impossible to realize.

The first successful English and French settlements did not take root in the New World until the first decade of the seventeenth century. During the next century and a half, the two nations gradually expanded their colonies and competed for the trade and allegiance of various Indian tribes. As their empires spread across the eastern third of North America, the English and French managed to thwart similar attempts by Holland and Sweden to establish their own North American colonies, and to contain the Spanish at the frontiers of northern Florida and eastern Texas. Wars between the French and English in Europe increasingly became entangled with their imperial rivalry in North America. In all, the French and English fought five wars that involved their duel for supremacy in the New World. The first was the Huguenot War (1627–1629), followed by the League of Augsburg or King William's War (1689–1697), the Spanish Succession or Queen Anne's War (1702–1713), the Austrian Succession or King George's War (1744–1748), and the French and Indian (1754–1760) as it is called in the United States or Seven Years' (1754–1763) War as it is called in Europe for the duration of the fighting there.

Versailles and Whitehall were the respective palaces for the French and British governments, which shared the same policies for exploiting their respective empires. Mercantilism was their grand strategy. Mercantilism recognizes the symbiotic relationship between military and economic power: success in one enhances the other. The key is the government's deft management of the economy, by which in a virtuous cycle industries are developed, exports promoted, competitive imports blocked, markets expanded, technologies mastered, the bourgeoisie enlarged, colonies seized and exploited, tax revenues enhanced and reinvested in industries and arms, and thus the kingdom further enriched and empowered. Imperialism is essential to mercantilism;

colonies supply the natural resources and markets that are often underdeveloped or nonexistent in the kingdom. Most of the profits from such policies are reinvested in more of the same, while the rest bolster the army and navy so that they can capture more colonies and protect more trade routes.

Mercantilism was the organizing principle of the age. To varying degrees both kingdoms mastered it, though Britain much more successfully than France. By the mid-eighteenth century, France had a population of twenty-five million and Britain six million. Only a fraction of each population was wealthy and skilled enough to contribute substantially to a market economy; most were peasants who lived from hand to mouth. Yet, despite having a population but a quarter that of France, Britain was more entrepreneurial, scientific, inventive, bourgeois, and, in a word, worldly. The difference is unsurprising. As an island realm, Britain depended on the sea for much of its defense and wealth. France, threatened by potential enemies on its long eastern and southwestern frontiers, just as naturally concentrated on continental politics and gave but fleeting thoughts to its interests elsewhere. Though both kingdoms had colonies around the world, the gap in dynamism between them was nowhere more pronounced than in North America. The two empires could not have differed more in character and geography. Each of the fourteen American colonies made money for the British empire. New France, in contrast, perennially drained rather than enriched French wealth, and thus French power.

France developed a cluster of settlements in the St. Lawrence valley and Acadia (Nova Scotia) during the seventeenth century and in the lower Mississippi valley during the early eighteenth. Elsewhere throughout the Great Lakes and upper Mississippi valley, the French "empire" consisted of a score of isolated trading posts and missions inhabited by several hundred traders, soldiers, and priests. By the 1750s, there were just over 70,000 subjects living in New France, of which 63,000 were in Canada and Acadia, and 4,000 whites and 5,300 blacks in Louisiana. The French did not conquer their empire, they rented it. Beyond their settlements and aside from wars against the Iroquois, Fox, and Natchez, the French largely paid for the right to trade with the Indian tribes. Fur and fish were the backbone of New France's economy. The settlers lived a subsistence existence; their harvests were often threatened by war and weather. Indeed, only annual subsidies from Versailles kept New France alive. France's empire cost far more than it was then worth.[2]

In contrast, the British had conquered their empire through war and with settlers, along with a vital but unpredictable ally, smallpox. By the 1750s, except for the Iroquois and Cherokee, the few surviving tribes along the frontier were but fragments of their former selves and cowed by British power. Over 1,304,000 Americans—1,062,000 white and 242,000 black—were squeezed between the Atlantic and Appalachians in fourteen (the thirteen that became the United States along with Nova Scotia) colonies. Each of the colonies was, to greatly varying degrees, economically diverse and generated wealth for England. Many of those Americans were increasingly restless for the wealth and land they could reap west of that mountain wall. In this they were usually backed by their respective colonial governments, most of whom had claims as far as the Mississippi—and some even to the Pacific Ocean!

Though their settlements remained far apart, the French and English claims in North America overlapped in several regions, most importantly in Acadia, the Great Lakes, the Ohio valley, and the southeast. The French had a stronger legal claim since they had arrived first to plant their flag and exploit those lands. The English, however, had an enormous economic advantage. Their trade goods were better made, more abundant, and less expensive than those of the French. This was ever more evident after the British established the trading post of Oswego on Lake Ontario's southern shore in 1726. Increasing numbers of Indians paddling down from the upper Great Lakes traded their furs at Oswego rather than Montreal. During the 1730s and 1740s, daring American traders pushed west into the Ohio valley as far as Lake Erie's southern shore and in the southeast as far as the lower Mississippi River. Though the French chased them out during King George's War, the traders trickled back as soon as the fighting stopped.

In Acadia the conflict was over how to interpret the 1713 Treaty of Utrecht, by which France granted that region to England. The French claimed that Acadia stopped at the Chignecto Isthmus; the English demanded land all the way to the St. Lawrence River. In 1749, the English disembarked two thousand settlers to found Halifax as the first step in eventually overwhelming in numbers the fifteen thousand French Acadians living on both sides of the isthmus. In 1750, the French and British built forts on either side of the Chignecto Isthmus. This was the only point along their two-thousand–mile frontier where their flags flew in sight of one another. For now the British would only protest the presence of a French fort on land they claimed as their own and demand yet another loyalty oath from the Acadians under their control.

Another tenet of the Utrecht Treaty was just as controversial. Article 15 granted England sovereignty over the Iroquois Federation, the six tribes of which straddled the watersheds draining west into Lake Ontario and east into the Hudson River across central New York. The English, however, used that tenet not only to claim dominion over the Iroquois, but over every tribe that the Six Nations had ever conquered or tried to conquer. If accepted that would have extended the British empire as far west as the Mississippi River. But the French rejected the claim, as did the Iroquois. The Iroquois at once proudly asserted their independence from either power, while addressing envoys from both as "father" or patron, implying a vague submission.

After King George's War ended, American traders again led pack trains across the Appalachians to garner Indian furs. But those traders competed not only with the French but with each other. Virginians and Pennsylvanians each asserted their own land claims to the upper Ohio River valley. They tried to legalize these claims by negotiating treaties with factions of tribes in the region. The British government did not mediate the dispute between the two colonies, but instead asserted its own claim to the region and then granted land to any company that would settle there. In 1749, Virginia's Ohio Company won the first bid. It would receive two hundred thousand acres to start and another three hundred thousand acres after it built a fort and settled one hundred families in those lands within seven years.

The conflicting claims between England and France were supposed to be resolved by a boundary commission established by the 1748 Aix-la-Chapelle Treaty. But the English and French commissioners were deadlocked for years as each side asserted claims unacceptable to the other. The French based their claims on prior discovery and a watershed theory of ownership whereby the Appalachian Mountains would split the two empires. The British used the Utrecht Treaty's Acadian and Iroquois tenets to demand all lands below the St. Lawrence, and Lakes Ontario and Erie west as far as the Wabash River. Thus did the commission exacerbate rather than mediate tensions.

By 1754 the frontier was primed to explode into another war. The spark turned out to be a race between the Ohio Company and the French to reach the Ohio River forks and built a fort there. The Ohio Company won and erected a small post there in January 1754. Over six hundred French and Indians and eighteen cannon paraded before the fort on April 17 and that display of massive force was enough to force its surrender. The defenders were paroled. The French renamed the post Fort Duquesne. Meanwhile, with orders from Virginia's governor to retake the fort, Lieutenant Colonel George Washington led about three hundred Virginians toward the Ohio forks. In May his small force was encamped at Great Meadows, about halfway between the British post at Wills Creek and Fort Duquesne. Learning of a French patrol lurking in the region, Washington led a small force and ambushed it. They killed ten, including the patrol's commander, Ensign Joseph Coulon de Villiers, de Jumonville, and captured twenty-two others. Only one Frenchman escaped to carry word to Fort Duquesne. The fifth and final war between the British and French empires for North America had begun.

WARFARE IN THE EIGHTEENTH CENTURY

Technology limited and shaped strategy and tactics in the eighteenth century as thoroughly as it has throughout the rest of history. Troops moved only as fast as sail, paddle, hooves, or feet could carry them. The ability to damage the enemy extended only as far as the musket and cannon shot of that era. And, of course, as in any war, logistics straight-jacketed strategy. Problems of transportation, communication, production, and storage limited the ability of monarchs to mobilize their kingdoms' people, industries, and agriculture for war.

Eighteenth-century warfare was largely fought by professional armies and navies whose ranks rarely comprised more than 2 percent of the population. Nearly all campaigns occurred during the summer, when forage and crops were most abundant. Months of preparations were followed by weeks of maneuver, which might be punctuated by a battle or siege.

Warfare during the four previous wars between Britain and France in North America was far more limited than in Europe. Neither side sent over more than small numbers of regulars. Strategy, such as it was, consisted mostly of large-scale raids of provincial frontiersmen and Indian auxiliaries against enemy settlements. Such raids ideally served two interrelated needs: they disrupted the enemy's raids and kept Indian allies enthused with plunder and scalps.

Invasion attempts were few. New France never had the manpower to conquer the American colonies; at best it could simply contain the restless Americans east of the Appalachians. Though potentially capable of doing so, the British government never seriously tried to conquer New

France during the first four wars between them. An exception was the Walker expedition Britain sponsored in 1711 to take Quebec, but that ended in disaster. Whitehall tended to regard colonial initiatives with a mixture of disdain, embarrassment, and fear that they presaged greater autonomy among those distant subjects: Quebec had been returned after the three Kirke brothers led a flotilla that captured it in 1629, as had Louisbourg after New Englanders successfully besieged it in 1745. All in all, North America was but a sideshow to Europe's conflagrations. A seemingly unspoken agreement allowed both sides to leave colonial defense in the hands of those subjects leavened with scattered companies of British regulars or French marines.

Shortly after the colonies were established, Britain's settlers outnumbered their French counterparts by a ratio of nearly twenty to one, but that advantage was never realized on campaign. New France's settlements were far more compact and closer to the frontier. Most Canadians lived in the narrow St. Lawrence corridor between Montreal and Quebec. Communication and transportation along that river was well established and possible by either boat or sledge in all but the most severe weather. Thus Canada's militia and marines were much more easily mobilized and dispatched against the enemy. In contrast, Britain's North American colonies were strung out over a vast distance. Only the settlements in New England and New York were directly threatened for the most part. The frontiers of the middle colonies, such as Pennsylvania and Virginia, saw more raiding during the French and Indian War, but on the whole the southern and middle colonies were quiescent. British settlements were also largely within fifty miles of the Atlantic Ocean, and so beyond the reach of even the most audacious raiding party.

Topography also limited warfare. Only a few corridors broke the wilderness that buffeted each empire and each presented the traveler— let alone an army—with an extremely challenging journey. Even the route between Albany and Montreal, the easiest and most direct, took weeks to paddle and portage. The British trading post of Oswego on Lake Ontario was vulnerable to French attack; a further advance to Albany, however, would require crossing 220 tough miles up the Onondaga and down the Mohawk watersheds. No other town of any strategic importance was accessible on the other frontiers. The Connecticut and Kennebec river valleys were French raiding routes, but they led to isolated settlements. Fort Duquesne became the base for raids against distant scattered settlements in the Susquehanna and Shenandoah valleys. The Fort Toulouse to Savannah corridor had military potential, but it remained unused. Though the French never had more than a score or so of men at Fort Toulouse and it would seem to be easy picking, the southern colonists avoided any campaign for fear of marching into lands controlled by the Creek Indians.

Since the French rallied more Indian allies, they also dominated those corridors. Only St. Lawrence Bay offered the British, with their naval superiority, a means to reach the heart of the French empire with minimal resistance. Travel by sea could be precarious, however: a storm wrecked the 1711 Walker expedition. When the British arrived before Quebec, they faced a citadel perched on towering bluffs manned by thousands of Canadians.

Climate was yet another force that shaped warfare. South of the Appalachians, winter began later and ended earlier, thus allowing river transport to the front for as much as a month longer. While the St. Lawrence froze over from December to March, even America's northernmost ports remained ice free most of the winter. Canadian freezes and storms often destroyed seedlings or harvests, making the colony dependent on massive grain imports from France just to survive. Harvests in the British colonies were not only abundant enough to feed the Americans but usually there was enough left over for export to Britain's Caribbean colonies. The British, however, never capitalized on these advantages in any of the wars. Their campaigns lumbered into motion long after the French had reinforced and supplied their frontier forts or launched their own campaign. Abercromby's 1758 campaign would be no different.

Albany was the only strategic objective the French had the remotest chance of reaching. But Montcalm's victories at Oswego in 1756 and Fort William Henry in 1757 captured only the jumping-off points for Albany. The ever-cautious Montcalm refused to follow up his victories even with a march against the ill-defended next step toward Albany, Fort Edward—a mere fourteen miles from Fort William Henry. A French offensive anywhere else along the frontier was useful only to the extent that it diverted the British from their own offensives.

The British for their part also failed to distinguish between primary and secondary strategic objectives. Rather than mass their resources to strike at Quebec, the key to destroying New France, the British frittered away their superior numbers with three or four offensives each year aimed at objectives on the French empire's periphery. Numbers, of course, were not enough to win. The French succeeded in defeating most of those offensives in the early years of the war with better tactics, assistance from their Indian allies, and the weather. By 1758, however, the British had massed enough troops, supplies, and experience to successfully capture forts Louisbourg and Duquesne, and destroy Fort Frontenac, thus seizing the strategic initiative. Those results were not inevitable. Each of those successful campaigns could have turned into defeats had each side made different decisions. The British would not sail to Quebec until 1759, five years after the war broke out.

North American warfare had become a hybrid, with characteristics from each continent.[3] Field battles and assaults on fortified lines were fought with regular regiments lined up facing each other. The only difference was that rangers and Indians replaced cavalry on the flanks. Large-scale wilderness battles were less common and mostly won by the French. Artillery played a secondary role in field battles or assaults.

Sieges, however, were indistinguishable from those of Europe. Parallel trenches were dug ever closer to the enemy fort, batteries were emplaced, and the bombardment begun. Sieges worked. Every siege during the French and Indian War succeeded except Levis's of Quebec in 1760. No forts were carried by storm; all were surrendered. A request to talk by one commander to his enemy was announced by flying colors that resembled the enemy's flag. Thus the British signaled their intention by flying a white flag and the French a red flag.[4]

After a successful siege, the victor had two options: he could either parole or imprison the defenders. Paroled garrisons headed back to their towns to live off their own country's provisions. They usually could return to the front only after a similar number of enemy troops had been released. The trouble was that paroled prisoners could and at times did violate their paroles. In 1757, Britain's North America commander, Major General John Campbell, Earl of Loudoun, refused to honor Fort William Henry's surrender agreement, which paroled the fifteen-hundred-man garrison, because after the surrender the Indians massacred a hundred or so men, and carried off hundreds more into captivity. Loudoun freed those paroled troops to fight again. That would lead to a heated exchange of letters between Loudoun's successor, Abercromby, and Canada's governor Vaudreuil in 1758.

Logistics were a constant headache for any commander. For each soldier in the field, ten other people were required to keep him there. Quartermasters had to requisition crops from farmers, and clothes, arms, munitions, barrels, ropes, tools, wagons, and dozens of other goods from manufacturers. It then took vast numbers of teamsters, laborers, and rowers to get those supplies to the various fronts. Hundreds of small boats were essential to transporting the troops and their supplies back and forth on Lake George. Flat-bottomed bateaux were ideal for hauling supplies while round-hulled whaleboats more swiftly conveyed troops, though each carried both.

The British slowly adapted to the challenges of North American warfare. In 1757, Loudoun required each regiment to train for fighting in forest and field alike, and to form a light infantry company. In the 1758 campaign, Abercromby distributed ten rifles to each regiment's best shots and had those men act as skirmishers. Even more importantly, he took the advice of his second in command, General Howe, to shorten coats and jackets, trim hat brims to two inches and hair nearly as short, and to brown shiny musket barrels, all to lessen the burden and visibility of the troops. In 1759, General Amherst would order regiments to form two instead of three ranks in the field, thus stretching thin red lines further to protect their flanks and ideally engulf those of the enemy. On the Plains of Abraham before Quebec in 1759, General James Wolfe would order his men to cram extra powder and two balls down their musket barrels for an even more murderous discharge.

But by 1758, the nature of changes in warfare went beyond British adaptations. The war's scale and intensity were starkly different than they were four years earlier. Montcalm recognized this: "the nature of war in this colony has totally changed. Formerly the Canadians thought they were making war when they went on raids resembling hunting-parties—now we have formal operations; formerly the Indians were the basis of things, now they are only auxiliaries. We now need other views, other principles. I say this; but the old principles remain."[5] Montcalm's aide, Louis de Bougainville, also noted the change: "Now war is established here on the European basis. Projects for the campaign, for armies, for artillery, for sieges, for battles. It is no longer a matter of making a raid, but of conquering or being conquered. What a revolution! What a change . . . townsmen, bankers, merchants, officers, bishops, parish priests, Jesuits, all plan this [war], speak of it, discuss it, pronounce on it."[6]

Regular troops were the backbone and muscle of most campaigns. The relative numbers of those troops rather than topography had the most important impact on each side's strategy. British naval supremacy intimidated the French from sending over troops numerous enough to defend the empire, let alone win the war. In all only 5,000 French troops would slip past the British blockade, while the number of redcoats in North America eventually reached 30,000. With their inferior numbers, the French annually could at best hold the line while mustering enough troops and supplies for a limited offensive against the British.

Although French forces generally adapted to North American warfare more readily than the British, there were similarities. Neither kingdom had standing armies, only standing regiments, the largest peacetime military unit. Armies were tailor-made from the list of regiments for specific campaigns and then disbanded after the work was done. The French often had two to four battalions per regiment while the British mostly had only one; the 60th Royal American was an anomaly with its four battalions. Each British battalion ideally numbered about 850 men in twelve companies—ten regular companies, one light, and one grenadier. French battalions numbered 556 troops in thirteen companies—twelve fusilier (line) and one grenadier. Sometimes the best fusiliers were formed into a piquet or light company.

In both armies the battalion's largest and toughest soldiers were picked for the elite grenadier company, which might be held in reserve or split into two platoons with each anchoring a flank. Sometimes army commanders concentrated all their grenadier battalions into one battalion for special assaults or even entire campaigns. The power of those concentrated grenadiers, however, was often offset in two ways: the battalions were weakened by the loss of their grenadier company, while a specially formed grenadier battalion needed time to learn to march and fight together as a cohesive unit.

Another similarity was that most regiments were not the "King's own" but instead owned by a lord who defrayed the cost of recruiting and supplying it by selling officers' commissions and receiving state subsidies. The system reduced the government's duties and costs at the price of professionalism. Those who could afford to buy a commission were rarely the best qualified. Neither side had an officer training program. Officers picked up their trade through haphazard observations, experiences, and, if they were especially motivated, reading ever more numerous books on the subjects of waging war and serving as an officer.[7]

While their abilities varied enormously, officers strove to at least look the part. They wore white wigs or powdered their hair with flour; gold lace scrolls adorned sleeves, cuffs, shoulders, and hats; silver gorgets or tiny breastplates dangled on their chests from ribbons dyed the regimental colors. An officer was partly paid with extra rations depending on his rank, which he in turn sold on the black market. A British colonel, for instance, got six times his soldiers' daily rations, which provided him a steady extra income. Many a colonel pocketed the pay from nonexisting men on his regimental list. In all, the criticisms Prime Minister Pitt leveled at British officers characterized every army of the era: "Want of Application to Geography, the different Arts of War and Military Discipline; their Insolence to the inferior Officers, and Tyranny over the common Men . . . [Their] Extravagance, Idleness, and Luxury . . . few seem to be affected with any other Zeal than that of aspiring to the highest Posts, and grasping the largest Salaries."[8]

As for strategy and tactics, there was a certain amount of democracy among the highest officers. Before and during campaigns, strategy and tactics were debated in councils of war chaired by the commander. After a consensus was reached by all present, a general usually, though not always, simply ratified the course of action decided upon. Thus could he take credit for victories and spread blame for defeats.

Sound intelligence, as always, was essential to formulating strategy and tactics. Deserters and prisoners were important sources, though they tended to exaggerate their army's numbers upward and morale downward. Scouts rarely got close enough to the enemy to count heads, let alone ascertain plans. The best source of intelligence was from Indians who traveled among native villages and army camps, even those whose warriors were on the opposite side. They provided word of enemy initiatives, political factions within a particular tribe, the number of potential warriors, and so on. The pro-British Mohawks and pro-French St. Lawrence Iroquois frequently traded delegations, mostly to negotiate promises that they abstain from killing each other should they meet on the battlefield. Intelligence of British strategy was often inadvertently or deliberately spread by American newspapers. These would reach Canada via American and Canadian smugglers, whose profits soared as the human costs of the war escalated. The British lacked the same means of intelligence—no newspapers were being printed in New France.

TURNING RECRUITS INTO SOLDIERS

Recruiting and training soldiers was an endless task in every regiment. Desertion, sickness, and battle thinned their ranks. Most recruiting occurred during winter, when the regiment was quartered. Officers scoured the markets and taverns for fresh faces willing to take the king's shilling or livre.

By the mid-eighteenth century, most regiments in both armies had adopted the kingdom's standard cut of uniform and color. Shirts were linen while coats, waistcoats, and breeches were wool, a sensible choice for durability and warmth but stifling during a hot summer. The French coats, shirt, knee breeches, and leggings were greyish white; those of the British troops red—hence their respective nicknames "whitecoats" and "redcoats."

Line companies wore black felt cocked hats; grenadiers wore tall mitres with the regiment's insignia and scrolls embroidered in silk, silver and gold. In the French army custom dictated that only grenadiers and sergeants sported moustaches; all other troops were supposed to be clean shaven. Regiments were distinguished by different colored facings and cuffs. Flag bearers and drummers wore the reverse colors of their regiment; thus if a French regimental facings were blue they would sport blue uniforms with greyish white facings.

There were exceptions. Each side employed regiments, often foreign, with uniforms as distinct as their traditions. The Swiss Karrer companies at Louisbourg wore red uniforms with blue facings. The three Highlander regiments sent to America, the 42nd Black Watch, 77th, and 78th wore plaid kilts instead of breeches (the Crown abolished the tartan after the failed rising of 1745). The knee breeches of British royal regiments were blue rather than red. The 80th Light Infantry wore light brown uniforms without facings and carried muskets "browned" by a chemical process that darkens the shiny metal and slows the rusting process. Though New France's colonial troops tended to wear the same colored uniforms as the regulars, each American colony was free to select its own colors. Virginia, New Jersey, Massachusetts, and most Pennsylvania regiments chose blue with red facings, though a few Pennsylvania units wore green uniforms. At first the rangers wore hunting clothes; by the summer of 1758 they were uniformed in dark green uniforms.

Of course those uniforms were the formal, parade-ground version. With but one annual issue of clothes, the cost of which was deducted or "stopped" from each soldier's payroll, that appearance got steadily more ragged, especially after a hard campaign. Captain John Knox was amused at a returning woodcutting party, which looked "as droll and grotesque . . . as a detachment of Hungarian or Croatian irregulars, occasioned by the length of their beards, the disordered shape of their hats, and the raggedness of their partly-coloured cloathing; for some had brown, others blue watch-coats (buckled around their waists with a cartouch-box strap) and some were in their threadbare uniforms; in short they had very little of the British regular in them. . . . [They] lay aside the uniformity of the clean, smart soldier, and substitute . . . the slovenly, undisciplined, wood-hewer, sand-digger and hod-carrier."[9] Troops tended to go native; they replaced worn-out shoes with moccasins, adopted Indian style wool or leather leggings, and encased their feet with thick layers of flannel during the winter to ward off frostbite. When soldiers received their new clothing, they usually paid a seamstress to convert their old ragged uniform into a waistcoat or breeches, with the scraps fashioned into a forage cap.

GUNS, GERMS, AND SURVIVAL

The French and British shouldered different muskets. The standard French musket was a .69-caliber, eleven-pound 1746 design manufactured at St. Etienne or Charleville. Though the marines were supposed to be equipped with the same model, many still carried a lighter 1729 musket made at Tulle. The standard British musket was the .75-caliber fourteen-pound Long Pattern in use since 1717, with such notable revisions as steel ramrods in 1724, and locks that were improved in 1729, 1734, 1741, and 1743, with most regiments that fought in the French and Indian War probably armed with the latter. The musket's nickname, "Brown Bess," was not documented until 1785.[10]

Loading consisted of half-cocking the musket, removing a cartridge from the box, biting off the end, pouring some powder into the pan and snapping it shut, pouring the rest of the powder down the barrel along with the ball and paper to hold it, and ramming it home. All that remained was to full-cock and pull the trigger.

A ball shot from a musket's unsighted smoothbore barrel had an effective range of a hundred yards. Unless the "fire at will" order was shouted, troops fired by platoons, with the second rank alternating with the first to fire and load. A well-trained soldier could get off three or even four shots a minute. Ideally a regiment could project a continuous storm of lead balls toward the enemy.

Contrary to popular belief, few provincials carried a rifle. Though German immigrants introduced rifles to Pennsylvania in the 1740s and probably earlier, it would not be until the 1760s that rifles were a common sight on the hunting trail. A rifle's accuracy was offset by its greater expense, loading time, and inability to mount a bayonet. None of the French or British regiments initially sent to North America had any rifle companies. During Abercromby's 1758 campaign, however, rifles were available, ten to a regular regiment's best sharpshooters. But just what those riflemen did and how well they did it remains unknown.

In eighteenth-century warfare, musket balls inflicted about 80 percent of the battle deaths and wounds, followed by cannon shot with 10 percent. Wounds from bayonets, swords, spontoons, and other weapons were relatively few. All of these weapons inflicted gruesome wounds. Cannon balls tore off limbs or pulverized bodies. Musket balls shattered bones and organs. Bayonets caused an especially vicious three-sided wound that was hard to sew shut. Yet a soldier had a good chance of escaping a battle unscathed. Casualty rates usually ranged from 2 to 10 percent in a typical battle. The battle of Fort Carillon was bloodier than most with the British and French suffering casualties of 11 percent and 13 percent, respectively.[11]

Germs were many times deadlier than weapons. In the filth of an army camp or hospital, infections festered in even slight wounds of any kind, and they often rapidly transformed into gangrene. Dysentery, scurvy, and a cornucopia of other diseases ravaged the ranks, especially the provincial troops who lacked experience in maintaining a disciplined regimen of personal hygiene. The longer the troops remained camped in one place the more human and animal waste littered the ground and fouled the streams. The diseases and stench were nowhere worse than in a hospital—four of every ten men placed in a hospital died. At least one disease could be combated. Though the sanitary practices and drugs had not yet developed to combat dysentery, scurvy was relatively easily treated with spruce-beer, a concoction "made of the tops and branches of the Spruce-tree, boiled for three hours, then strained into casks, with a certain quantity of molasses. After the mixture cooled, it was ready for use."[12]

Soldiers rarely spent more than a few days under fire in the typical campaign, unless they were participating in a protracted siege. Most of the time they marched and camped or simply camped for day after monotonous day. Idle hours could be devoted to cards, rum, and dalliances with the women among the camp followers. The British private made twenty shillings a month, the French private five sous, eight deniers.[13] Soldiers could supplement their pay by woodcutting—two shillings and a gill of rum for a cord in the British army. Soldiers could be billeted in civilian homes if they were available, but once established settlements were left behind it was typical for half a dozen or more to cram into a wedge tent for shelter and intermittent sleep. Food was usually abundant if dull. In the British army, a "soldier's allowance per week is seven pounds of beef, or, in lieu thereof, four pounds of pork, which is thought to be an equivalent; seven pounds of biscuit bread, or the same weight of flour; six ounces of butter, three pints of peas, half a pound of rice; and this is called seven rations."[14] French soldiers got daily rations of a half pound each of salt pork and peas, and a pound and a half of bread.[15]

Winter was a soldier's worst season, especially if he sheltered in a tent rather than a building. He shivered away the short frigid days and seemingly endless nights in a constant battle against frostbite and scurvy. The troops spent much of their time chopping and hauling wood and huddled around the smoky fires. Summer brought its own problems. Soldiers were plagued by clouds of maddening mosquitoes whose bite caused virulent fevers and made "a person's head, face, and neck so swelled and inflamed as not to have a feature distinguishable." For protection, soldiers "wore long linen trowsers, with crape or green gauze nets sewed to our hats, which hung down loose before and be-hind, with a running string at the bottom to gather it round the neck."[16]

Incessant military drills were just another monotony. Nearly all officers hoped to convert human beings into automatons who would obey any order instantly and unthinkingly. They were only partially successful. When drills failed to maintain discipline on or off the battlefield, the offi-cers imposed cruel punishments. The accused might suffer being flogged—dozens or even hundreds of lashes—with a cat-o'-nine tails or a multistranded, lead-tipped whip, or by having to run a gauntlet of troops slashing with ramrods, or by straddling a log with weights attached to his legs. These punishments might lay up the miscreant for weeks in agoniz-ing pain and sometimes crippled him for life. The hangman's noose and firing squads greeted those caught deserting or assaulting an officer. The readiness to inflict such vicious punishments varied with the fortunes of war. When recruits were scarce and casualties heavy, officers reduced penalties or turned a blind eye to minor infractions. Disciplinary mea-sures, ironically, were probably harshest during peacetime.

Despite the similar tactics, training, and organization, was there any difference in the temper of British and French regulars? Some thought so. In his journal, Captain John Knox observed that the French

> ran down to the precipice with a ridiculous shout and manned their works. I have often reflected upon the absurdity of this practice in the French, who entertain a high opinion of their own discipline and knowl-edge in the art of war; there is nothing that can be more absurd than such noise in engaging an enemy . . . it . . . must tend to defeat all regularity

and good order among themselves, because their men are thereby confused and are rendered incapable of paying attention to their officers or
their duty; it is a false courage. How different, how nobly awful and expressive of true valour is the custom of the British troops! They do not
expend their ammunition at an immense distance; and, if they advance
to engage or stand to receive the charge, they are steady, profoundly silent and attentive, reserving their fire until they have received that of
their adversaries, over whom they have a tenfold advantage; there are
cases where huzzahing may be necessary, but those are very rare; the
practice is unmilitary in an army or body of regulars; and experience
plainly shows us that the troops who, in perfect silence, engage an enemy,
waiting for their first fire, will always preserve a superiority.[17]

Exactly how exaggerated these differences were is difficult to assess.

THE BRITISH ARMY

Each of Britain's American colonies enjoyed a degree of prosperity, despite being bound by mercantilist laws to trade only with England for
most goods; none needed to be subsidized. The colonies competed endlessly among themselves for parliamentary perks, trade, and western
claims. The race between fur companies based in Virginia and Pennsylvania to dominate the upper Ohio valley was a major reason war broke
out in 1754.

To the French and most other European rivals, Britain's government
seemed surprisingly weak to manage such a wealthy and expanding
empire. George II was a constitutional monarch whose powers were
limited by the 1689 Bill of Rights and 1701 Act of Settlement. A cabinet
of ministers debated and implemented policies, with the duty for imperial affairs split between the Board of Trade and secretary of state for
the Southern Department. The king ratified cabinet decisions. The cabinet then had to receive approval from parliament, with 558 House of
Commons members and roughly 250 members of the House of Lords.
Though the Whig Party dominated, party loyalty or principles were
largely abstractions. A vote in parliament tended to be determined by a
politician's personal interest in the affair, in which the pecuniary usually superceded the philosophical; vote buying was endemic.

Political power in the colonies was equally diffuse. Though most colonies had a governor appointed by the king, real power to tax, promote, and obstruct lay in the legislatures, elected by property owners. The colonies had to submit their laws to parliament for approval—except for Maryland, Rhode Island, and Connecticut, which were proprietary rather than Crown colonies. The colonies employed agents in London to lobby parliament, the cabinet, and the king.

In each colony, the governor and elected legislature engaged in a perpetual tug-of-war over policy and privileges. This conflict was especially pronounced during wars. The governor was trapped between Whitehall's demands to aid the war effort and the legislature's demands for protection and other government services at little or no cost to taxpayers. Each colony formed its own "committee of war" to mobilize resources; the committees varied considerably in their efforts. Not surprisingly, the northern and middle colonies, which were the closest to the fighting, made the largest contributions while the southern colonies made the smallest.

Whitehall tried but largely failed to coordinate these colonial war efforts. British generals complained bitterly over the miserliness and ingratitude they experienced in North America. General John Forbes captured that anger when he lambasted the "villany and Rascality of the Inhabitants, who to a man seem rather bent upon our ruin . . . than give the smallest assistance, which if at last extorted is so infamously charged as shews the disposition of the people in its full Glare."[18] General Loudoun provoked American animosities when he demanded that Americans open their homes to the redcoats or he would force their entry at bayonet point.[19]

British officers and troops provoked many of the same resentments that would explode into revolution less than a generation later. Benjamin Franklin observed that after a typical march, the British army "plundered and stripped the inhabitants, totally ruining some poor families, besides insulting, abusing, and confining the people if they remonstrated. This was enough to put us out of conceit of such defenders if we had really wanted any."[20] In 1758, Prime Minister Pitt alleviated some of the simmering anger by promising to reimburse the colonies for some of their expenses. Whitehall did eventually reimburse the colonies for 1,544,830 pounds, or about 40 percent of their expenditures. Massachusetts's expenses of 818,000 pounds were the largest of any colony; it received 352,000 pounds back from parliament.[21]

American contempt for the British army and its generals extended beyond their heavy-handed methods for mobilizing supplies and men. North America has also been rightfully described as "the grave-yard of British military reputations."[22] British generals dispatched to North America during the French and Indian War emerged from a long swath of mediocrity (Loudoun, Forbes, Amherst, Murray, and, yes, Wolfe) or outright criminal incompetence (Braddock, Webb, and Abercromby) that stretched between Marborough and Wellington. Despite such deplorable role models, American commanders actually proved to be more able than the British. William Johnson, John Winslow, Robert Rogers, and John Bradstreet outshone their British counterparts when given independent commands, even if George Washington did not.

Though British officers and their men tended to scorn colonial officers and troops alike, the Americans proved to be just as able as the redcoats when the shooting started. Indeed, aside from the regular army triumphs at Louisbourg in 1758 and the Plains of Abraham in 1759, American troops supplied most troops in victories at Fort Beausejour, the Onondaga River, Lake George, Fort Frontenac, Fort Duquesne, and Fort Niagara. Yet the regulars received the lion's share of the laurels. As Ben Franklin pointed out, rather than give credit where it was due, the British regulars would, when present with colonial troops, "claim all the Honor of any Success, and charge them with the Blame of every Miscarriage."[23]

Many of those regulars were American themselves. The king authorized the first independent companies in 1696. The 42nd Regiment (not to be confused with the 42nd Highlanders) was created in Georgia in 1737. During the French and Indian War three more regiments were formed in the colonies, the 50th and 51st, which were captured at Oswego in 1756, and the 60th Royal Americans, whose four battalions fought in nearly all the later campaigns. Between 1754 and 1760, over eleven thousand Americans joined regular regiments or independent companies. That recruitment often caused resentment, as indentured servants abandoned their masters for a different kind of servitude. When Pennsylvania passed a law in 1756 that forbade the recruitment of servants, parliament promptly responded by amending the mutiny act so that disrupting recruitment was a capital offense, though it did promise to compensate owners for any losses.[24]

Seven regular regiments—the 27th, 42nd Highlanders, 44th, 46th, 55th, 60th (1st and 4th Battalions), and 80th—would charge the barricade before Fort Carillon on July 8. The backgrounds of those regiments differed widely. The 27th, 46th, and 55th were raised in England, the 60th and 80th in America, the 44th in Ireland, and the 42nd in Scotland. American recruits swelled the ranks of all the regiments formed across the Atlantic, while British and Europeans joined the 60th and 80th. All the regiments but the 42nd were relatively young and inexperienced in combat. The 27th, the 44th, and 46th were founded in 1751, the 55th and 60th in 1757, and the 80th in 1758. Three were special regiments: the 42nd was Scottish Highlander, the 80th was the British army's first light regiment, and, although the 60th was a regular regiment, its troops were trained to load and fire from the ground and cover. The history of the 42nd and 80th will be explored in depth, along with the improvised ranger battalion of six companies.

The 42nd was the oldest, the largest, and the sole Highlander regiment in Abercromby's army. It would suffer nearly half of all British casualties at Fort Carillon. Few regiments in British military history have won as many battle laurels or suffered as many casualties. The first independent companies were formed in 1667 to "watch" the Scottish frontier. That duty, combined with their dark tartans, won them the name the "Black Watch." It was not until 1739 that those independent companies were joined into the 43nd regiment, which was redesignated the 42nd in 1749. The Black Watch fought at Fontenoy in 1745, returned to Scotland that year, and fought at Culloden in 1746.

With Lieutenant Colonel Francis Grant in command, the 42nd arrived at New York in June 1756. For the next two years the Black Watch would see no action. In 1757 it was attached to Loudoun's aborted Louisbourg campaign and spent the summer at Halifax before returning to New York. In 1758, three new companies joined the 42nd, bringing its companies to thirteen and its strength to nearly thirteen hundred troops. Only ten of those companies would embark on Lake George. Two others guarded Fort Edward and the third was at New York while the campaign took place.

It was an elite regiment from the beginning. Only the physically toughest and largest from the best families were accepted into its ranks. Those clan loyalties created bonds impossible to duplicate in other regiments. Their uniforms certainly conveyed their elite image. The uniform was a scarlet jacket and waistcoat, with buff facings and white lace, plaid kilt, and dark blue bonnet with a border of red, white, and green. In addition to a musket, the men carried a broadsword or claymore and often a pistol or two. On July 22, 1758, in recognition of its years of loyal service, George II designated the 42nd Black Watch as the "Royal" Highlander Regiment of Foot. He and Britain would only learn a month later that, as he signed that edict, the 42nd's remnants were recovering from the worst losses in its history.[25]

Today the rangers are the best remembered British unit in that war. Ranger units were organized as companies rather than regiments. The first two ranger companies were formed in 1756. Their success led to the creation of ten companies by 1758. The rangers' reputation as wilderness fighters every bit the equal of the French marines and Indians owes much to their leader, Robert Rogers. During the war, he led over fifty raids or scouting missions.[26]

Despite—or more likely because of—their successes, Rogers and his rangers had their critics. Like nearly all regular officers, Lord Loudoun had mixed feelings toward those troops, which he found as exasperating as they were indispensable. Although most rangers were skilled woodsmen and courageous fighters led by skilled officers, their discipline tended to dissolve when they were confined to a fort. Captain General Cumberland replied to Loudoun's complaints by ordering him to "Teach your troops to go out upon scouting Parties: for till regular officers are with men that they can trust [and they] learn to beat the woods & act as irregulars, you will never gain any certain intelligence of the enemy, as I fear, by this time you are convinced Indian intelligence & that of rangers is not at all to be depended on."[27]

Yet nothing was done until December 1757, when Lieutenant Colonel Thomas Gage offered to raise a regular light infantry regiment that would be trained in ranger skills without any of their alleged vices. Loudoun eagerly wrote Prime Minister Pitt how

Gage made an offer of raising and clothing at his expense a regiment of 500 rangers at the same pay with the troops, if His Majesty should be graciously pleased to appoint him colonel of that corps. As by this plan, I should both make so great a saving to the public by reducing the pay of the rangers from seventeen pence, halfpenny sterling, to sixpence and their clothing. And at the same time have a corps of rangers that would be disciplined, and have officers at their head on whom I can depend which, except for a few, is not the case at present. And, as by this plan, if it succeeded I should be independent of the rangers and from thence be able to reduce their expense, besides which, as I am obliged to increase the rangers, it is necessary to have an officer at their head by whom I can communicate the order to them and to be answerable for their being executed.[28]

Loudoun enthusiastically embraced Gage's plan and took the liberty of helping him recruit and equip the troops until Whitehall sent its approval. When he took over as North American commander in chief, General James Abercromby was just as supportive of Gage's efforts, granting him 4,300 pounds to form the 80th Light Infantry with an authorized strength of five hundred troops. Abercromby wrote that the light infantry "would discharge all the functions of rangers in a short time, better than those at present in your pay, so that in the end some such plan would be a great saving." But later Abercromby had second thoughts. Fearing that Gage might not be spending that money wisely, he asked Major Gordon of the 27th and Lieutenant Duncan of the 44th "to examine the said account with the vouchers to see that the sum is properly vounched."[29] The officers did so and found nothing amiss.

Meanwhile Gage made rapid progress filling the 80th's ranks. It was not hard to find volunteer officers or enlisted men. He handpicked his own officers along with ninety-six volunteers from other regiments to serve as noncommissioned officers. Six companies would be ready by the time Abercromby's army embarked on Lake George. Yet they were still unseasoned. The 80th's companies would follow Rogers's rangers, who remained unchallenged as the army's scouts and advanced guard.

Finally there were the fourteen provincial regiments, including six from Massachusetts, four from Connecticut, and one each from New York, New Jersey, New Hampshire, and Rhode Island. Recruiting for provincial regiments was never easy, but it was relatively better received than recruiting for regular regiments. Recruiting began in February or March when the governor issued the colonel's commissions for each regiment. The colonel himself usually did little recruiting. Instead he handed out officer commissions and let them do the work. Those provincial recruiters had two advantages over their regular counterparts. Rather than enlist for six years, each provincial regiment only formed for a strictly contracted nine-month or twelve-month service. As if this were not incentive enough for those who felt compelled to serve as long as it did not last too long, provincial pay was twice that of regular army pay, and there was an enlistment bonus. Rank would be granted according to the number a man recruited: fifty recruits made a captain, half that a lieutenant, and fifteen an ensign. Those "officers" naturally recruited in their own communities, so companies tended to be tightly knit socially if not militarily. If recruiters failed to fill the regiment's ranks, the governor could use the 1754 Act for Levying Soldiers to order a draft from militia units. Draftees could hire a substitute if they paid a fine to the colony ranging from five to twenty pounds. A legal contract bound volunteers and draftees alike for a limited service. Thus few hesitated to head for home if the army violated the agreement and kept troops beyond the time limit.[30]

The militia provided a huge pool of manpower for the regular and provincial regiments, as well as defended their homes. All able-bodied men from sixteen to sixty in every town or county were required to belong. Since most militia spent little more than one or two days a year at drill, their quality as soldiers was abysmal. Those on the frontier had to drill more often and at times might find themselves desperately trading shots with a French and Indian war party.

It might be imagined that serving a common king against a common enemy strengthened bonds between British and Americans. Actually it exacerbated their differences. British gentlemen officers who, as members of the nobility or untitled wealthy bought their commissions, resented rubbing shoulders with American officers who were often elected by their men and could come from the humblest of lives. To minimize such unpleasantries parliament passed a law in August 1754 in which royal commissions superceded colonial ones, so that a British lieutenant could outrank an American colonel. The law provoked deep resentments among American officers, many of whom, including Washington, resigned rather than submit. Washington and many others were enticed back into the ranks when King George II decreed in November 1754 that provincial officers were beneath a regular officer of the same rank but above all others below. The abuses, unfortunately, continued despite the decree. Pitt understood that the animosities between regular and colonial officers undercut army morale and colonial respect for the Crown. On December 30, 1757, he reissued the order that all regular officers were only superior to provincial officers of equal rank but had to follow orders of those above them.

Some of the resentment rubbed on the different motivations that drove the British and Americans into battle. The British fought for their king and empire, the Americans, sometimes literally, for their homes and colony. Governor Dinwiddie of Virginia bluntly complained to George Washington about the "idle argument which is often used, namely, you are defending your Country and property, is justly look'd upon as inapplicable and absurd. We are defending part of the Domain of Great Britain."[31] Ever more Americans could not have disagreed more.

THE FRENCH ARMY

Like Britain, France fought the Seven Years' War with a dearth of able leadership on the battlefield. None among the ranks of that era's French generals could step forward beside a Turenne or Saxe of old or Napoleon and his best marshals to come. The mediocrity of the French generals was compounded by their inability to pick their second. When an army was formed, the king appointed two men to lead it, a general who determined strategy and an intendant who organized and supplied the troops. Politics rather than proficiency usually governed both choices; competition rather than cooperation usually fouled the subsequent relationship between the general and intendant. Fortunately, Louis XV's choices for his commanders in New France—Jean-Armand Dieskau, Baron de Dieskau (1755), Louis-Joseph de Montcalm, Marquis de Montcalm-Gozon de Saint Veran (1756–1759), and François-Gaston de Levis, Duc de Levis (1759–1760)—were as good as his choices to head his armies in Europe were largely disappointing.

Though the French generals did not have to squabble with an intendant—since the forces were deemed too small to need one—they did have to bow to the governor-general. Each general had his own conflicts with Governor Pierre de Rigaud de Vaudreuil, who had no significant military experience but remained a fervent armchair strategist nonetheless. Vaudreuil, after consultation with the general and his staff, drew up the year's campaign plans and sent a stream of orders to his field commanders. As if having an amateur Canadian dictating to professionals was not irritating enough to the proud French, the command structure was further skewed by the different ministries charged with administering the colony. The Marine Ministry was in charge of New France and its governor-general, while the War Ministry controlled the army and marine forces in the field. The marine and war ministers tended to bicker just as badly as the governor and general, or the marines and soldiers.

Marine companies first arrived in New France in 1683 and were dispersed to guard forts and towns. Each company then ideally numbered fifty troops and four officers; they were uniformed in light-grey leggings and coats with blue facings, cuffs, and knee breeches. Over time Canadians composed nearly all the marine officers and troops alike. By 1754 ninety marine companies protected New France, of which thirty were in Canada, twenty-four on Isle Royale, and thirty-six in Louisiana. The war brought changes to the marines. A March 14, 1756, decree raised company strength to sixty-five men. On March 15,

1757, Versailles dispatched ten more marine companies to Canada. In July 1757, ten companies were formed into the first marine battalion; a second battalion of eight companies was formed in 1760. Those forty companies posted to Canada were reinforced during the war by several Louisiana companies, who served mostly at Fort Duquesne. Unfortunately, the marines tended to be poorly armed because they were supplied with muskets rejected from the royal arsenals.[32]

The marines were excellent light infantrymen and experts in wilderness warfare and survival—matched in the British army only by the American rangers. However, like the rangers, the marine tradition of independence, initiative, and victory sometimes led to a relaxed and even disdainful attitude to military protocol and authority. In 1751, Governor Duquesne imposed strict discipline and drill on the marines, which he hoped would transform those frontiersmen into professional soldiers. Those hopes apparently went unrealized. Montcalm found the marines "a troop knowing neither discipline nor subordination. Within six months I would make grenadiers of them, and now I would carefully abstain from placing as much dependence on them as the unfortunate M. de Dieskau did, by having given too much ear to the confident talk of Canadians."[33] The French officers ascribed the discipline problem as arising from the marine officers' tendency to remain aloof from their men: "Canadian officers, though courageous, knew hardly anything of their profession. . . . They hardly knew their own troops, who were always billeted with the habitants. Even if they were together in their postings, they all thought of their own petty interests, which created conflicts between officers & soldiers. Isolation & their limited means for enforcing discipline rendered the latter insubordinate. Often they were not in the wrong."[34]

The best-trained Canadian soldiers were gunners. As early as 1698 an artillery school was established at Quebec to which each marine company sent one man, who eventually returned to his unit. In 1750 a special cannonier-bombardier company was formed in Quebec, followed by another in 1757. They were uniformed in blue coats with red cuffs, facings, and breeches. Armed with muskets, they could also serve as grenadiers. The artillery commander during the war was Captain François Marc Antoine Le Mercier.

During the war Versailles sent twelve battalions of army troops to New France. The first battalions of six regiments arrived in May 1755— La Reine, Guyenne, Bearn, and Languedoc at Quebec, and the Bourgogne and Artois at Louisbourg. In 1756, the second battalions of the

Royal Rousillon and La Sarre regiments reached Quebec. The Berry Regiment's second and third battalions set foot in Quebec in 1757. The first battalions from the Volontaires Etrangers and Cambis regiments reinforced Louisbourg in 1758.

A French battalion had a grenadier company of 45 men and twelve fusilier companies of 40 men each, for 525 altogether. Volunteer or piquet companies were often raised from the ranks for special missions. A warrant issued by Montcalm on February 25, 1757, allocated an extra 10 men to each company, but none of the battalions ever filled that quota. Though man for man the soldiers may not have been as tough as the marines, they were much better disciplined and paid twice as much. That, and their fondness for Canadian women, provoked animosities between French soldiers and marines as contentious as those afflicting British and American troops.

The French battalions at Fort Carillon boasted nearly a century of heritage and combat experience over their British opponents. The 24th La Reine (1634), 34th La Sarre (1651), the 37th Royal Roussillon (1657), 53rd Languedoc (1672), Guyenne (1684), 71st Berry (1684), and 72nd Bearn (1684) fought in every war that engulfed France after their respective foundations. Although all those regiments wore the grey-white uniforms, the facings of the La Reine, Guyenne, Berry, and Bearn were red, and those of the La Sarre, Royal Roussillon, and Languedoc were blue.[35]

Then there was the militia (*milice*), composed of all able-bodied men from sixteen to sixty years old, except nobles (*seigneurs*) and members of religious orders. Militia companies were organized by parishes; each parish had at least one and some several companies, depending on its population. By 1758 over 15,000 men were on the militia rolls. Though Canadian militia were all as disorderly and unready for war as American militia, Montcalm tried to use "them with good effect, though not in places exposed to the enemy's fire. They know neither discipline nor subordination, and think themselves in all respects the first nation on earth."[36]

Theoretically, France was governed by an absolute, divine monarch who decided all. In reality Louis XV's powers were nearly as restricted as those of George II. The king might have had the final formal word, but his surrounding official and unofficial advisors tugged him in different directions. Among these none was more influential than his mistress, Jeane-Antoinette d'Etoiles, Marquise de Pompadour. She could sweet-talk Louis into reshuffling his state council and even override its decisions. Ministries of war, foreign affairs, marine (colonial affairs and the navy), and treasury administered France;

each minister intrigued to push his own interests at the expense of rivals. Still other forces crimped Louis XV's power. The thirteen regional parlements or courts wrangled with him over religious and taxation issues. Louis XV was locked up in a courtly etiquette that demanded his display before the nobles from his morning rise to his nightly rest. In between, the king's courtiers besieged him with demands for favors and often none-too-subtle mockery.

But the greatest limit on the king's power was France itself. Economically and militarily France could not protect the vast empire it had acquired over the centuries at such an endlessly expensive cost. Most French manufacturers, entrepreneurs, and naval commanders simply could not compete against their British rivals. British companies seized market shares from the French during peace and ravaged French shipping during war. Against this combination of commercial and naval might Louis XV and his ministers were nearly helpless.

France's problems were exacerbated in the wilderness empire on the opposite side of the Atlantic.[37] New France might appear to have enjoyed an administrative advantage over the fourteen squabbling American colonies, each with its assertive elected legislature, tax-hating populace, and weak governor. A governor-general ruled New France, with powers over defense, justice, and most decisions; an intendant served as his prime minister and took care of daily administrative problems. No legislature or independent court existed to challenge his rule.

Unfortunately, those powers tended to corrupt those who held them. New France's administration was one massive kleptocracy in which each official took a cut proportionate to his rank. Officials fattened their incomes not just from bribes gleaned from every transaction, but from goods received from false invoices, salaries from false names on muster or administrative rolls, or gifts from false numbers at Indian councils. François Bigot, the intendant since 1748, was the kingpin of the corruption machine, or "Great Society" as it was called. The biggest money-maker was to overcharge the king for goods and services. Bigot's front company at Bordeaux, Gradis et Fils, would sell him goods duty-free, which he in turn resold to the king at bloated prices. From 1756 to 1758 alone, Bigot and his machine billed Versailles for 23 million livres worth of goods that cost only 11 million livres, and this at a time when New France teetered at the brink of starvation, its soldiers lacked enough munitions and provisions, and the Indians complained angrily over the miserly gifts received from the "Great Father."[38]

The corruption appalled the French officers serving in New France, although surely they were acquainted with similar practices reigning at Versailles. Their outrage was provoked not only because the thievery was more obvious in New France, but because it clearly debilitated the war effort. The deputy commissary general, Captain Jean Baptiste Doreil, bluntly asserted that the "ineptness, intrigue, lies, and cupidity will in a short time destroy this Colony, which costs the King so dearly."[39] Montcalm castigated the Canadian officials who "were all hastening to make their fortunes before the loss of the colony; which many perhaps desire as a veil to their conduct. . . . I have often spoken of these expenditures to M. de Vaudreuil and M. Bigot; and each throws the blame on the other."[40]

Corruption worsened a myriad of other problems plaguing New France. A century and a half after its establishment, New France had a population of only seventy thousand people to exploit that vast territory from the Appalachians to the northern Rockies and the Gulf of Mexico to Hudson Bay. New France as a whole was a perennial drain on the kingdom, by 1753 owing 3,495,675 livres to Versailles and other creditors. The source was a perpetual trade deficit with France. In 1753, for example, New France exported 1,719,683 livres worth of goods and received 5,202,461 livres worth of imports, for a deficit of 3,482,778 livres. Only fish consistently made a profit. Nearly all other endeavors, including the fur trade, usually lost money. Smuggling to the American and Caribbean colonies alleviated some of the shortages experienced by nearly everyone in New France. In such a restricted, subsidy-dependent economy, prices were three times or more those in France. Except for the wealthy elite, most people lived hand to mouth. New France's society and economy was a miniature version of those in France.[41]

INDIAN ALLIES

The fulcrum of power for the French and British empires was supplied by the native inhabitants of North America. Each tribe was a rope in a continental tug-of-war between the two empires. Depending on circumstances, the French and British pulled at the village leaders and followers either gently with presents, harshly with threats, or some mix of the two. For a century and a half the French had mastered the art of thriving in a wilderness in which the native peoples vastly outnumbered them.

To gain furs and converts the French had to understand Indian tongues, customs, and the power balance within and among the tribes. The French empire in North America rested on the ability of its officers, traders, and priests to make the tribes dependent on manufactured goods and to play them off against one another. When war broke out in 1754, most Indian tribes sided either enthusiastically or reluctantly with the "Great Father," the French.

Whereas the French trod lightly across the land, the British trampled it. An Iroquois chief captured that difference at a 1755 council: "Brethren, are you ignorant of the difference between our Father [the French] and the English? Go and see the forts our father has created, and you will see that the land beneath their walls is still hunting ground, having fixed himself in those places we frequent only to supply our wants; whilst the English, on the contrary, no sooner get possession of a country than the game is forced to leave; the trees fall down before them, the earth becomes bare."[42] British diplomacy was further skewed by the tendency of each colony to pursue its own interests with the Indians. Diplomats tended to denounce their rivals from other colonies along with the French. The Indians, not surprisingly, tended to distrust all the competing colonial agents and their abundant promises.

The French, however, did not have a monopoly over Indian loyalties. Every tribe was split among pro-French, pro-British, and neutral factions, whose respective numbers and powers varied considerably with the fortunes of war. No tribe was more divided than the Iroquois, whose six nations stretched across central New York State from the Mohawk valley to the Genesee River. The eastern bands, especially the Mohawk, leaned toward the British while the western bands, especially the Seneca, favored the French.

Both the British and French shared a powerful upper hand over the Indians, who had long ago become dependent on them for gunpowder, lead, and, to a lesser extent, all other trade goods. But here the British had one advantage: their trade goods were less expensive, better made, and more abundant. French victories during the war's early years nullified that British advantage. But later, as the British blockade bit more harshly into the supply ships sailing to Canada, the French gifts grew ever more stingy. As the war swung against France in 1758, increasing numbers of warriors stayed home while others made their way into the British camp. This would be evident during that year's Fort Carillon campaign, where the British actually fielded more Indians than the French.

Indian diplomacy involved days of long, eloquent speeches combined with generous gifts to "cover the dead" and convince the skeptics that the supplicant was truly a "Great Father" worthy of being followed. Wampum strings, or multistranded belts of purple and white beads made from quahog or whelk clamshells, played an important role in diplomacy. The more elaborate the belt, the greater the diplomatic impact because of the scarcity and thus value of each bead, especially the purple ones. The envoy would present the belt with a plea for war or peace. Depending on the emotions of the moment, the belt might be graciously received, disdainfully spurned, or even ground under the heel of an enraged chief.

Indians went to war not as tribes but as individuals. Even when a council of chiefs reached a consensus for alliance, each man of that tribe was free to do as he pleased. War leaders might be nominated by the chiefs or simply declare their intentions to lead any "brothers" who might join them. Even if a sizable number took to the war path, those allies could be a double-edged sword. Once in the field the French and British often found themselves dependent on their Indians, not just as guides and warriors but even as strategists and tacticians. Many a frustrated frontier leader echoed Captain Louis Antoine Bougainville's resigned lament that the Indians "determine the route, the halts, the scouts, and the speed to make, and in this sort of warfare it is necessary to adjust to their ways."[43]

Indians were also at best fickle allies. Their bloodlust could be satiated by victory or soured by defeat, and either way could set them packing for home. Dreams, too, might spur them to immediate action or be interpreted as a bad omen of a pending disaster that must be avoided at all costs. Yet when Indian warriors sprung an ambush they could be terribly fierce:

> At the very instant they surprise the enemy, they fire & very rarely fail to shoot their men down. They immediately rush forward, axe in hand, throw themselves on their adversary & . . . give him an axe blow to the head. If he flees, they throw it at him so that it sticks in his back, at which they are very skilled. As soon as the man is felled, they run up to him, thrust their knee in between his shoulder blades, seize a tuft of his hair in one hand &, with their knife in the other, cut around the skin of the head & pull the whole piece away. . . . Then, brandishing the scalp, they utter a whoop which they call the "death whoop." When fighting, they utter the most frightful yells they can manage, in order to give themselves courage & to intimidate the enemy. If they are not under pressure & the victory

has cost them lives, they disembowel [the dead enemy] and smear the blood over themselves. Although they find these atrocities repugnant, they nonetheless commit them in order to steel themselves to the slaughter & induce themselves in a kind of rage.[44]

For prisoners the horrors had only just begun. Bound tightly they were hustled away toward the nearest friendly fort or village. Tomahawks bashed in the skulls of those who faltered. If the Indians had suffered dead in the battle, they might torture one or more of the prisoners when they felt they were safely beyond pursuit. Occasionally a captive might even be butchered and eaten if the party had exhausted its provisions, although most cannibalism served religious rather than nutritional needs. At a fort they might replenish their supplies by selling some prisoners to the commander, if he were willing to buy. Otherwise the prisoners were dragged on to distant villages. A runner sent ahead informed the inhabitants that the party was near and the fate of its members. Armed with clubs, the villagers would make two parallel lines between which the prisoners were forced to run. Most barely survived that gauntlet of blows; the exhausted stumbled and were beaten to death. The survivors were dragged into the council lodge. Those families who had suffered a death could choose one among the prisoners; they could then either assuage their grief by torturing that victim to death or adopt him to replace the lost beloved.

Few French or British lost much sleep over paying for or directly participating in such gruesome warfare. Bougainville vividly captured the moral dilemma: "The cruelties and the insolence of these barbarians is horrible, their souls are black as pitch. It is an abominable way to make war; the retaliation is frightening and the air one breathes here is contagious of making one accustomed to callousness. . . . What a scourge! Humanity shudders at being obliged to make use of such monsters. But without them the match would be too much against us."[45]

British and French agents were as busy as ever in 1758 trying to seduce each tribe to its side. But the Indians had wearied from four years of death from battle and disease, and the dearth of goods. Most stayed home with the belief that it was better for the white men to destroy each other. The Fort Carillon campaign would be the only wilderness struggle during the war in which the Indians played no significant role.

CHAPTER 3

Grand Strategies and Commanders

I am convinced of the extent and great weight of this command.
—Abercromby

For myself, I am tired of working miracles and of not being listened to.
I shall demand my recall at the end of the campaign.
—Montcalm

GRAND STRATEGY

The 1758 Fort Carillon campaign reflected French and British grand strategies, which in turn were rooted in the asymmetrical power of those nations. When the war opened in 1754, France had 180,000 men under arms, six times more than the 30,000 Britain possessed. During the subsequent conflict, France and Britain boosted those numbers to 330,000 and 140,000, respectively. Though only a fraction of those huge forces would be sent to North America, the British committed far more than the French: 30,000 to 5,000. The primary reason for that disparity lay in the British navy. In 1754, the British fleet had more than twice as many warships as the French, 130 to 57. Throughout the war, while the British fleet steadily expanded, the French fleet just as steadily eroded from defeats on the high seas and blockades of their home waters. With British warships sailing each spring to blockade the St. Lawrence, the French dared not send more than enough troops and supplies across that ocean gauntlet to keep Canada alive.

Geography and history explain the differences over power and strategy. As an island kingdom, Britain could afford to maintain a small army as long as its fleet remained larger than that of any rival. That mix

57

of arms had worked well for seven centuries: no successful invasion of Britain had taken place since 1066. Britain's reliance on sea power and aversion to large standing armies was reinforced a century earlier, from 1642 to 1660, when civil war then Cromwell's dictatorship ravaged the country. In contrast, France faced potential enemies along its long eastern frontier from the English Channel to the Mediterranean Sea, and in the southwest across the Pyrenees Mountains. A large standing army was thus essential for French security. Different manpower pools further contributed to each kingdom's mix of land and sea forces: the population of France in 1755 was twenty million, Britain's a mere six million.[1]

The fate of nations often depends on more than traditional policies rooted in geography and history. Leadership is often the crucial element. Military genius is a rare and fleeting phenomenon. None of the men whom Whitehall and Versailles dispatched to command the armies in their respective new world empires will ever be ranked among the Alexanders and Napoleons of history. As judged by the results of their campaigns, their talents varied, with the French quite competent and most of the British less so. But all the generals on either side were held back by their rancorous squabbles with colonial governors. Deficiencies and constraints on leadership would be especially evident in 1758.

BRITISH STRATEGY

British strategy traditionally centered on maintaining a fleet large enough to shield the nation from invasion and, as it developed its empire, to protect its colonies in North America, the Caribbean, and India. In North America, despite the frequent wars with France before 1756, Whitehall mostly defended its own colonies rather than trying to conquer those of France. The only exception was grabbing Nova Scotia as part of its spoils in the 1713 Treaty of Utrecht, which ended the War of the Spanish Succession. In Europe, the goal was to sidestep getting sucked down into the quagmire of a continental war. That was best done by playing off the great powers against one another, then backing the weaker coalition against the stronger and propping it up with gold rather than troops. Only one spot on the continent was deemed worth fighting for: the low countries of Holland and Flanders. These were deemed the most likely jump off for an invasion of Britain after France's northern ports. When France or another great power threatened to overrun that region, Britain usually sent in an army. That parsimonious strategy, however, was complicated with the inauguration of the Hanoverian dynasty in 1714. From then on, Kings George I (1714–1727) and George II (1727–1760) pressured the cabinet to commit British troops against any threat to their ancestral home.

After coming to power in December 1756, Prime Minister William Pitt revolutionized British strategy from containing to conquering the French imperial threat.[2] To that end he sought to bog France down in an unwinnable war in Europe while Britain's armies, fleets, and privateers systematically picked off ever more of Versailles' ill-defended colonies, trade, and ships. He would soon boost the annual subsidies to Prussia's Frederick II and other German allies to two million pounds, raise and deploy enough troops to recapture northern Germany and Hanover, and mount large-scale raids on the French coast. Those efforts helped distract Versailles from what the British were doing in distant seas and lands, especially North America.

For better or worse, Pitt's North American strategy at first continued that of his predecessors. Instead of concentrating his forces against Canada's heartland in the St. Lawrence valley, he chose to strike at several far-flung targets on the empire's periphery. In 1758, three armies would be mustered and marched or sailed against Forts Carillon, Louisbourg, and Duquesne. Major General James Abercromby would lead the largest army, 6,500 regulars and 20,000 provincials, against Fort Carillon. Major General Jeffrey Amherst was given the Louisbourg mission, with 14,000 regulars and 600 rangers. Finally, Brigadier General John Forbes would command 2,500 regulars and 5,000 provincials against Duquesne. In all, Pitt intended to hurl nearly 50,000 troops against the French that year.[3]

Pitt's strategy could be criticized for several reasons. Victory might have been swifter and more certain had British power been concentrated in an attack on Canada's heartland rather than its periphery. The armada amassed against Louisbourg could have sailed against Quebec instead. Once the St. Lawrence River was firmly blocked, the rest of Canada would suffocate. Instead, the campaigns against Louisbourg, Carillon, and Duquesne simply diverted resources from that crucial objective. Similarly, Pitt's hope for 25,000 provincial troops was too ambitious. The colonial assemblies would strain to provide only about half that amount. Of those that were raised, most would do little or no fighting; all would consume enormous amounts of expensive supplies. A better use of provincials would have involved mustering just enough to

protect supply lines and haul provisions; any more than that weakened
rather than strengthened the war effort.[4]

Further, Pitt did not just need a strategy, he needed a competent
commander in chief to realize it. After four years of defeats, Whitehall
despaired of finding the right man. In 1755, the first general sent over,
Edward Braddock, blundered into a battle on the Monongahela River,
which cost him his life and devastated a British army. His replacement
in 1756, Massachusetts governor William Shirley, was not only an amateur but was whispered to be corrupt as well. He was recalled before he
could prove himself to his backers or detractors. James Campbell, the
Earl of Loudoun, was a professional soldier who spent 1757 avoiding
any offensive against the French. By the end of 1757, the French had defeated nearly every attack on their imperial frontier; the British had
captured only the Chignecto Isthmus in Nova Scotia.

ABERCROMBY

Pitt's choice of James Abercromby made much more political than military sense. Then fifty-two years old, James Abercromby had so far displayed a thoroughly undistinguished career. He was born in 1706 to a
wealthy family in Glassaugh, Scotland, during an age when enough
money could take the most undeserving to the heights of military
power. His career began at the tender age of eleven, when his father
bought him an ensign's rank with the 25th Foot. He eagerly purchased
a captainship that opened with the 1st Royal Scots Regiment in 1737
and then a major's rank in 1742. During the War of Austrian Succession
he first served as commissary of musters on Lieutenant General St.
Clair's staff in Flanders. On April 16, 1746, he was promoted to lieutenant colonel. He spent little time with his regiment that year. St. Clair
tapped him to serve as quartermaster general in the failed expedition to
take Port l'Orient in Brittany. In April 1747 he was wounded in his first
and only battle until then, a sortie from Hulst in the Netherlands which
was besieged by the French. He was promoted to colonel on December
18, 1755, and major general on January 31, 1756, when he was sent to
America to serve as second to Lord Loudoun. He commanded the second brigade in that year's aborted expedition against Louisbourg.
When Loudoun's inertia proved too much for Pitt's ambitions, Abercromby stood waiting in the wings.

How did someone with such a lackluster career rise so far so fast in the British army? The fortuitous mingling of political connections and wealth explains the phenomenon. The Abercromby family held a seat in parliament which the general himself occupied for a few of his younger years. More importantly, the Abercrombys firmly backed both the Newcastle and Cumberland factions, which were so powerful that Pitt himself had to bow before them. Historians differ over which politician or faction was more important. Francis Parkman asserts that Pitt "recalled Loudoun, for whom he had a fierce contempt; but there were influences which he could not disregard, and Major General Abercromby, who was . . . an indifferent soldier, though a veteran in years, was allowed to succeed him."[5] Stanley Pargellis believes that Newcastle, with whom Pitt jointly governed at this time, was more influential in elevating Abercromby: the "chief claim to consideration . . . was Newcastle's political indebtedness" to Abercromby.[6] L. B. Namier is among those who argue that Newcastle's powers may have been spent by this time; William Augustus, the Duke of Cumberland—the army commander and heir to the throne—may have been just as important.[7] And then there was King George II, whose insistence that seniority was sacrosanct would make the choice of Abercromby inevitable.[8]

Character and leadership are entwined. Lawrence Gipson's portrait of Abercromby offers several insights, describing him as a: "kindly, tactful man, he was far removed from the tough, hard-bitten military type; he was not in the most robust health . . . he had begun to feel the weight of these [years] prematurely. Nor was he a born fighter: He lacked the spirit, the quick wit to size up situations instantaneously and to act decisively to take advantage of any opening presented by the enemy, and he also wanted the aggressiveness that characterizes without exception any great military leader."[9]

A perceptive French observer described Abercromby as "a man of more courage than resolution, more of sense than of dash or of objectives; age has lessened in him the fire necessary for the execution of great undertakings. He reflects sufficiently, operates slowly and with too much precaution. He expresses himself with difficulty, talks little, writes better than he speaks."[10] Abercromby did not lack intelligence. He wrote clearly about the complexities of his office. He immersed himself in details and managed them quite well. Nor was he immune to advice, especially from his close friend, Massachusetts governor Thomas Pownall. Abercromby profusely thanked Pownall "for the many kindly hints & suggestions [he had] been so good as to furnish . . . I shall not fail," Abercromby wrote, "to put them into practice."[11] Loudoun captured the essence of the man who would replace him: "Abercromby is a good officer, and a very good second man anywhere, whatever he is employed in."[12] The Duke of Cumberland, who commanded all British land forces and was the king's second son, agreed: "The character you give Abercromby is that which I always had of him."[13] Historian Stanley Pargellis was also succinct: "As second in command, Abercromby proved himself an obedient and trustworthy officer. . . . He incurred no one's dislike; he won no one's admiration."[14] It is a pity that Abercromby did not stay the "second man." John Shy writes that he embarked on a study of the 1758 campaign "in the hope that, in the course of my research, I would find evidence that Major General James Abercromby was really a very good army commander. Unfortunately, he was not."[15]

Any fair-minded investigation cannot help but reach the same conclusion. Indeed, Abercromby would prove to be murderously unfit for an independent command. In light of his decisions in the Carillon campaign, it is jarring to read his assertion "that too much attention cannot be given to whatever concerns the health of the troops," and that to that end he was "ever studious to inform [himself] . . . of whatever they may want or stand in need of, for their preservation."[16] In retrospect, he was mindful of everything, perhaps, except the harm of being ordered into a slaughtering field.

But no one could have predicted that. If Abercromby was clearly no military genius, why should anyone have questioned his competence? He had ably served on the staff of St. Clair and Loudoun during campaigns which failed from a lack of initiative rather than strategic or tactical blunders. It was hoped that Abercromby would muster the necessary drive to fulfill his mission. Only time would tell whether the trust in him was justified.

On December 30, 1757, George II issued "our trusty and well beloved" Major General James Abercromby his commission to be commander in chief of His Majesty's forces in North America. The king's instructions were quite specific. Abercromby was empowered to order each governor to provide a certain number of troops, transports, supplies, and Indian gifts. Indeed he was to make clear to the governors that "the execution of our designs may not be retarded by any slowness of the levies to be made in their respective provinces." Likewise Abercromby should coordinate his policies with the northern and southern

Indian superintendents, and "cultivate the best harmony and friendship ... with the chiefs of the Indian tribes." He was also ordered "to cultivate a good understanding and correspondence with" the naval squadron commander in North American waters, especially to suppress the smuggling trade between the Americans and French. He could issue temporary commissions to fill officer vacancies, to be approved later by Whitehall. George II conferred upon Abercromby one more honor—he was named colonel of the 60th Royal American Regiment.[17]

In a separate letter, George II addressed the conflict in rank between regular and provincial officers. Acting on Pitt's firm advice, the king reissued a November 1754 decree that all provincial generals and colonels would rank below a regular colonel but above all other regular ranks. At the rank of lieutenant colonel and lower a provincial officer would be below, by one rank, a regular officer of the same rank. In other words, a provincial lieutenant colonel was inferior to a regular lieutenant colonel but superior to a regular major, and so on. George II also promoted Colonels Forbes, Stanwix, Howe, Whitmore, and Lawrence to the rank of brigadier general for as long as they served in North America.[18]

The prime minister supplemented the king's instructions with his own. Pitt offered Abercromby his "congratulations" and assured him of the king's "firmest reliance on your zeal and abilities." He also enclosed a circular letter he had sent to the governors in which he issued their respective provincial troop quotas for 1758.[19] To the governors of New York, Massachusetts, New Hampshire, Rhode Island, and New Jersey, Pitt justified the switch in commanders. He claimed he had "nothing more at heart than to repair the losses and disappointments of the last inactive and unhappy campaign, and [sought] by the most vigorous and extensive efforts to avert by the blessing of God on his arms, the dangers impending on North America."[20] Then came his call for 20,000 troops to join Abercromby's regulars in invading Canada by way of Lake Champlain. Provincial regiments would rendezvous at Albany or some other spot designated by the commander in chief. The ultimate objective was Montreal. The king would provide all arms, ammunition, tents, boats, and provisions, while the provinces would pay and clothe their troops. Pitt asked the governors to collect all firearms in their provinces in order to supplement those sent over from England.

Pitt left nothing to chance. Transports were needed to convey troops, ordnance, and supplies to Louisbourg. To curb intelligence leaks and gain vessels, Pitt authorized Abercromby to impose an embargo on all North American ports as soon as possible "to continue until such time as all the transport vessels with the troops, the train, the stores, and all the other requisites for the siege of Louisbourg shall be actually sailed for Halifax."[21] Pitt elaborated or repeated his instructions in letters on January 9, 11, and 27.

But most importantly, Pitt made the object of Abercromby's campaign crystal clear to the general: "an invasion of Canada, by the way of Crown Point [Fort St. Frederic], in order to proceed, if practicable, to an attempt on either Montreal or Quebec, or both."[22] Amherst, in turn, was expected to sail on to Quebec, if possible, after taking Louisbourg. Any surviving French forces would be trapped and crushed between the armies of Abercromby and Amherst.

On March 4, the HMS *Squirrel* dropped anchor at a New York wharf bearing the orders of George II and Pitt to Abercromby. They reached the general's headquarters at Albany on March 7. The promotion at once gratified and humbled Abercromby. To Pitt, he declared that had he had "nothing so much at heart, as to comply herewith to the utmost of my power and abilities." He asked Pitt to "express my sentiments of gratitude to the King for so distinguishing a mark of His Royal favor and confidence in me, and to assure my Master, that altho I do not think my self equal to so important & extensive a command, yet no endeavour shall be wanting on my side to convince His Majesty of my zeal for the service."[23]

Two days after receiving his orders, Abercromby left General Howe in command and set forth for New York. Heavy snows delayed his carriage; he arrived at noon on March 13. He met that day with Governor DeLancey to plot mobilization and strategy. So far he had been prompt in reporting to his assignment. Yet he seems to have viewed his new duties with resignation rather than enthusiasm. To his confidant Governor Pownall, he requested "the continuance of your friendship & assistance in this extensive & difficult command." A few days later he wrote that "it gave me no less concern, than it occasioned surprise in me, as I am convinced of the extent and great weight of this command."[24]

As for the man Abercromby was slated to replace, Lord Loudoun, he was in Boston planning that year's campaigns when Pitt's terse orders arrived on the 10th, relieving him of command: "the King has judged proper that your Lordship should return to England."[25] Very mixed feelings must have beset Loudoun as he wrote to Abercromby to discuss the transfer of power. The letter was void of any sentiment or even congratulations. As ordered by Pitt, he would soon depart for New York to deliver to his successor all of his correspondence, instructions, and other documents of his headquarters. He then wrote of some minor issues, including pay for carpenters sent to Albany, the transfer of five companies of 60th Royal Americans and Lieutenant Colonel Henry Bouquet to New York, and the mustering of a Cherokee war party against the hostile Shawnee, Delaware, and Mingo Indians striking the Virginia and Pennsylvania frontiers.[26]

Pitt had optimistically called for the campaign to begin on May 1. For reasons not entirely his own, Abercromby would not actually get his offensive underway until two months later.

HOWE AND JOHNSON

Abercromby would prove his worth as an administrator, but two other leaders were essential for implementing the 1758 Lake George campaign. One was Lord George Augustus, Viscount Howe. Pitt would have preferred to appoint a much more obviously competent officer, such as Howe, to command His Majesty's forces in North America. But he dared not yet challenge the army's rigid seniority system and the political factions in Whitehall and parliament. Acting on continual reports of Howe's vigorous leadership, Pitt named him brigadier general in North America on December 29, 1757. Howe was elevated with the largely unspoken understanding that his dynamism and bravery would allow him to rule the army under Abercromby's benevolent reign.

Howe was born in Ireland around 1724 or 1725, making him either thirty-three or thirty-four in 1758. His intelligence and connections got him an excellent education at Westchester and Eton. He became an ensign in 1745 in the 1st Foot Guards, the year Prince Charles led the Stuart revolt. His regiment had just departed from London, when word arrived that Cumberland had crushed Charles at Culloden. In 1747, Cumberland picked him as one of his aides for his campaign in Flanders; the British defeats at Laufeldt and Lettingen were Howe's baptisms by fire. He learned from the victorious French commander Marechal Maurice de Saxe the importance of speed, surprise, marches around the enemy flank, and the massing of troops in attack against the vital points of the enemy's line. Howe shared his lessons with all who would listen. His views found an influential audience as he enjoyed the patronage of some of Britain's most powerful leaders, including Cumberland and Newcastle.

In an army where officers tended to believe that discipline in the ranks depended on fear of the lash, Howe was a soldier's officer, one who never let his nobility prevent him from squatting around smoky fires, breaking bread and cracking jokes with his men. He tirelessly saw to his troops' comforts before his own, slipped away on patrol with the rangers, and had a cheery word for all. His troops adored him "for his robust Soldier-like Constitution, his bold, enterprising Spirit, and every other military accomplishment; with how much Care he has been forming his regular Troops to the Method of Bush-fighting all Season, so that he has now, it is said, made them as dexterous at it almost as the Rangers. . . . His Soldiers love and fear him, and are willing to comply with his Commands, because he first sets them an Example."[27]

Despite his popularity and patrols, Howe had not yet witnessed more than glimpses of North American warfare. He first set foot in the continent at Halifax in 1757 as lieutenant colonel of the recently formed 60th Royal Americans, which was to take part in that year's aborted Louisbourg campaign. On September 28, 1757, he received command of the 55th.

A bullet would cut Howe's life short before battle tested his tactical skills. We will never know how the Fort Carillon campaign would have turned out had he lived a week longer. What is certain is that George Howe was a brilliant and courageous leader, an English version of the American Robert Rogers.

Yet another exceptional leader was Sir William Johnson, the Indian superintendent for the northern colonies.[28] Irish-born Johnson came to New York in 1738 to manage his uncle Peter Warren's tenants in the lower Mohawk River valley. His business and diplomatic skills made him popular not just with the tenants but with the neighboring Mohawks as well. He eventually became a powerful land owner. New York named him a militia colonel and Indian agent. The Mohawks adopted him as Warraghiyagey, "The Doer of Great Things." On April 14, 1755, Braddock appointed him Indian superintendent and commander of the expedition to take Fort St. Frederic on Lake Champlain. Johnson's campaign got no further than the south shore of Lake George where his provincial troops defeated an attack by Major General Jean-Armand, Baron de Dieskau, and his French, Canadian, and Indian force. Johnson himself caught a musket ball in his thigh and resigned his command to concentrate on Indian affairs.

The endless duties and frustrations of serving as Indian superintendent were stressful enough for a healthy man. Johnson was plagued by severe and at times debilitating chronic illnesses. In late 1757 he was confined to bed for seven straight weeks with agony so horrendous that he could not even turn over. Even after he was able to rise in December, a pain gnawed at his side.[29] To lighten his burden Johnson tried to shed his duty as militia colonel, arguing to Governor James DeLancey that "I have been so much harassed these three years past & now again so soon after my late & severe illness that it has impaired my health to that degree that I doubt I shall never be able to endure much fatigue. Therefore I hope you will appoint another to the command of the regiment who has better health & abilities."[30] DeLancey rejected the request. Johnson recovered. Within four months he was again in the field at the head of four hundred warriors. Rallying that number was no easy task.

While the Canadian Indians were said to be mustering for the French, rumor had it that the Iroquois were debating whether to swing behind the British. They would hold a council at Onondaga in the spring to decide the matter. In late December William Johnson was asked to attend; a formal invitation would arrive. Johnson reasoned that the Iroquois would not have invited him if a strong consensus for joining the British did not already exist.[31]

Johnson promised Abercromby he would enlist warriors for that summer's offensive but would not know how many until the Onondaga council was concluded. If the council agreed to alliance with British, Johnson would expect to field between 400 and 500 Indians. Neutrality would yield around 300. But if the Iroquois chose to join France, the British could expect no more than a handful.[32]

On April 26, 1758, the Oneida chiefs Canaghquayeson and Nicolas strode into Fort Johnson, the home of William Johnson, in the lower Mohawk valley, with wampum belts in hand. The Iroquois council at Onondaga would meet in twelve days and Johnson was invited to appear as the Mohawk sachem Warraghiyagey. Johnson was uncharacteristically optimistic about the council, believing that the Iroquois would announce their alliance with Britain. To tip the balance in Britain's favor and rally as many Indians as possible, he asked Abercromby to supply him an appropriate amount of Indian gifts.[33]

Johnson never made it to the council. A raid by Oswegatchie Iroquois against German Flats in the lower Mohawk valley killed thirty-two settlers and closed the road to Onondaga. Johnson mustered the local militia and Howe marched with the 46th from Schenectady. But the Indians were long gone by the time the troops arrived at the smoldering ruins and bloated, mutilated corpses.

Johnson soon received word that the Onondaga council had broken up inconclusively. Another council would be held a month or so later to redebate the issue. Nonetheless, Johnson dispatched runners with belts to each tribe, calling on them to send him warriors. Together they would march against the French. Johnson would not have any idea how many Indians would accompany him to Abercromby's camp until after the campaign actually embarked.[34]

FRENCH STRATEGY

France's strategy was the reverse of Britain's. Versailles struggled to hold the line in North America and win in Europe. From spring 1754 to summer 1758, that strategy was very successful. French forces in North America staved off every British thrust. In Europe, French armies captured Minorca and Hanover in 1756; they would hold the former but lose the second. While Versailles could continue to send large armies against Hanover, there was little more that could be done for North America given the massed sails and guns of British sea power. As the British naval blockade tightened, Versailles reasoned that to send more troops to North America might well mean to lose more. New France would have to fend for itself.

Most French ministers shared the War Ministry's January 1758 assessment that New France's ability to survive another year was bleak. That year the British would likely mass ten times more troops in North America than the French would. At best, the French could muster no more than thirty-four hundred regulars, twelve hundred marines, and six thousand militia. In the entire colony, there were only two trained engineers and eighty-six gunners. All but a handful of Indians had deserted from the French due to a lack of presents and deaths from battle and smallpox. No frontier fort was thought capable of fending off a siege for more than three weeks. Provisions and munitions were critically low.

Faced with these realities, Versailles was forced to wrestle with an ever more basic question: Was Canada worth saving? The War Ministry acknowledged that many people believed "that the preservation of Canada is of little importance to France. Some allege that it costs the King a great deal, and that it will eventually cost more; that it yields nothing, or next to nothing."[35] The report goes on to present the argument that the wealth poured into Canada was diverted from that which could have been used to develop France itself, and that the colony was so vulnerable that the English would eventually take it. Versailles would confine itself to treating New France "as a desperate disease is treated, in which the sick man is supported by cordials until he either sinks or a crisis saves him; that is to say, to send thither only what is absolutely necessary so as to be able to try and make a defense."[36]

Yet reasons were cited for holding Canada. France had a moral duty to prevent Canada from falling into the hands of Protestant heretics. Canada's lands were vast and its riches largely unknown; someday it could reap enormous wealth for France. Not all of Canada's enterprises lost money; its fisheries annually produced huge wealth for France that would be lost if the colony were lost. Even if Canada always cost more than the wealth it created, it forced the English to divert enormous wealth to defend their North American colonies as well. If the English took Canada, they could then sail on to capture Louisiana and the Caribbean sugar islands, and from there eventually seize Spain's Mexico.

After mulling over the issue, the War Ministry's staff threw up its hands. The king should decide New France's fate. Louis XV ordered his ministers to continue to defend his North American empire. The War Ministry then addressed the question of whether Canada could be defended or even reinforced. Here again, the ministers offered alternatives. The British naval blockade made the problem of delivering supplies, which were essential to Canada's survival, vexing: "To send succors in divisions is to run the risk of losing all in detail; to send them together, is to expose ourselves to a general action and to lose all at once."[37]

Finally there was the question of Canadian loyalty. It was understood that the "people of Canada must naturally be quite tired of the war." Many had perished while the remainder "have not time to increase their property or even to repair their houses; a portion of their subsistence has been wrested from them, many have been without bread for 3 months, the troops that incommode them are quartered on them." As if all that were not reason enough to oppose the war, "they are told that the English offer them freedom of religion, furnish them with goods at a cheaper rate and pay liberally for the smallest service. These ideas are spreading."[38]

In the end, Versailles chose to send just enough troops, supplies, and goods for the Indians to keep New France alive. It did resolve some small problems. It approved Montcalm's proposal to divide the militia into three ranks and assimilate the best grade into the regulars and marines. It nodded to other specific steps that Governor Vaudreuil had taken or proposed for Canada's defense. Versailles assumed that if Canada fell, Louisiana would soon follow. With British naval superiority, Louisiana was deemed indefensible. Yet French forces were empowered to retreat to Louisiana if conquest were imminent. To prevent New France from being "wholly sacked, the inhabitants dispersed or destroyed, the Colony irrevocably lost to the King," the power to surrender was given to the governor. As for strategy, Versailles left that up to the governor and general to decide.

But that decision gave rise to another problem: each man despised the other. Getting such diametrically opposed individuals to forge a common strategy was among the greater challenges facing New France. Who were these men that held Canada's fate in their hands, and what drove them apart?

Pierre de Rigaud de Vaudreuil de Cavagnial, Marquis de Vaudreuil, served as governor from June 23, 1755, until he surrendered New France on September 8, 1760. Ironically, that colony's last governor was the first actually born there. Born in 1698, and the son of a governor himself, he was named governor of Trois Rivieres in 1733, where he served until 1742; he was then transferred to Louisiana. He served as Louisiana's governor until 1753, when he was recalled to Versailles. There Louis XV tapped him to lead New France on January 1, 1755. It was a good political, if not military, choice. Vaudreuil knew little of war; his only taste of it was to lead a bloodless campaign against the Fox Indians in 1738.

His inexperience would soon become quite evident, especially to the French officers who served in Canada. The perceptive if not unbiased Louis Antoine de Bougainville pronounced Vaudreuil a mediocrity who was "limited, without talent, perhaps free from vice, but having all the faults of a petty spirit, filled with Canadian prejudices, which are of all the most foolish, jealous, glorious, wishing to take all credit to themselves. He no more confides in M. de Montcalm than in the lowest lieutenant."[39] Indeed, for three years, from 1756 to 1759, Vaudreuil lost no chance to take credit for every victory and criticize Montcalm for every setback, even though the governor never left the safety of his mansions at Montreal or Quebec for the front.

MONTCALM

In 1756, the general whom Louis XV had tapped to replace Dieskau was Louis Joseph de, Marquis de Montcalm. The king had "concluded that a better choice could not be made than of our dear and well beloved, the Marquis de Montcalm, Major-General in our armies, considering the proofs he has given us of his valor, experience, capacity, fidelity, and affection to our service in the different engagements and other commissions entrusted to his care."[40] Those were more than the king's sentiments; the flowery praise for Montcalm was largely true. At age twelve, he received his first commission, though his first battle did not come until Philipsburg in 1734, when he was twenty-two years old. Many more followed; by 1756 he had fought bravely in eleven campaigns and suffered five wounds.[41] In Canada, his officers and, for a while, Indian allies seem to have adored him. Commissary General Andre Jean Baptiste Doreil described Montcalm as having "political as well as military talent; a statesman and a man of detail, a great worker, just, . . . clear-sighted, active, and having nothing in view but the public good; in a word, a virtuous and universal man." The general seems to have adapted quickly to North American warfare, including Indian diplomacy: "He knows how to deal with Indians, to attach them to him, and to make them act according to circumstances. They know him, love him, respect and fear him."[42]

Yet Montcalm had his critics as well. An anonymous officer described him as

full of talent, but ambitious beyond measure; more brilliant in consequence of the advantages of a cultivated memory, than profound in the sciences appertaining to the art of war, the first elements of which he did not possess, that General was ill-equipped to the command of armies; he was, besides, subject to transports of passion which had produced a coolness towards him even among those whom he had obliged, and who, by circumstances, ought to have the same interests as he. I will add, that though brave, he was in no wise enterprising; he would, for example, never have attacked [Oswego], had he not been, as it were, forced thereto by the reproaches of the timidity he exhibited, made by M. de Riguad [the governor's brother], a man, it is true, of limited mind, but full of bravery and boldness and accustomed to range the woods; and he would have abandoned the siege of Fort [William Henry], at the very moment he undertook it, had he not been reassured by the firmness of the Chevalier de Levis. To this mediocrity, in the talents necessary to a military man of his rank, he united a very grave defect in a General: indiscretion. More occupied in the care of giving brilliancy to his eloquence than with the duties his position exacted, he could not prevent himself making his plans public long before they were to put in execution; and that he had a grudge against any one, was sufficient to make him unceasingly mangle the reputation of

such a person in unseemly terms, even in the presence of the domestics,
and consequently of the troops. Tis by such remarks as these, which at bottom he did not intentionally circulate, that he made M. de Vaudreuil lose
the confidence of the soldier, the farmer, and even the Indian.[43]

Conflict between men as proud as Vaudreuil and Montcalm was inevitable. Differences in temperament, experience, culture, and strategy
mixed with bloated egos to poison their relationship. The battles began
shortly after Montcalm stepped ashore in 1756 and only grew worse
with the passage of time. Under any circumstances it would have been
rankling for a veteran with three decades of experience to receive orders from someone who had never heard a shot fired in anger. But to
Montcalm, Vaudreuil's orders were not only amateurish, they were also
frequently nonsensical, contradictory, and downright insulting. Vaudreuil persisted despite Montcalm's repeated calls on him to desist.
Typical was this plea: "What need have you, Sir, after my three years
service under your orders, to prescribe to me useless or minute details
which I should blush to prescribe to the lowest captain."[44]

Another sore point was how to divvy up the few reinforcements or
supplies that reached New France. The ever-tightening British blockade
netted ever-larger portions of everything sent across the Atlantic from
France. What little that did arrive had to be apportioned among the colonists, soldiers, and Indians, and then split again within each group.
Deciding who got what was the governor's privilege. Even the slightest
whiff of favoritism sparked bitter resentments. Montcalm and his officers complained that Vaudreuil shortchanged them on replacements by
diverting too many to the marines rather than the army. The army battalions were the backbone of New France's defense, they argued, yet
were understrength and allocated a mere fraction of the troops needed
to fulfill their duty. In a diplomatically veiled complaint in July 1758,
Doreil explained to Marine Minister Perienc de Moras that "only 328 recruits have arrived; of these, the Colonial recruits have received 98. I
have embodied the other 230 into our battalions. . . . I still require about
550 men to complete them."[45]

Why would the governor deprive the army? The French officers believed that "Vaudreuil, jealous no doubt of the glory that the Marquis de
Montcalm has acquired, would, without affecting it too much, fain have
deprived him of the means of succeeding in making a good defense."[46]

Then there were the letters Vaudreuil sent to Versailles castigating
Montcalm and the other French officers. Disingenuousness was one of

Vaudreuil's more annoying calling cards. When confronted, he denied either penning or dictating those letters, thus abdicating responsibility for anything in them that might be critical of others.[47] Could he possibly believe that Montcalm and his officers, who were informed by supporters at Versailles of Vaudreuil's blistering criticism of them, would not believe that he wrote or read every report sent back to France? And if true, it would have been a bizarre admission for someone entrusted with New France's fate.

The feud threatened to undermine Canada's defense. In early 1758, Marine Minister Moras scolded both the governor and general for putting their egos before their duty to the Crown and Canada. He politely warned Montcalm that he had

> good inside intelligence on what reigns between you and M. Vaudreuil, [and] I would strongly hope that whatever that involves would be subordinated to devotion to the King. . . . It is very difficult to prevent your split feelings from not affecting operations . . . I am confident that the wisdom and righteousness of your feelings along with your brilliance with which you always reproach M. Vaudreuil will not affect the glory of the King's arms or the future of the colony. . . . I have already exhorted M. Vaudreuil to have the same feelings for you that I desire you to have for him.[48]

A cipher was enclosed with the letter to permit the uninhibited exchange between the minister and general over the intimate details of operations and administration. Moras did not explain whether he was more worried about their letters being intercepted by the spies of the British or Intendant François Bigot. Regardless, the marine minister's efforts failed to inspire a lull, let alone peace in the war between the general and governor. But their battles would soon be overshadowed by one even greater.

74

CHAPTER 4

Preparing for Campaign

*Their officers, with very few exceptions, are worse than their men. Nay some
of them (the officers) have actually deserted and shammed sick, and we were
always much longer in getting them out to their duty than their men.*
—James Abercromby on provincials

*God knows we do not wish to disparage the value of the Canadians . . . In the
woods, behind trees, no troops are comparable to the natives of this country.*
—Louis Antoine Bougainville on provincials

BRITISH LEADERSHIP

James Abercromby had his work cut out for him. Massing troops and
supplies and acquiring the means to transport them to distant fronts is
a challenge for any military commander. In North America's vast wilderness these problems would be especially difficult to surmount. Nor
were his problems merely logistical. Abercromby was also expected to
wear the hats of military strategist and diplomat. To get the soldiers,
weapons, and other items that he needed for his summer campaign he
would have to squeeze them from the governments of fourteen miserly,
cantankerous provinces. To gain the assistance of Indian allies, he
would have to constantly polish the chain of friendship with a score of
fickle, demanding Indian tribes. Having done all this, he would have to
coordinate three offensives against the enemy, and he would have to organize and lead one of those campaigns.

To accomplish this dizzying array of tasks, Abercromby had a staff
of only ten officers. Captain James Abercombie and Captain James
Cunningham served as his aides-de-camp, Captain Francis Halkette his

brigade major, Lieutenant Colonel John Bradstreet his quartermaster, John Appy both his secretary and judge advocate, Robert Leake his commissary of stores and provisions, James Pitcher his commissary of musters, Robert Webster his provost marshal, James Furnis his royal ordnance comptroller, and, most important of all, Abraham Mortier his chief accountant. Abercromby issued warrants once or twice a week to Mortier to pay off various contractors. During 1758 other officers would be temporarily posted at his headquarters, including engineer Captain Matthew Clerk, who would play a crucial role in the campaign.

When it was in his interest to do otherwise and he could get away with it, Abercromby did not adhere to every letter of his instructions. Pitt had assigned Bradstreet as deputy quartermaster to Forbes's campaign; Captain Joshua Loring would take Bradstreet's place as head of the bateaux corps in Abercromby's army. Instead Abercromby chose to retain the brilliant if mercurial Bradstreet and assigned the less accomplished John St. Clair to Forbes. Loring was detached to Amherst's campaign to help organize his transport fleet. Abercromby explained to Pitt that Loring "was not capable of commanding so large a body of bateau men as we shall have occasion for. I have again been obliged to leave this charge to . . . Bradstreet who . . . knows best how to deal with them, which is no easy task, for they are an unweildy & unruly set."[1] As for other personnel, the respective duties of Leake and Furnis extended to all British forces in North America, but Abercromby used them primarily for his own campaign.

BRITISH MOBILIZATION

Abercromby's role as commander in chief of all armies was at once eased and complicated by the reality that Pitt made many important strategic decisions for him. Most important were decisions with regards to troop disposition. In all, Pitt hoped to muster 51,142 troops for the 1758 North American campaigns. To conquer Louisbourg, Major General Jeffrey Amherst would receive 14,215 troops of thirteen regiments, along with 600 rangers. Major General John Forbes would lead 1,880 regulars in three regiments and 5,000 provincials against Fort Duquesne. Fifteen hundred troops would remain in Nova Scotia.[2]

Major General James Abercromby's army would be the largest. Originally that army was to have 9,447 regulars and 20,000 provincials, but the actual numbers fell short in both categories. The ordnance, however, did arrive as promised. The army would pack enormous heavy fire-power: 6 twenty-four pounders; 6 twelve pounders; 4 five-and-one-half-inch howitzers; 2 ten-inch mortars; 2 eight-inch mortars; and 20 four-and-two-thirds-inch mortars. Accompanying those guns would be 800 rounds of round shot and 50 rounds of tin-case shot for each twenty-four pounder; 400 rounds of round shot and 100 rounds of tin-case shot for each twelve pounder; 300 rounds of shells for each five-and-a-half-inch howitzer; 300 rounds each for the ten- and eight-inch mortars; and 1,000 rounds for the four-and-two-thirds-inch mortars. In addition, there were entrenching tools for one thousand men; 10,000 one-bushel sandbags; 20,000 one-half-bushel sandbags; 1,000 hand grenades; and the "proper ministers and attendants." Twelve thousand of the provincials would be provided with muskets—with wood rammers and bayonets in tanned leather—360 halberts, 240 drums, and 12,000 cartridge boxes, 200 rounds of powder and shot for each musket, and 4,000 tents. Presumably the 8,000 troops who did not receive a King's musket would have to provide their own. Just transporting all the ordnance assigned to Abercromby to Lake George and beyond would be daunting enough. But first it had to be assembled at English docks and sailed to New York.[3]

Pitt had scheduled Abercromby's campaign to begin on May 1. There was simply no way Abercromby could depart so early, even if he marched with only the troops, supplies, and equipment on hand. But collecting all that ordnance in England took months. Pitt was unable to get the supply fleet to set sail from Spithead, England, until the first week of April. The first ships arrived at New York six weeks later. As the convoys of ships dropped anchor at New York, the supplies had to be disgorged onto the wharfs or transferred to lighter ships to sail up the Hudson to Albany, consuming even more time.[4] Moving supplies from New York up the Hudson River to Albany was relatively easy, but getting them to the army gathering at Fort Edward was drawn out, tedious work. Heavy rains turned the upper Hudson River into a torrent, the roads and trails into quagmires; they swept away the few bridges over side streams. As if the swift current was not difficult enough to row against, three sets of rapids on the Hudson River demanded long portages. At Fort Edward supplies were transferred to three hundred wagons and ox teams for the fourteen-mile haul to Lake George.[5]

Given his personality and outlook, as Abercromby immersed himself in organizing his campaign, it was inevitable that he would issue orders that would rankle the Americans. His first important act as commander in chief occurred on March 15 when he sent a circular letter to the governors, calling on them to fulfill their orders from the king and his prime minister. He asked them to furnish his army with 20,000 provincial troops as soon as possible. He also imposed a shipping embargo, to be continued until further notice. He was especially concerned about the fitness of the provincial troops. To avoid the "indifferent ones" of previous years, Abercromby asked the governors to employ an inspector who would ensure only the best men were enlisted. Each man should bring his own musket along "with a powder horn, shot bag, and case for the lock of his gun, and also . . . a good blanket." Those men without muskets would be supplied with the Crown's firearms.[6]

As the governors received that year's troop quotas, they began the laborious, expensive, and frustrating toil of rounding up those men, arms, and supplies, and dispatching them to the front. Each governor reported on his relative progress to Abercromby. Some were more diligent in doing so than others. Not surprisingly, most of Abercromby's correspondence was with the provinces whose troops would join his own army—New York, Massachusetts, Connecticut, New Hampshire, and Rhode Island. The letters Abercromby dispatched merely echoed orders previously sent to those governors by Pitt. The practice of Pitt rather than the commander in chief issuing orders to the provincial governors was potentially inefficient. Presumably the commander in chief would be more familiar with each province's ability to provide troops and the needs of each campaign for those troops.

Nonetheless, the governors were soon wrestling with their assemblies to fulfill Pitt's orders. New York was the first to comply. Governor DeLancey received Pitt's instructions on March 4, convened the assembly on March 9, and made a speech before the united assembly and council the next day. On March 14, the day after Abercromby arrived and met with DeLancey, the council voted to raise 2,680 troops. On March 15, the legislature approved the council's measure, along with a bounty of ten pounds for every volunteer. That same day DeLancey issued an embargo on shipping. Despite this prompt and enthusiastic response to Pitt's orders, DeLancey complained that "the country is drained of many able bodied men, by almost a kind of madness to go a privateering, many enlist in the battoe [sic] service, and numbers are necessarily impressed for waggoneers [sic] to carry up provisions."[7]

It was one thing, however, for a provincial governor to promise a certain number of troops, and another for the colony to actually muster and deliver them. New York promised 2,680, but ultimately delivered only 650. Massachusetts governor Thomas Pownall asked his assembly to raise 7,000 troops as "a noble example" to the other provinces, but the colony delivered only 2,009.[8] The other colonies also fell short of what their governors had pledged: Connecticut promised 5,000, delivered 4,550; New Hampshire promised 800, delivered 740; Rhode Island promised 1,000, delivered 960; Pennsylvania promised 3,000, delivered 2,727; and Virginia promised 2,000, delivered 1,868. New Jersey did send all the 1,000 troops promised, but this was but half the number called for by Pitt. Angry at not receiving compensation for contributions in previous years, Maryland and South Carolina initially refused to provide any troops, but eventually they assembled 227 and 127 respectively. Thus of the 20,000 troops originally called for by Pitt to support Abercromby, the provinces promised 22,480 and delivered 13,858.[9]

The excuses offered for the shortfalls varied. As mentioned, Maryland and South Carolina initially refused to provide any troops, but eventually relented and assembled some. Other provinces also protested, yet promised to supply a large portion of their quota. Then there were the provincial assemblies that wanted to satisfy Whitehall, but simply could not afford to pay for what Pitt demanded.

New Jersey offered only 1,000 troops, short of the 2,000 called for by Pitt. Governor John Reading wrote Abercromby a short, perfunctory letter expressing his assembly's concern that they had received no compensation for their previous contributions and thus hesitated to commit any more troops and supplies unless Whitehall could guarantee reimbursement. Abercromby fired back a letter assuring Reading that compensation would eventually arrive. In the meantime, New Jersey had to contribute its share like the other provinces. Reading did not reply.[10]

New Hampshire also authorized a number less than Pitt's quota. Governor Benning Wentworth promised Abercromby he would try to convince the assembly to raise its contingent from 800 to 1,000 men, but was pessimistic about his chances. Want of money was the worst problem, followed by want of arms and other equipment. Abercromby allowed the New Hampshire troops also to rendezvous directly at Fort Edward rather than Albany.[11]

Massachusetts's delivery fell far short of Pownall's promise. Massachusetts would supply no more than 2,009 troops to Abercromby, less than one-third of those promised. The reasons were financial and manpower limits rather than political protest. Pownall confessed that "the real truth is in attempting to raise 7,000 men, we have overreached our strength."[12] The Massachusetts troops would collect at Worcester before marching west to Fort Edward, rather than to Albany. Every regiment had to muster at least 500 armed and equipped troops before it could march.

As if to compensate for the shortfall, Pownall did all he could to ensure that those troops mustered not only got to the front but behaved like soldiers. He issued strict orders to his officers regulating their organization, discipline, equipment, and behavior on the long march to Fort Edward. The troops were divided into messes of six men. Each mess was issued a tin kettle and hatchet, which the men took turns carrying. One man from each mess would be elected to secure rations. Each soldier received six pence sterling worth of provisions each day. Every fifty men would be allotted a wagon in which to haul their heavy equipment and provisions. The troops would be assembled for morning and evening roll calls. Each regiment had a surgeon and two assistants, known as mates. The pace of any march should allow the rear to keep up with the front. An advance guard with scouts forward and on the flanks would spring any ambush. A rear guard would prevent straggling and desertion. Special care would be taken when marching through defiles.

Pownall did not hesitate to mix religion and war. He ordered each colonel to "see that his regiment observes a constant and regular performance of Divine Service in the field. By making your regiment better men, you make them better soldiers." The governor believed that religious devotion "will soon diffuse itself into the whole economy, and will be plainly seen in their persons, their cloaths, arms, accoutrements, their conduct, diligence, obedience, and even in their courage, of which this Spirit is the firmest and most lasting foundation."[13]

BRITISH SUPPLIES

Mobilizing troops was just the first step. Even more challenging was feeding them—over an 180-day period twelve thousand men devoured 10,920 barrels of flour, 6,240 of salted pork, 650 of rice, 1,950 of butter, and 14,625 of peas. Shipping those provisions to the front was as challenging as gathering them from hundreds of sources. Bradstreet informed Abercromby that in his estimation, accumulating a month's worth of supplies for the provincial troops would "take three weeks for a thousand bateaux, eight hundred wagons and oxcarts, to transport the 5,760 barrels of provisions necessary, each barrel to be handled five separate times."[14] Complicating that dilemma was yet another. There was a manpower tradeoff in the sense that every man armed with a musket would be one less available to act as a teamster or bateau man to convey supplies to the front.

Each governor appointed agents who scoured the countryside for provisions. Rhode Island governor Stephen Hopkins's actions were typical. He wrote Abercromby that he had

> issued warrants to the sheriffs of the several counties in this colony to take into their custody all such beef, pork, flour, bread, and rice as are to be found . . . and to keep it safely and ready to be delivered . . . to the contractors or their agents, whenever they demand it. . . . Your directions shall be complied with in regard to setting the price so that neither buyer nor seller may have reason to complain. . . . And if any here shall be desirous of carrying their provisions to New York . . . proper care [shall be] taken that they give sufficient bond for landing it there and they return certificates before their bonds be given up.[15]

As for payment, the Crown promised to split the costs of raising troops with the provinces. If the provinces handled the troops' pay and clothing, Whitehall would take care of the arms, tents, and provisions. But it took much more than that to equip men for war. Before requisition officers placed their orders they had to know whom to bill, the king or provincial government. Abercromby received many letters like that from the three Connecticut quartermasters, asking such specifics as who would pay for such essentials as kettles, utensils, medicines, surgeons, and muskets collected from the population, whether swords should also be gathered; and to whom they could apply to receive compensation for the previous year's expenses.[16]

There were rarely enough muskets available to arm all the troops. Those provincial troops supplied with the king's arms often tried to take them home as compensation after the year's campaign was up. The regular officers tried to stem the illegal outflow; provincial officers tended to turn a blind eye to the thefts. Those who brought their own muskets into the field demanded compensation should they be lost or damaged. Abercromby promised to compensate them. But the commander chastised those provincial governors who failed to collect more muskets for their provincial troops. He expressed his astonishment to New Jersey governor John Reading that "no arms are to be found within your province when . . . it is known almost to everyone that few if any of the people of this continent are without arms."[17]

Abercromby complained bitterly to Pitt that the arms shortage was entirely contrived "because the provinces knowing my distress, make a handle of it to retard their troops from joining me, alleging that men without arms can be of no service, wherefore I have been obliged to direct them to impress arms, but how far they will comply with this so necessary & unavoidable measure, I will not venture to say."[18] That was not the only source of irritation to the general. Like all British officers, he deplored the reality that among the American troops "every captain [was] . . . a shopkeeper & sutler which proved not only a disgrace but ruin to the provincial troops." Apparently those shopkeeper officers tended to supply their troops from their own stores and charge the government bloated prices.

The general had other complaints. He was not impressed by the quality of the men the colonial legislatures and recruiters had dredged up. He expressed his displeasure that the "provinces scarcely began to raise a man till the middle of April. Many of those that joined us were hired in room of others, who should have gone, & others draughted or forced out of the militia."[19]

Although officially the rangers were considered regulars, Abercromby distrusted and disliked them; he dismissed them as mercenary, mutinous, and ill-disciplined. The general acquired that view from his aide, Captain James Abercrombie. While accompanying a ranger patrol in November 1757, Abercrombie was astonished that they took potshots at game "within hearing of the French sentries," that officers and men slept at their posts, that when engaged they took cover and fired in the air rather than at the enemy, and that they had mistaken Lake Champlain's South Bay for a beaver pond.[20] Although it was unfair to judge the ranger companies by the actions of one patrol, that is what the captain did. And, as for that "beaver pond," the rangers may just have been having some fun at the incredulous English captain's expense.

The general was sorry to hear such criticism "because last year they were a useful and well behaved body & generally succeeded well when they went out in small parties." Upon reviewing the captain's report, Abercromby favored completely reorganizing the rangers. Only the best woodsmen would be retained and the troublemakers dismissed. Regular officers would replace the provincial officers. Abercromby presented his advice to Lord Loudoun, who did not follow through with the recommendations. Neither did Abercromby himself when he became commander in chief.[21] Although Abercromby may have despised the rangers, he found Robert Rogers indispensable: "so necessary and useful a man, that I should be extremely sorry to part with him. . . . Without him those four [ranger] companies would be good for nothing. . . . We can only depend on him for any sort of intelligence."[22]

The regular regiments were just as unready for campaign. Empty ranks had to be filled. Recruiting officers scoured taverns and markets to find those willing to take the king's shilling. Abercromby asked Governor Pownall to have published in the newspapers a notice calling on all officers on leave to rejoin their units and issuing a pardon for all deserters if they too returned to their regiments. The four New York independent companies received orders to "level" their ranks or reassign the troops until each company enjoyed roughly equal strength. Surgeons also were needed. Abercromby issued James Napier orders and 200 pounds sterling and 16 shillings to hire sixteen more surgeons for six months, and an additional 120 pounds sterling to pay for the transportation of their baggage and forage for their draft animals.[23]

BRITISH WATER TRANSPORT

A huge flotilla of boats was needed to transfer supplies north to Fort Edward and transport the army along the surface of Lake George. Before leaving Albany for New York, Abercromby ordered his deputy quartermaster, Lieutenant Colonel John Bradstreet, to gather the boatmen and builders and construct the flotilla. A conflict must have exploded with the pugnacious Bradstreet. On April 4, Abercromby wrote Bradstreet announcing that he was replacing him with Captain Joshua Loring as soon as that officer completed his mission of organizing the whaleboat flotilla for the Louisbourg campaign. Although the general would later go back on the threat, the animosities would only worsen.[24]

The shipping embargo contributed to the war effort in several ways. The embargo not only helped keep intelligence and supplies from reaching the enemy. A portion of those hundreds of idle ships could be requisitioned as transports. To that end appraisers had to be appointed to inspect the ships and reach a just price for their lease. The ships would then be cleared of their existing cargo and refilled with troops, ordnance, and supplies. Pennsylvania governor William Denny was the first to announce an embargo. One by one the other provinces followed.[25]

The embargo harshly penalized shippers. Some petitioned their colonial government for permission to ignore it. Few were allowed to do so. At least eighteen ships at Philadelphia and fourteen at New York were pressed into the king's service as transports. Most likely several dozen more were impressed in other American ports. At times the procurement was heavy-handed. Connecticut interests accused Colonel Simon Fraser and troops of the 78th as "having carried off a ship from New Haven illegally and by military force." Fraser wrote Governor Fitch that he had acted solely according to the law. When the owners had refused to sell, Fraser had had a sheriff issue him a warrant by which he had confiscated the ship. By another warrant Fraser had obtained the repairs, provisions, and sailors necessary to sail it. Upon paying off the workers and issuing a receipt to the owners, Fraser had departed with his troops aboard the ship bound for Halifax. With the Louisbourg expedition successfully under way, Abercromby lifted the embargo on May 22. It had lasted about six weeks and mostly delayed rather than destroyed profits.[26]

Six weeks after he received his promotion, Abercromby could write Pitt that the various campaign preparations were slowly but surely taking shape. Yet there were deficiencies. It appeared as if every province would fall short of fulfilling its troop quota. But the worst problem was money. Pitt had still not clarified all the details of just who would pay for what.[27] If nothing else, however, Abercromby had proven his worth as an administrator.

FRENCH LEADERSHIP

Abercromby's troubles in preparing for that year's offensives paled before those faced by Vaudreuil and Montcalm. With New France's winters lasting half the year and a cramped growing season, Canadians could not grow enough food to feed themselves, let alone the five thousand extra unproductive mouths billeted among them. Every inhabitant of New France, from the governor to the most wretched peasant, nervously awaited the spring convoy filled with grain and other supplies that kept the colony alive. The arrival of those supply ships was erratic enough in peacetime. In war, delays and losses of many ships was inevitable. As the British blockade steadily tightened, ever fewer ships managed to get through. Every spring those French and Canadians living along the St. Lawrence would strain to catch the first glimpse of the supply ships; their anxious wait would last longer than usual in 1758.

Throughout the winter the government doled out grains and salted meats from its warehouses in ever-declining rations, leaving all the subjects and soldiers pinched with hunger, lethargy, and despair. The first cut in rations occurred on November 1, 1757; each soldier would receive a half pound of bread and quarter pound of peas daily and six pounds of beef and two pounds of cod weekly. Then on November 25 rations were cut to four pounds of bread, two pounds of peas, three pounds of beef, three pounds of horsemeat, and two pounds of cod stretched over eight days. That winter Vaudreuil and Montcalm agreed to distribute the troops among the farmers. The "soldier is much better off in [cantonment]. . .than in town; the farmers are obliged to feed him, like themselves, at 10 sous per day, which the contractor pays."[28] By late March the warehouses were almost empty. On April 1 Governor Vaudreuil sliced the daily fare even thinner, with soldiers allowed a measly four ounces of bread per day and civilians only half that.

By mid-May, War Minister Belle Isle received the alarming report from Montcalm's headquarters that

> all resources are exhausted and we are on the eve of the most cruel famine, unless the succors which we are expecting from our Monarch's bounty and liberality arrive within fifteen days at the most. . . . The supply of animals is beginning to fall. The butchers cannot furnish a quarter of the beef necessary for the . . . inhabitants . . . though they pay an exhorbitant [sic] price for it; without fowls, vegetables, mutton, or veal, we are on the want of dying of hunger. . . . The mechanics, artisans, and day-laborers, exhausted by hunger, absolutely cannot work any longer; they are so feeble that tis with difficulty that they can sustain themselves.[29]

Intendant François Bigot did dip into the treasury at his command, purchased twelve hundred horses, and sold them for food at a discount to the population. The conversion of all those horses from potential draft animals into a source of food would stymie the army from undertaking a significant campaign against the enemy.

While the king's subjects may have complained about their hunger and other shortages in private, only a few dared to publicly protest. In Quebec a mob of housewives paraded in vain before the headquarters of the lieutenant general of police. In Montreal, Montcalm just as vainly protested to Vaudreuil the cutbacks for his soldiers. The governor wearily explained that nothing more could be done, the warehouses were bare.[30]

Or were they? The food shortage was partly artificial, attributed by Montcalm to "bad government: ignorance, a lack of foresight, and grand greed." He condemned the Canadians who "only take care of those things they immediately need; they commit huge expenses and then neglect the work they have begun. They lack foresight." The priests too warranted condemnation as the "great depleters of Canada who refuse to donate any grain despite edicts of the government and bishop."[31]

The lack of food had military implications as it drained a soldier's energy to march and fight. But that was not the only shortage. Gunpowder was perennially scarce both because Versailles did not send enough and New France used so much: "there is no country where so much of it is consumed, both for hunting and distribution among the Indians; burning of powder is equally a passion among the Canadians, but I think we gain thereby in the day of battle by the correction of their aim in firing."[32]

Given these shortages it is not surprising that morale and discipline among the troops suffered. Montcalm worried that

> discipline is becoming relaxed in spite of my care and severity. The recruits arrived last year are a collection of bad boys. The soldiers to be subsisted must necessarily be dispersed among the farmers. There he lives in quasi independence, out of sight of officers or sergeants. The Canadian settlements are not contiguous like the houses in the villages of France; they are at a great distance from each other. I have had sixteen soldiers belonging to our battalions tried this winter either by the ordinary tribunals or court martial. Three of them have been shot for desertion, two condemned to the galleys for mutiny against their sergeants; the rest for theft. The Colonial troops have not furnished fewer painful, but necessary examples.[33]

Montcalm faced an insurmountable dilemma. There were at once too many soldiers to feed and too few to fight. As of April 20, 1758, the French army in Canada numbered 3,781 troops, of which the La Reine Battalion had 465, La Sarre 499, Royal Rousillon 508, Languedoc 474, Guyenne 508, the Berry's 2nd and 3rd battalions 811, and Bearn 516. Those battalions not only had fewer troops than their British counterparts but were well below their official strength by 449 troops, which would have brought their ranks to 4,230.[34]

In their various dispatches to Versailles, Montcalm and his subordinates continually explained their plight and pleaded for more supplies and troops. That spring General François Gaston de Levis presented their dilemma to War Minister Antoine Rene Voyer d'Argenson de Paulmy: "We are always in the same position; we wait with much impatience the arrival of the vessels and the supplies from France. We cannot decide anything about our operations; all depends on the movements of our enemies and the means at our disposal."[35] But Versailles faced its own dilemma: France's war in Germany. It had few troops or supplies it was willing to divert for the perilous sail across the Atlantic. Even if the troops evaded British warships and arrived safely in Canada, they simply became additional mouths Versailles would be responsible for feeding.

Despite all the food, troop, and discipline shortages, Montcalm painted an idyllic picture of relations among the French, colonials, and Indians: "Our troops live in the greatest concord with the Canadians and Indians. Our officers conduct themselves with politeness towards the one and the other. . . . The slightest appearance of wrong on the part of our officers is immediately punished with great severity."[36]

Here Montcalm glossed over a serious problem—most French and Canadians thoroughly despised each other. Each party had characteristics that rankled and often incensed the other. The French heaped upon the Canadians accusations of ill-discipline, corruption, and incompetence. Montcalm's aide-de-camp, Louis Antoine de Bougainville, tried to be diplomatic when he wrote that "God knows we do not wish to disparage the value of the Canadians. . . . In the woods, behind trees, no troops are comparable to the natives of the country."[37] His frustrations got the better of him in May 1757 when he bristled at a report brought by "a courier from Carillon. During the winter there was at this post disorder, pilferage, vexations, and all that which goes with command by a Canadian."[38] The Canadians, in turn, accused the French of snobbery, arrogance, and a heavy-handed insensitivity to their values and customs. Assistant Chief of Staff Pierre-Andre Gohin, Comte de Montreuil, admitted that the "Colonial officers do not like those of the regular army."[39]

Snobbery played a role. Montcalm thoroughly approved of his troops settling in Canada. The colony had many unfulfilled needs, the most important of which was for more enterprising settlers and soldiers. Quite pleasing to Montcalm was how "our soldiers appear to relish their sojourn in this Colony. Many marriages continue to be contracted; several have taken up lands to clear, without marrying and without being discharged from military service."[40] Yet, it was one thing for common soldiers to fall in love with local girls and quite another for his officers to do so. The idea of his aristocratic officers mingling with the locals disgusted the general and he did all he could to discourage such liaisons. Despite his efforts, two officers did gain his reluctant permission, but only because of extraordinary circumstances. Captain de Bellau of the Guyenne Regiment married the Montreal mayor's daughter, an acceptable choice. The penniless Lieutenant de Miltiere of the Languedoc Regiment hooked another wealthy local girl; besides, he "is well liked by the Indians whom he often accompanies on an expedition, and has easily learned the Iroquois. The Marquis de Vaudreuil proposes to transfer him, some day, with his rank, to the Colonial troops."[41]

More than snobbery may have spurred Montcalm to meddle so much in the love lives of his officers. Melancholy and boredom afflicted him as he neared his forty-seventh year. His military duties were light during winter in a snowbound land where the troops were dispersed among the inhabitants and the enemy was far away. The general remained in Quebec until February 20 when he departed for Montreal, reaching that city on February 22. He found Montreal's parochial, corrupt, backbiting social elite just as tiresome and claustrophobic as that of Quebec. Immersion in the whirl of social events at once relieved and highlighted the tedium. He confessed all this in chatty letters to generals Bourlamaque and Levis, mixing gossip and news of social events like balls, dinners, and Mardi Gras with instructions and information over discipline, supplies, strategy, promotions, and diplomacy with the Indians. He preferred to "spend nearly all my evenings in my room; it's the place here I am the least bored and I enjoy the most pleasure."[42]

At times the general bit his lip in irritation at real and imagined slights from his nemesis, the governor. To handle Vaudreuil, Montcalm admitted that "I promise him everything, I agree with him over everything, and I don't divulge anything." In this the general was simply treating the governor as did all others: "Between us," he confided to Bourlamaque, "Vaudreuil is little obeyed by the Canadians who indulge him."[43]

But there was one area where Montcalm could not restrain his tongue. The proud general was the governor's subordinate, and thus subject to implement whatever strategy Vaudreuil devised. Yet the general did not hesitate to debate the governor passionately with what to do about the British offensives that would threaten Canada with invasion later that year.

Vaudreuil submitted his first plan for 1758 to Montcalm in January.[44] Citing the enemy threat on all fronts, especially against Fort Carillon, the governor proposed a bold course of action whereby he would split the French forces into two. Montcalm and Bourlamaque would lead the bulk of the army to Fort Carillon while General Levis headed an elite force of 3,500 men—including 400 marines, 400 picked soldiers, and the rest of the Canadians and Indians—into the Mohawk valley via the St. Lawrence, Lake Ontario, and Oswego River route.

Levis's offensive had four objectives. First it would prevent the enemy from reestablishing itself at Oswego on Lake Ontario. It was also hoped that a march through the Iroquois lands with so large a force would inspire many Iroquois warriors to join the French, or at the very least prevent them from aiding the British. Levis's advance would ravage the settlements and destroy any forts as it advance toward Schenectady and British supply lines on the Hudson River. Finally, that large a force advancing on Abercromby's rear might just spook the general into splitting his forces and delaying his own advance.

If the advance by Levis went as planned, Montcalm should then advance south from Fort Carillon with most of the army and colonial troops for a decisive battle against Abercromby. Regardless, Montcalm should conduct an active defense with constant large-scale raids on the enemy's supply lines, although, the governor added, the general was permitted to act as he saw fit depending on circumstances. For his part, the governor promised to gather as many Indians as possible and send them to Montcalm, but he cautioned the general against putting much faith in their staying in the field for any length of time. Any operations, of course, depended on receiving enough supplies. Thus until those arrived, the army's essential task was to conserve the dwindling provisions left in the storehouses.

Vaudreuil's plan made Montcalm and his officers shudder.[45] They deemed it not bold but reckless. In his reply, Montcalm's pen dripped with fiery sarcasm. He skewered one after another of Vaudreuil's proposals as so laden with contradictions and illogic "that it must have been a mistake of his secretary."[46] His central argument was that it was ludicrous to split one's forces in the face of a superior enemy. As for his own operations, he pointed to the difficulties of mounting even limited attacks against the enemy's supply lines. He blasted as suicidal the governor's order that he lead his army against Abercromby "for an affair general and decisive." As for the thrust into the Mohawk valley, by the time Levis had gathered enough supplies and bateaux, it would be far too late to relieve any pressure on Montcalm. Even if Levis was able to begin his campaign earlier, the 3,500 troops Vaudreuil had allocated him were at once too many to feed, arm, and transport hundreds of miles and too few to defeat the British should Abercromby split off half his troops against him. Word would soon reach British ears of such a large force rowing on its long route up the St. Lawrence, into

Lake Ontario, up the Onondaga River, and then down the Mohawk. With the advantage of interior lines, Abercromby could march against an underdefended Fort Carillon and take it before dispatching part of his army back to defend the Mohawk valley. Montcalm insisted that 500 Canadians and Indians could achieve the same result of rallying the Iroquois and threatening Albany more quickly and less expensively, while allowing the French and Canadian forces to concentrate at Fort Carillon against Abercromby. He concluded by accusing the governor of ulterior motives, implying that he was deliberately weakening Montcalm's army so that he would suffer a humiliating defeat.

Though Vaudreuil ignored Montcalm's objections, he would later admit that his plan had a flaw.[47] He had allocated enough troops to Levis to fulfill his mission but could only spare two months' worth of provisions for that many men. If a large number of Iroquois joined Levis, the campaign would be shortened—unless they could capture significant amounts of enemy supplies. As it happened, circumstance would kill Levis's expedition before it started.[48]

Having determined the strategy, the governor left it up to Levis and Montcalm to work out the details. Levis naturally was eager to embark on his first independent command. By spring he devised "a campaign plan . . . that I presented to messieurs Vaudreuil and Montcalm; they found it good and allowed me to execute it if circumstances permitted."[49]

Montcalm began to flesh out the details of his assignment. He would have to plan Fort Carillon's defense and his army's supplies with the colony's chief artillery and supply officer, Captain François Marc Antoine le Mercier, who had considerable experience at and around Fort Carillon. Unfortunately, Montcalm harbored nearly as much contempt for Mercier as for the governor, although he was more restrained in expressing himself to his subordinate when they exchanged terse communiqués in March. Montcalm's criticism of Mercier's proposals was polite but pointed. He admitted that when Mercier "presents only the roses I reply with thorns."[50] The general ended his letter with the double-edged statement that "the talents of M. Le Mercier are so well known that one can be worried in this regard."[51]

Vaudreuil fulfilled his role, counseling with Indian delegations and issuing orders to each parish militia captain to ready his men for the approaching campaign. The militia was to gather in Montreal no later than May 20. As for the regular troops, that winter the La Reine, Languedoc, and Berry battalions were billeted in or around Quebec, while the Bearn, La Sarre, and Royal Rousillon sheltered in or around

Montreal. Most troops were scattered in private homes; only the La Reine and seven companies of the Bearn enjoyed barracks. Montcalm admitted that "nothing is better than trying to prolong the sojourn of our battalions with their hosts for as long as possible."[52]

La Reine was chosen as the first battalion to move. In addition to already being concentrated in one place, it had nearly exhausted all its provisions but could find enough at Fort Carillon to sustain itself. With the dearth of supplies it would be another six weeks before the other battalions could be sent. La Reine received its orders on May 5 to proceed to Fort Carillon; it did not embark until May 14. Between May 8 and 15, about 230 gunners and sappers commanded by Captain Lotbiniere and Lieutenant Fiedmont also set off for Fort Carillon. It would take La Reine battalion nearly a month to get all its troops, supplies, and equipment from Quebec to Fort Carillon. As for the other battalions, the governor and general achieved a rare accord that for now they should stay put.

The St. Lawrence was usually not difficult to row up, but a combination of a heavy snowmelt and fierce west winds made traveling its waters exceptionally difficult that year. Conditions on the Richelieu River were equally challenging. The flotilla of bateaux drew provisions first at Chambly then portaged around the falls there to Fort St. Jean. The spring thaw had turned the road through the lowlands between Chambly and St. Jean into a swamp, making progress even slower and more miserable than usual. Further, Bigot's policy of slaughtering horses for sustenance over the winter had reduced the number of available draft animals. The easiest stretch of the journey lay on Lake Champlain from Isle aux Noix to Fort Carillon.

As the mobilization slowly unfolded, Vaudreuil and Montcalm immersed themselves in their work. Only occasionally did one raise his head to toss some barely veiled slight at the other. All along they seesawed between pessimism and optimism, between action and passivity; when one was up, the other—almost responsively—was down. Montcalm admitted as much. By early May, the governor's earlier enthusiasm began to falter as starvation and the British blockade worsened. Montcalm observed that "Vaudreuil has started to believe that we will be unable to mount a single expedition this year. . . . The more Vaudreuil seems to believe in inaction this year the more angry I become and the more I want to act, and I demand only six weeks with which I promise to achieve grand results or at least avoid anything bad."[53]

Strategy, of course, depends not just on one's own capabilities but on the enemy's intentions and capabilities. Information is a vital component of military and political power. Both sides gleaned as much intelligence as possible from prisoners, deserters, scouts, spies, and newspapers, and then rigorously analyzed it, separating the kernels of truth from the chaff of lies, exaggerations, and rumors.

French intelligence was usually adept at discovering British intentions. By March 1758, Montcalm and Vaudreuil had learned the broad outlines of the assault that would be unleashed against them that year. The interrogation of seven rangers captured during the Battle on Snowshoes yielded important information. Not only did those prisoners reveal a planned but eventually aborted winter campaign against Fort Carillon, they also passed on news of summer offensives against Forts Louisbourg, Duquense, and Carillon. That was partly confirmed when the French got their hands on a copy of the New York government's act of March 24, 1758, authorizing funds to underwrite 20,000 provincial troops to accompany Abercromby's regulars "to invade the French possessions in Canada."[54] Then on May 7, Montcalm got a detailed look into that year's British strategy from a gregarious captain of the 27th who was among those men captured by Langy's raid.[55]

Meanwhile the French and Canadians prayed for the supply fleet to evade the British blockade and safely dock at Quebec. It was not until April 15 that the ice imprisoning the St. Lawrence broke up and ships were free to set sail or drop anchor. Yet another excruciating month of quasi-starvation and anxiety would pass before, on May 19, cheers broke out along Quebec's ramparts as eight supply ships and a small British prize vessel escorted by the frigate *Sirenne* rounded Isle d'Orleans and sailed toward the city. An ecstatic crowd packed the quai to learn that eight thousand barrels of flour were stacked in those ship holds. Not only was the famine's end in sight, but an impatient Governor Vaudreuil could now launch his campaign.[56]

Those ships carried more than supplies. French spies in London had learned the details of that year's British strategy for North America and had sent it back to the ministries in Versailles, which in turn relayed it to Montcalm and Vaudreuil on the first supply ships. Three days after the ship reached Quebec on May 19, a courier with a packet of dispatches and intelligence reports from Versailles, reached Montreal. The ominous news chilled the commanders with "reasonable fear."[57] The British were planning a massive three-pronged assault with fifty thousand troops on New France, with Louisbourg, Duquesne, and Carillon the primary targets. Several weeks later, that news was reconfirmed with new details when Lieutenant Wolff, leading thirty soldiers and six Indians took three prisoners, one an ensign of the 55th, and killed seven near Fort Edward; the prisoners revealed what was now widely known in the British camp. Within days of returning to Fort Carillon, Wolff would be dispatched on a much more peaceful mission on a prisoner exchange to Fort Edward.[58]

With the arrival of supplies and armed with ample intelligence, Vaudreuil and Montcalm were eager to act. But they would have to wait a little longer. Another heartbreaking delay occurred when a "northeaster continued with such violence for eight days that it was impossible to get anything out of these vessels the whole of that time. At length, the wind having moderated, some sloops were loaded with provisions for Chambly and Montreal to be thence distributed to the different points of operation."[59]

While enough supplies had arrived to alleviate briefly the hunger of the army, little trickled down into the hands and mouths of sixty thousand civilians. The famished population would have to await the next supply convoy. As of June 16, only twelve of the thirty-six ships that had sailed from Bordeaux had arrived, and none from Rochelle, Bayonne, or Marseilles. The eight thousand barrels of flour that were unloaded would not last the summer. What little had arrived took weeks to disperse. On June 17, starvation provoked a riot among housewives in Montreal. On June 20, six more ships arrived from France loaded with provisions. One came from Rochefort, and two each from Bayonne and Bordeaux, along with a frigate packed with munitions and food. If it was rationed and distributed properly there was now enough food on hand to succor the population until the crops were in. But that year's harvest threatened to be as miserly as ever: "Little has been sown for want of seed; and sowing was scarcely completed when the land was inundated with rain, which has continued for nearly a month. It is since cold, and now freezes at night so hard as entirely to destroy all the vegetables . . . the result is an advance of prices so horrible as to entail suffering on the most comfortable."[60]

Indian loyalties were as erratic as the weather and supplies. Across New France the natives were restless, and some were outright defiant. The most important reason was the lack of French gifts to buy the Indians' allegiance. That was made clear at a May 20 council between Montcalm and prominent Iroquois chiefs, who tried "to communicate to him the disposition of their brethren." Some were loyal to the French, others to the English, but the latter, they assured him, would be "easy to bring . . . back, if provisions and supplies arrive soon."[61] The problem was not confined to the St. Lawrence valley Indians. By early 1758 at Fort Duquesne, "the Indians, to whom large presents cannot be made as the stores are empty, begin to dislike going out to fight."[62] Every frontier post faced the same problem—the storerooms were bare and without gifts the Indians refused to budge.

Versailles was well aware of the dilemma. Like their British counterparts, they despaired over the trials in rallying the Indians and their usefulness: "English presents, our poverty, our prodigious inferiority— what motives to abate their ardor! Besides being independent, never making two expeditions consecutively, even should the first have resulted only in raising one scalp; ill qualified for defense; afraid of death; what benefit can be expected to be derived from them?"[63]

Exacerbating these problems was the smallpox epidemic that had burned like wildfire through the tribes the previous year. The first epidemic afflicted those Indians present at the capture of Fort William Henry that August. Smallpox festered among many of Colonel George Monro's defenders. After the surrender, when the Indians surged into the hospital and hacked those sick men to pieces, they inadvertently infected themselves. They then carried the smallpox virus along with their loot and scalps back to their distant villages. The irony was that by massacring helpless soldiers the Indians brought mass death upon themselves.

Further afield in New France, the news of relations with the Indians was dismal:

> everything is quiet at Fort Duquesne where considerable provisions are expected from Illinois; nothing new from the forts at Presq'isle and Riviere au Boeuf. The commandant of Detroit is dying; the Five Nations rarely go to Niagara; there is a little fermentation and discontent against us among the Indians of St. Joseph, the Miamis and the Weas. The Folles Avoins have killed eleven Canadians at the [Fort la] Bay; missed the commandant and pillaged a storehouse. A great many Indians have died at Michilimakinac. The commandant of Louisiana writes that they have had no ships from France for two years, and that he is greatly embarrassed, having nothing to give the Nations.[64]

It increasingly looked as if the French and Canadians would have to fight nearly alone against the British onslaught. As the battalions received fresh supplies they were sent to the front. From May 31 through June 10, the two Berry battalions and the Languedoc Battalion were transported from Quebec to Fort Carillon. The La Sarre battalion embarked for Fort Carillon on June 16, the Royal Rousillon on June 18, and the Bearn on June 21. Of the French commanders, Colonel François-Charles de Bourlamaque was the first to set off, leaving Montreal on June 12 and reaching Fort Carillon with the Languedoc Battalion on June 15. During his sojourn at Montreal, Bourlamaque organized supplies and transport for his troops and conferred frequently with Vaudreuil and Montcalm. Meanwhile, by mid-June, Levis had gathered at Lachine 1,600 troops, including 400 soldiers, 400 marines, and 800 Canadians. There they awaited Indians and Vaudreuil's order to proceed.[65]

The arrival of supplies and departure of the battalions to the front did little to alleviate the gloom that pervaded amongst the French and Canadians alike. All were aware of the vast British armies and fleets massing against parts of Canada that year. Many feared that they could not hold out much longer. Deputy Commissary General Doreil reckoned that Montcalm's "position will be critical; men and means will be few, and if the reports of the prisoners are to be credited, those of the enemy will be considerable. Far from being able to act offensively on that frontier, I shall consider the campaign very brilliant if we are able to maintain our position."[66]

Montcalm himself lapsed into pessimism. The dearth of troops, provisions, and pay spurred him to issue on June 19 a report to Vaudreuil which politely insisted that the governor fulfill the army's needs. Two days later he sent the governor his plans for moving his army and supplies to Fort Carillon's defense. In both messages he blasted Vaudreuil's scheme to send Levis and 3,500 men to the Mohawk valley and requested that they be dispatched instead to Fort Carillon.[67] Montcalm's criticism at once angered Vaudreuil and stiffened his commitment to his plan.

Vaudreuil fired back. At ten o'clock in the evening of June 23, Montcalm was preparing for bed when he received the governor's latest communiqué. What he read must have set his blood pressure soaring and kept him up late scribbling a reply. It was the latest of Vaudreuil's ambiguous and often contradictory orders that Montcalm had endured over the previous years and which exposed the general to varying degrees of criticism no matter what he did. The most troubling tenet of the June 23 message was the clause that seemed at once to urge him to attack Abercromby's army and yet avoid a large battle.[68]

In his reply, Montcalm lamented that it was bad enough to have to defend Fort Carillon against such overwhelming enemy forces "without you burdening me with an instruction, the obscurities and contradictions whereof appear to render me responsible for events which may happen and we must anticipate."[69] The general declared he would not leave for the front until the governor signed an unambiguous order that would govern that summer's campaign. Montcalm then submitted a document to that effect and demanded Vaudreuil's signature.[70]

Vaudreuil grudgingly caved in to Montcalm's demand. Montcalm's response to him held nothing remarkable; it countered each point of Vaudreuil's instructions and then committed both the governor and general to unambiguous duties in response to the summer's likely scenarios. Most importantly, Vaudreuil gave Montcalm the freedom to retreat to Fort St. Frederic if Fort Carillon's defense proved impossible. Thus did Montcalm score a personal victory before he embarked for the front on June 24. All that appeared to lay ahead was an ignominious retreat before overwhelming odds. It is doubtful that the ever-pessimistic general departed with thoughts he was about to win the greatest military victory of his already distinguished career.

CHAPTER 5

Wilderness War

The death of one man was the ruin of 15,000.
—Francis Parkman

NEW YORK TO FORT EDWARD

By the beginning of May, Abercromby was nearly ready to launch his own campaign to capture Fort Carillon. On May 5 the general and his staff set sail up the Hudson from New York to their new headquarters at Albany. They arrived six days later. There they were exasperated to discover that the army was short of everything, including bateaux, provisions, munitions, troops, and especially muskets.[1]

Finding arms for the volunteer regiments that trudged into camps around Albany or Fort Edward epitomized the Sisyphean travails of organizing the campaign. Abercromby sent a long list of muskets, bayonets, cartridge boxes, gunpowder, screws, lead, and other essentials to Ordnance Comptroller James Furnis at New York to procure. Furnis forwarded the request to Boston contractor Thomas Hancock, who managed to buy two hundred muskets and ship them to Albany. But that shipment filled a mere fraction of the need. Abercromby then went so far as to ask Governor James DeLancey to gain the New York council's power to confiscate the people's muskets. The council bluntly rejected the notion.[2]

The shortage was seemingly relieved by the arrival in early June of a large shipment from England. Now the number of muskets exceeded the number of provincial soldiers demanding them. Learning of the shipment, New Jersey governor Francis Bernard, who had just replaced John Reading, asked for enough muskets to arm his regiment so that it could be dispatched to the front. The elation turned to despair when it was discovered that the muskets were poorly made and apt to blow up in a soldier's face when he squeezed the trigger. DeLancey eventually ordered the weapons stored in a New York City warehouse where they would be saved for only the gravest of emergencies.

Abercromby was back nearly where he had begun. How was he to arm all the provincials? That problem was partly alleviated when Pitt's convoy, loaded with 10,000 muskets, 4,000 tents, and artillery, dropped anchor at Albany on June 19.[3]

Over 1,500 bateaux were needed to haul supplies and troops on the Hudson River and Lake George waters. Building and manning that many vessels was a Herculean task, brilliantly surmounted by Deputy Quartermaster John Bradstreet. By late May Bradstreet had amassed 450 bateaux and whaleboats at Lake George alone, but he lacked crews. Abercromby authorized him to recruit among the provincial regiments. With the inducement of a boatman's higher wages, volunteers slowly filled Bradstreet's corps. But he would need three times as many boats to carry all the troops, supplies, and artillery earmarked for the campaign. Abercromby learned of numerous bateaux on the Mohawk River and asked Governor DeLancey to issue him the power of impressment. DeLancey granted it and Abercromby got those boats. But like the Hydra's heads, new problems arose for every one solved. Reports of a French warship on Lake Champlain prompted Abercromby to implement plans to counter it. He ordered Captain Joshua Loring to gather shipwrights and seamen to build and man two warships on Lake Champlain once the army had captured Fort Carillon.

As Abercromby and his staff gathered troops and supplies at Albany, they forwarded them to General Howe at Fort Edward. Concentrating 17,000 troops around Fort Edward would be a logistical and sanitary nightmare. Governor Thomas Pownall of Massachusetts offered a partial solution. He suggested cantoning the New England provincial troops on their respective frontiers until four or five days before the campaign opened. That could alleviate the congestion at Fort Edward while simultaneously protecting Massachusetts's borders. Abercromby thanked Pownall for the offer but ordered him and the other governors to forward the troops to Fort Edward immediately "as we do not know what may happen."[4]

After the Massachusetts volunteers finally mustered, they numbered 2009, less than one-third of the 7,000 troops Pownall had promised. Those troops did not set off for the frontier at the same time. A mutiny by Colonel Fowles's regiment at Marblehead was quelled non-violently—the ringleaders were left behind. Then, despite Pownall's strict orders, many men fell out on the long road from Worcester to Fort Edward. Pownall and his officers worried about the fate of those stragglers and despaired at being unable to help them. The troops were not the only ones who strayed. Colonel Timothy Ruggles, the regiment's commander, abandoned his men and took a different route. Learning of the incident, a furious Pownall advised Abercromby to make an example of Ruggles. But the general was too busy to officially reprimand the colonel. Then word got back to Pownall that some officers had engaged in a drunken spree upon reaching Fort Edward. Once again the governor was filled with shame and anger. He apologized to Abercromby "that my officers had behaved in so irregular a manner." He also noted the number of stragglers left on the march, including the sick and lamed, deserters, and miscreants, and promised to retrieve them.[5] Though every provincial regiment experienced similar problems, no governor took them more personally than Pownall.

Each provincial regiment that marched into Albany tended to linger there until the last moment. More than the relative comforts of eighteenth-century civilization kept them there. They could plead the military necessity of awaiting their promised muskets, tents, and other essentials. But perhaps more than anything, the proud provincial officers tarried to minimize the amount of time they would be subordinated to regular officers of the same rank.

These delays irked Abercromby. In early June he sent orders to General John Stanwix at Schenectady to travel to Albany and roust the provincials. Stanwix came as ordered but failed to budge the stubborn Americans. Indeed they stayed put even after the muskets and other supplies arrived. John Appy wrote that "they could not have no further excuse to delay their march; yet it was still a few days before they all set out. . . . Their dilatoriness, and the constant trifling demands they make, of sundries not provided by His Majesty, and that with no other view than cloaking their tardiness, is almost incredible, to those who have not the opportunity of being an eyewitness to it."[6]

Poor discipline on the march or in isolated camps was bad enough. Tensions were compounded whenever citizens and soldiers mixed on a large scale. Albany was among those American towns where the mix could be explosive. On the evening of May 21, a sentry challenged three citizens who strolled toward him. What happened next was a tragedy: "The sentry called twice to him that he must fire if he not answer. [Burgen] Hufsen replied he might fire & be damned upon which the sentry actually fired & wounded Hufsen so severely that he died a few minutes thereafter. The coroner's inquest found it willful murder" and the sentry was arrested. Hoping to reduce the charge to manslaughter, Abercromby wrote Governor DeLancey requesting that he order the Albany magistrate to turn over the sentry to be tried by court-martial. The general's sympathies were thoroughly with the sentry, whose trial would deprive the king "of this man's service & those who must attend his loyalty in the ordinary course of law."[7] The governor honored the general's request. The subsequent court-martial acquitted the sentry, at once bolstering military authority and further poisoning relations between civilians and soldiers.

As one regiment after another marched north from Albany to Fort Edward, the lower Mohawk valley became ever more vulnerable to attack. Rumors spread that Rigaud Vaudreuil, the governor's brother, was massing several thousand troops and Indians at Oswego for a sweep down the Mohawk valley that might threaten Albany. On June 17, Abercromby ordered General John Stanwix to gather 2,600 provincial troops and the four Independent regular companies and two ranger companies at Schenectady. He was then to march them up the Mohawk valley to German Flats, the western-most large settlement in the region. En route he should scatter 1,000 of those troops in small detachments at various hamlets. Even without being executed, Vaudreuil's plan had succeeded in diverting troops from Abercromby's campaign.[8]

Abercromby hoped that Indian allies would soon partly fill his army's shortfall caused by the absence of Stanwix's command. On June 4, he met with Indian Superintendent William Johnson at Albany. He revealed the details of his campaign and asked him to rally as many warriors as possible. Johnson promised to do so but said he would need enough gifts to underwrite his diplomacy. Abercromby issued the necessary voucher. Johnson bought or ordered as many goods as possible and arranged for them to be hauled to Johnson Hall. He then headed home on June 7.

The general, meanwhile, although weakened by dysentery, reached Fort Edward on June 9. There he was greeted by Lord Howe and a parade of the 42nd, 44th, and 55th regiments, along with four ranger companies. While most of the general's staff had accompanied him to Fort Edward, several lingered in Albany. Most notable within this group were his secretary John Appy, who handled all correspondence with the governors; Captain Christie, the quartermaster general, who would supply provincial regiments as they arrived; and Captain Gordon, who would forward supplies and troops to the front, either by road or river.

The fifty-five miles from Albany to Fort Edward were vulnerable to enemy raiders. Companies of the 27th, 42nd, 46th, and 55th regiments were camped along the way, including 200 troops each at Half Moon, Stillwater, Saratoga, and Fort Miller at the Great Falls. Their officers kept them busy. The troops hauled supplies, bridged streams, felled trees, built forts, widened roads, and deployed guards and patrols.

Defending the links in that supply chain were onerous enough. But hauling supplies up the Hudson and around the portages was back-breaking drudgery. The river route included "three portages . . . whereof one is at times six miles in length, but never less than three. This is the rifts between the Half Moon and Stillwater. The next is up-wards of two miles above Saratoga, and the last five miles higher, op-posite to . . . Fort Miller . . . the first of [the series] is near three quarters of a mile long, and the other only 400 yards."[9]

FROM FORT EDWARD TO LAKE GEORGE

Slowly, steadily, the army massed at Fort Edward. When Colonel Frede-rick Haldimand's 4th Battalion of the 60th Royal Americans arrived on June 17, the army numbered 5,250 regulars. The regiments present in-cluded the 27th (650 troops), the 42nd (1,000), the 44th (850), the 46th (650), the 55th (650), and the 60th's 1st and 4th battalions (550 and 900, respectively). Also present was Thomas Gage's 80th (450 troops), Rob-ert Rogers's four ranger companies (300), and two companies of Stock-bridge Indians (80), and finally 2,550 provincials consisting of the New York regiment's three battalions (1,700 troops) and the New Jersey regi-ment (850).[10]

The same day that Haldimand's force arrived, Howe set forth on a two-day slow march to Lake George. Rogers and 200 of his rangers led the way, followed by the 44th, 55th, and New Jersey regiments, the Stockbridge Indian companies, 178 ox-drawn wagons packed with sup-plies, 90 wagons carrying bateaux, and 30 wagons carrying whale-boats. Each man carried ten-days worth of provisions. When his troops reached Lake George, Howe set them to work constructing two stock-ades just west of Fort William Henry's ruins. Other regiments followed. The 27th, 46th, and New York regiments marched from Fort Edward on June 18. The 27th remained at the night's halt at Halfway Brook (a point roughly midway between Fort Edward and Fort William Henry) to build a stockade. The rest of the regular and provincial regiments made the journey over the next ten days. The troops were not idle after their march. Howe busied them with light infantry tactics in the surrounding woods.[11]

At the Lake George camp it took several days to unload the wagons and rest the draft animals. With a large escort the wagon trains returned to Fort Edward where they were repacked with provisions, munitions, boats, and ordnance; some oxen dragged artillery pieces. That train departed for Lake George on June 27.

By June 29, the British army on Lake George had grown to number 6,370 regulars, including 124 artillerymen, rangers, and Gage's 80th Light Regiment. Of the 17,480 provincials promised, so far only 5,960 had arrived, including five Massachusetts regiments, Ruggles's (449 men), Doty's (869), Prebles's (525), Williams's (563), and Partridge's (442 light infantry), DeLancey's New York (1,715), Johnson's New Jersey (992), Fitch's Connecticut (475). The New Hampshire, Rhode Island, and three other Connecticut regiments would arrive within the next few days. By July 2, 7,510 provincials had massed at Lake George. Provincial volunteers swelled the ranks of Rogers's rangers to 700. Then there was the artillery: two brass twenty-four pounders, 4 iron eighteen pounders, 6 brass twelve pounders, and 6 brass six pounders among the cannon; 1 iron thirteen-inch, 2 brass ten-inch, 2 brass eight-inch, and 8 five-and-one-half-inch mortars; and 4 brass eight-inch, 5 iron eight-inch, and 4 brass five-and-one-half-inch howitzers. Three hundred and fifty rounds accompanied each cannon or mortar. If handled intelligently, all those troops and heavy guns would overwhelm any enemy before them.[12]

Abercromby issued a series of regulations to govern the 14,000 troops in camp and on the march. Some rules were amusing. On May 18, the general decreed that "officers do not, on any account whatever, send their servants or baggage in canoes, unless there is some person in the canoe who understands the management of it."[13] One can imagine soaked and trembling servants trying to explain to livid officers why their baggage was at the bottom of Lake George or floating down the Hudson.

The following day the general "recommended" that regimental commanders not bring their wives or mistresses on campaign. He imposed firm limits on women for men lower down the ranks. Regiments of 700 and 1,000 troops were allowed no more than three and four women each, respectively. Though the camp followers mostly washed clothes, some also relieved the men's more throbbing physical needs.

Over the next few weeks dozens of other regulations were posted and enforced. Gambling was strictly forbidden; the penalty for troops and camp followers alike was three hundred lashes. Even more serious was the spreading of "false alarms in camp, by discharging of firearms, by drawing of swords, by beating of drums, or by any other means."[14] A court-martial followed by the death sentence would greet violators.

WAITING TO EMBARK ON LAKE GEORGE

Abercromby impatiently awaited word on two key questions. One was the whereabouts of his Indian allies. On June 21, he wrote Johnson urging him to hurry to Lake George as soon as possible. Johnson's diplomacy was working but he needed more time. Indians had begun congregating at Fort Johnson in early June and impatiently awaited the offensive. Those Indians had to be fed, equipped, and entertained—an expensive and daunting task. The financial aid Johnson had been promised finally arrived on June 24: 1,397 pounds sterling arrived to pay the salaries of his employees and 3,200 pounds sterling worth of Indian gifts and equipment. But Johnson needed another week to complete his diplomacy and gather more Indians. He asked Abercromby for a specific rendezvous date and promised he could be at Lake George after a four-day march. A peeved Abercromby wrote Johnson that he hoped to embark his army on Lake George on June 26 and ordered the Indian superintendent to meet him there. Should Johnson not get there in time, the general would leave behind enough bateaux to transport his Indians to the army. On June 27, Johnson replied that he would soon arrive with at least 200 Indians and more would follow. He added, "I am as much perplexed as you are displeased by the delay, & your displeasure adds to my perplexity."[15] Deputy Indian Superintendent George Croghan arrived at Johnson Hall that same day with word that 100 Indians from the upper Susquehanna River villages would soon join them.

The other question nagging Abercromby and his men was just where were the French, and what were their intentions? British plans depended on knowing as much as possible about enemy plans. Intelligence received that winter had been encouraging. Deserters and Indians revealed that the enemy suffered severe shortages. But later reports were troubling. The French apparently were scheming a two-pronged offensive against Albany via Fort Edward and the Mohawk valley that summer. The most credible source of information was from James Campbell, an American from German Flats who was captured at the Oneida Carrying Place in March 1756 and managed to escape in March 1758. He observed that Canadian "provisions are very scarce & dear, particularly among the peasants . . . from whom the Governor has taken what he thought proper for the use of his army, and stored it in the King's magazines." But most important of all, he revealed that "there would be a large army march early against Fort Edward, & if successful to Albany. At the same time a small army would come down the Mohawk River by the way of Oswego and to Schenectady if possible."[16]

That was indeed Vaudreuil's plan, vociferously opposed by Montcalm and the other French officers. When he heard the report, General Howe was skeptical about the French ability to pull it off: "the enemy will meet with considerable obstacles in putting such a design . . . in execution." Yet he did not rule out the possibility: "Should their situation . . . be so desperate . . . they may make a desperate push."[17]

Throughout the spring and early summer Howe ordered Rogers and his men to stalk the forests around Forts Carillon and St. Frederic for more intelligence. In April, Rogers dispatched each of his four companies on a different mission. One scouted Lake George's west shore and another the east, a third the mountains between Lakes George and Champlain, and the fourth Wood Creek. But none brought back any prisoners or deserters. In early May, Rogers led an eighteen-man patrol as far as Fort St. Frederic; he returned with three prisoners.

Even more important information was divulged on June 8 when two French deserters from La Reine Regiment arrived at the Lake George camp with word that the regular battalions were either at or en route to Fort Carillon. Abercromby was eager to confirm this intelligence. Whatever misgivings he had towards the rangers, they remained his eyes and ears in the wilderness.

Howe ordered Rogers to set forth on an ambitious and dangerous mission. He was to lead 100 rangers, 40 troops of the 80th, and ten Indians up Lake George in five whaleboats to scout the landing place at the north end and the road to Fort Carillon, and discern the enemy's strength. The mission lasted a week. Toward Lake George's north end, Rogers landed his men, hid most of them, and then trekked with three trusted rangers to the top of 700-foot-high Rattlesnake Mountain (Mount Defiance), a mile west of Carillon. They counted three regiments camped before the fort, a hundred bateaux, and many other men just disembarked. In all, Rogers estimated there were about 4,000 troops. Then, "when I was returning . . . at the distance of about 300 yards, [the rangers] were fallen upon by a superior number of the enemy who had got between me and them. Capt. Jacobs, with the Mohegon [*sic*] Indians, run off at the first onset, calling to our people to run likewise; but they stood their ground and discharged their pieces several times, at last broke through the enemy, by whom they were surrounded on all sides except their rear, where a river divided them: they killed three of the enemy, but lost eight of their own party in this skirmish. My party rallied at the boats, where I joined them, and having collected all but the slain together, we returned homewards."[18] Rogers and his men returned to Fort Edward on June 20 with maps of the entire region embracing Fort Carillon between Lakes George and Champlain. After accomplishing that mission, Howe shifted the rangers' duty from gathering intelligence to screening the army from French and Indian raids and scouts.

The end of June also brought word from Indian scouts that the French had massed an army, bateaux fleet, and supply depot at Oswegatchie, about midway between Montreal and Lake Ontario. That force would soon row to Oswego and then head east toward the Mohawk valley. Although this latest report echoed earlier ones, Abercromby now dismissed the notion, arguing that the French would have to cancel that expedition when the British army embarked on Lake George. Nonetheless, he sent word to Brigadier General John Stanwix at German Flats to march 1,700 troops to the Carrying Place between Wood Creek (which is a tributary of the Onondaga River) and the Mohawk River, and fortify it against a possible attack. Abercromby's assessment would prove to be correct.[19]

COMMUNICATIONS BETWEEN THE COMMANDERS

The sparring between the British and French was not restricted to their troops in the field. Even their commanders traded shots, though with words rather than musket balls; poison lurked beneath the flowery prose. On April 24, Abercromby sent letters introducing himself to Vaudreuil and Montcalm as the new British commander in chief. He then asked them to ensure that prisoners of war would be treated humanely and eventually exchanged. He ended by denouncing the 1757 Fort William Henry capitulation during which the Indians had butchered one hundred or more prisoners before the French imposed order.[20]

On June 10, Lieutenant Wolff, accompanied by a drummer and twenty French troops, arrived from Fort Carillon under a flag of truce at the Halfway Brook camp that Howe commanded. Wolff carried Vaudreuil's reply to Abercromby. Howe sent the letter to Abercromby and retained the French delegation.

Vaudreuil promised his best efforts to "carry on hostilities with humanity and observe, as in Europe, the rules of public law as far as the necessity in which [we] are mutually placed to make use of Indians, will permit us." He also offered a means by which the two commanders at war with each other could exchange letters through a wilderness filled with war parties: "My orders to this officer in going to you are, to proceed by the most frequented route, not to leave it, and to have the English flag displayed. You will have the goodness to give orders on your side, to the officer you will detach to bring me [an] answer, not to turn from the most ordinary route, and to have a French flag hoisted; you may be convinced that he will be well treated and sent back to you under a good and safe guard."[21]

The governor's seeming dismissal of the Fort William Henry "massacre" enraged Abercromby. On June 25, 1758, just ten days before he would move against Fort Carillon, Abercromby wrote Vaudreuil a very strong letter declaring "null and void" the terms for Fort William Henry's capitulation. Those British troops who had been paroled with the promise not to serve until the same number of French prisoners had been released could fight once again. Abercromby then addressed existing negotiations over the exchange of captured officers, especially Colonel Philip Schuyler. King George II had involved himself in these negotiations. Having acquired "a true sense of the active zeal Colonel Schuyler has so often shewed for his service," the king sought his exchange.[22] Schuyler would eventually be released.

Meanwhile Lieutenant Wolff and his escort would be detained for the campaign's duration, thus allowing them to be eyewitnesses to British preparations. The raiding leader Wolff must have ached to be in the field fighting the redcoats rather than acting as a messenger. On July 9, he would have the grim satisfaction of watching their demoralized retreat.[23]

FRENCH PLANS

Abercromby's decision to detain Wolff would affect French plans. When Wolff and his troops did not return to Fort Carillon as expected

on June 23, Colonel François-Charles Bourlamaque correctly surmised the reason. The British army must be about to march. He dispatched Ensign Langy, 60 troops, and several score Nipissings, Al-
gonquins, and Iroquois down Lake George to spy on the British.
Three days later Langy was back at Fort Carillon, having captured 16
rangers without losing a man on an island a half-dozen miles from
Lake George's south end. Those rangers confessed that Abercromby
was about to head north with 20,000 to 25,000 troops, of which 6,500
were regulars. Bourlamaque hurried Langy, the Indians, and the prisoners north toward Montreal for interrogation by Vaudreuil and
Montcalm. Upon delivering the captives, Langy was to return immediately. His skills and courage were essential for Fort Carillon's defense. While the prisoners had substantially exaggerated the British
army's strength, the troops that Abercromby would lead north would
still outnumber the French by five to one. And for now those French
forces awaited their commander.

Accompanied by Captain Charles de Raymond and 400 marines and
militia, Montcalm left Montreal on June 25 at five o'clock in the morning. That force went to Chambly by bateaux, then marched along the
portage around the Richelieu River rapids to St. Jean, where they embarked in bateaux for the long row up Lake Champlain. On the evening
of June 27, the general and his party encountered Langy, the Indians,
and the captive rangers canoeing toward them. Upon receiving the latest intelligence, Montcalm urged his men to row more swiftly toward
Fort Carillon. Although the records are fuzzy, Langy seems to have sent
his captives on with their escort while he headed south with Montcalm
and his troops.[24]

Arriving at Fort Carillon at three o'clock on the afternoon of June
30, Montcalm was greeted by Bourlamaque, the troops standing in review, and a salute of twelve cannons. But any exhilaration Montcalm
might have felt at once again being in the field in such a beautiful setting soon dissipated as he interrogated several new ranger prisoners
who echoed earlier estimates of the size of Abercromby's army. His
army at Fort Carillon would double in size if Vaudreuil sent him in
time the 3,500 men, including 400 picked soldiers from the army battalions, from the thrust against the Mohawk valley—which Montcalm
condemned as a "Quixotic" and "chimerical" "venture that will
maybe cause the loss of the colony."[25] He fired off several letters to
Vaudreuil requesting that he recall Levis and send him to Fort Carillon as soon as possible.[26]

Fortunately Levis's force had not yet embarked up the St. Lawrence on that long, roundabout odyssey to the Mohawk valley. A week earlier, on June 22, Levis had received Vaudreuil's grudging approval to lead the 400 regulars from Lachine to Chambly, but he had had to delay the rest of his army's scheduled journey up the St. Lawrence on June 28. Vaudreuil agreed to wait until the severity of Abercromby's threat could be precisely determined. That, Levis diplomatically pointed out, would not of course be possible until Abercromby and his army appeared before Fort Carillon. And by then, he added, it would be too late. Vaudreuil conceded the point but remained skeptical. He had dismissed the various scouting and prisoner reports of 20,000 to 25,000 enemy troops preparing to march against Fort Carillon as gross exaggerations (though he seems to have kept the source of his alternative knowledge to himself). Montcalm wrote that he suspected Vaudreuil rejected those estimates as an excuse "to weaken the corps which was entrusted to me" in hopes that Montcalm would suffer a humiliating defeat.[27]

Vaudreuil reconsidered on June 29 when intelligence reports arrived from two vital fronts: Amherst's massive British expedition had succeeded in landing near Louisbourg and were besieging that citadel while Abercromby's army was about to embark for Fort Carillon. Although he scoffed at the latter report, he ordered Levis to take his 400 elite troops to Fort Carillon just in case.

Would Levis and his men arrive on time? On June 30, as he organized the regulars at Chambly, Levis sent word to Montcalm that "Vaudreuil had determined . . . yesterday in the evening to release my detachment. I had been of this opinion thinking that it was necessary to go even sooner . . . I am pressing Vaudreuil to send promptly to you all the aid that is possible and especially the Indians . . . Vaudreuil is determined to send you everything." If Levis was disappointed at the diversion of his expedition, he hid it. Several days earlier, on June 26, he seems to have resigned himself to that reality when he complained that "the lack of provisions retards our operations. We can only begin to open the campaign in the first days of next month. The troops are now marching to defend Lake George. For that I am destined to go in a little while." Now Levis feared he would not be able to reach Montcalm before July 10, and he pushed his men into an exhausting forced march and row to get there earlier.[28]

On July 2 the governor ordered his brother Rigaud to lead the rest of the troops at Lachine to Fort Carillon. Those troops would not arrive until after the battle. There were not enough boats on hand above the

Richelieu River rapids to ship the whole force, and it would take over a week to drag the necessary number of bateaux over the long portage around those rapids.[29]

Vaudreuil was right about the numbers, if not the timing, of Abercromby's offensive. Abercromby would lead only 17,000 men to Fort Carillon. All the same, that army was nearly eight times larger than any previous British force that had reached as far as Lake Champlain. Was it Vaudreuil's awareness of how small previous invasions had been that prompted him to dismiss the prisoners' accounts? Was it just gut instinct? Or were the French officer claims true that Vaudreuil wanted his rival Montcalm defeated? Regardless, Abercromby's army, if skillfully handled, would be more than large enough to overwhelm any French forces before it.

There was an ironic twist to the Indian raid Langy had led that had netted the prisoners. As many as 150 Indians had operated from Fort Carillon just days before Montcalm had arrived. But the general had no sooner set foot at Fort Carillon when nearly all those Indians set off for Montreal to demand the governor's ransom for the prisoners. Only 16 Iroquois, Ottawas, and Nipissings remained. They were not enough to adequately scout, let alone ambush and generally terrorize the enemy. Those few Indians got ever more demanding, larcenous, and homesick. The day after Montcalm arrived they insisted they be allowed to go home and only relented after he promised that other Indians would soon arrive. Together, he urged, they would attack the British. That seems to have provoked rather than assuaged them. An exasperated Montcalm wrote that they were "extremely insolent; they stole all our fowls this evening. They spirited off a barrel of wine and butchered several livestock, and we must endure it all. What a country! What a war!"[30]

FORT CARILLON

At Fort Carillon itself, the walls and bastions remained unfinished. There was much to be done and little time to do it. The site of future Fort Carillon was first occupied in August 1755 by General Dieskau, who left troops there while hurrying on to his disastrous attack on Colonel William Johnson's army at Lake George's south end. On September 20, 1755, Governor Vaudreuil ordered New France's head engineer, Lieutenant Michel Chartier, seigneur de Lotbinière, to design and supervise the construction of a fort where the Ticonderoga promontory juts southeast into Lake Champlain. The fort was first called Vaudreuil after the governor, and then, according to lore, the name was changed to Carillon because the beautiful sound of the water rushing down the La Chute River reminded the more poetically minded of a series of bells softly chiming.[31] The fort's exact location was about two hundred yards from the point's edge, where a seventy-five-foot cliff plunges down to the lake's cold waters. Over the next several years the forest on the peninsula would slowly be cleared to supply fortifications, buildings, fuel, and fields of fire.

Lotbinière based the fort's design on principles established by France's greatest military engineer and siege expert, Sebastien le Prestre, Marquis de Vauban (1633–1707). Fort Carillon was a fifty-four-toise by twenty-nine-toise (1 toise = 1.949 meters) rectangle with four triangular bastions. The Reine and Germain bastions pointed, respectively, northwest and northeast—the most likely directions of attack. Facing Lake Champlain were the southeast, Joannes, and southwest, Languedoc, bastions. The seven-foot-high walls were built of thick, squared oak logs laid atop one another in parallel rows fourteen feet apart with earth filling the space between. By 1756, thirty-six cannon, including twelve eighteen pounders, fifteen twelve pounders, and nine eight pounders, were mounted on the walls, with the heaviest concentration of firepower mounted on the La Reine bastion. Another ten cannons lacked carriages. Fort Carillon was surrounded by a dry moat five feet deep and fifteen feet wide. Inside the fort were three barracks and four storehouses.

The northeast bastion housed brick bread ovens capable of baking sixty loaves at once. A powder magazine was hewn out of solid rock beneath the Joannes bastion. The barracks, magazine, and cistern were constructed of stone. Starting in 1756, the fort's walls were gradually encased in stone blocks. The construction stone was taken from the fort's foundation and a quarry a mile away. The task was still undone when the French abandoned the fort in 1759. Important storehouses were located outside the fort in a palisaded village on the low ground between the fort and lake. Brick and lime kilns were nearby.

All inspectors agreed that Fort Carillon's "site is very good and susceptible of an excellent fortification; it is favorable in that the enemy can only open a trench on one side, where . . . he can be deprived of that advantage by removing down to the bare rock the trifle of earth that is lying upon it. The forts in this country are constructed only of pieces of timber, one over the other, in which cannon effects a practical breach

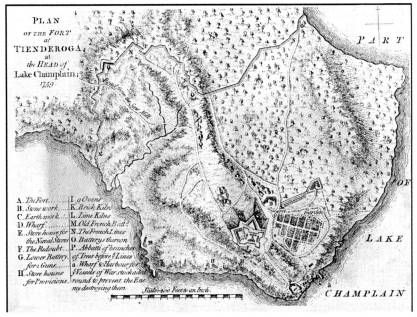

Map 4: "A Plan of the Fort at Tienderoga . . ."

A Set of Plans and Forts in America. London: Mary Ann Rocque, 1765

Courtesy of the Massachusetts Historical Society

with more difficulty than in stone; therefore the forts . . . will only be taken by force of shell."[32]

But there were flaws. The fort may have looked formidable from afar but weaknesses riddled it. One was its small size, only one-third that of the standard Vauban fortress. Only about 400 troops could be crammed into Fort Carillon's barracks. Likewise, only so many supplies vital to sustaining the garrison could be squeezed within the walls. Thus hundreds of provision barrels were stacked outside; these were not only exposed to storm and rot but could "be burned by any one man sufficiently bold, who the enemy may send during the drifting of snow . . . when a soldier on guard does not see twenty paces in front of him."[33] The two-story-high barracks extended above the fort's walls making it an easy target for enemy cannon. Further, the cistern was too small to supply the fort's needs, and the water was muddy and barely palatable. The magazine was so damp in the spring and fall that the powder had to be removed and stored outside the fort. And the fort did not cover all the ground and gullies that could approach it from the land side or even adequately command the lake.

Photo 1: Fort Ticonderoga viewed from Mount Rattlesnake (Defiance)
Courtesy of James P. Millard © 2006 America's Historic Lakes

Other defects were even more perilous. Fort Carillon was built with
its back to the lake and was overshadowed by two heights upon which
the enemy could plant batteries and shell the defenders into a quick
surrender. The first was a low plateau spread a half mile before the
fort. Though only about twenty feet higher in elevation than the fort,
the plateau not only offered a besieger a perfect firing range but also
severed the fort's overland retreat to Fort St. Frederic, a dozen miles
north. The other eminence stood about a mile southwest of the fort beyond the mouth of the La Chute River. The French considered the 850-
foot Mount Rattlesnake (Defiance) too steep, wooded, and remote to
pose any danger to Fort Carillon. They were wrong. But fortunately for
them, Abercromby would also neglect that mountaintop.

With a vigorous commander besieging Fort Carillon, retreat by its
defenders would have been nearly impossible. Artillery and manned
bateaux at Lake Champlain's narrows would have effectively sealed off
the only escape route. Fortunately for the French, they faced enemy
generals like James Abercromby, with his spasm of recklessness, in
1758 and timid Jeffrey Amherst the following year.

Even assuming the French could decamp and flee north to Fort St. Frederic before the British cut them off, their retreat could not end there. It was bleakly acknowledged by all that "Fort Carillon once taken, Fort [St.] Frederic would not stand an instant. The latter is built of stone so as to be incapable of resisting four cannon shot, which would be sufficient to tumble into ruins. All the country in its vicinity is flat and affords at every step an easy landing for the largest guns."[34] Either the British had to be stopped before they got within artillery range of Fort Carillon or Lake Champlain's southern end was theirs.

As if these gaps in the fort's defense were not serious enough, no significant fortifications stood between Lake George's north end and the two-and-a-half-mile road that started on the west side of where the La Chute River drained Lake George. The road extended north a half mile where it crossed the river by a pontoon bridge, ran slightly northeast nearly another mile where it recrossed the river by bridge above a sawmill powered by one of the five falls, and then veered sharply east the final mile to Fort Carillon.

Ticonderoga's successful defense ultimately depended on a complex of redoubts and entrenchments. In hindsight the main fort should have stood on the plateau with fortifications on Mount Rattlesnake, at the

Photo 2: Mount Rattlesnake (Defiance) viewed from Fort Ticonderoga

Courtesy of James P. Millard © 2006 America's Historic Lakes

cliff overlooking Lake Champlain, at Lake George, and at various easily defended points along the La Chute River road. Such a defense in
depth would have blunted attacks launched on both Lake George and
Lake Champlain while allowing the French to safely retreat north to
Fort St. Frederic should the British break through.

But as it then stood Fort Carillon was easy pickings, as all the French
officers posted there painfully acknowledged. Deputy Commissary
General Andre Jean-Baptiste Doreil articulated the bleak consensus:
"The enemy could land above Carillon without fighting, cut off the
communications of that fort with that of [Fort] St. Frederic and consequently with Montreal, and afterwards march against this last place,
leaving a third of his army to blockade those two forts and M. Montcalm. The general would have no other course to pursue, his provisions
being consumed, than to surrender. . . . The total loss of the Colony
would follow."[35] His assessment got grimmer the longer he stayed
there: "Fort Carillon is worthless. . . . An ignoramus constructed it—a
relative of M. de Vaudreuil. . . . Ineptness, intrigue, lies, cupidity will in
a short time destroy this colony which costs the King so much."[36]

The criticism from his fellow engineers would not prevent Lotbinière
in November 1758 from petitioning War Minister Belle Isle for a Cross of
St. Louis: "Tis a favor, I dare say, I have merited by the zeal I have en-
vinced on all occassions."[37] Belle Isle was not impressed—Lotbinière's
reputation had preceded him. In the margin of Lotbinière's letter, the war
minister wrote: "This account is filled with falsehoods and deception. . . .
He has only just been made Captain, even to the prejudice of some Sen-
iors, and is not in a position to expect, as yet, the Cross of St. Louis. He
has officiated as engineer; lacks not theory, but has little or no practice. It
is he who built Fort Carillon, which though tis worth nothing cost the
King so much and is not perfect. He did not impoverish himself by it; he
receives an income of 7 to 8 thousand livres since three years; he had
scarcely anything in 1756. He is a relative of the Marquis de Vaudreuil."[38]

All of the fort's flaws were readily apparent to Montcalm. He was appalled by Fort Carillon's cramped dimensions, half-finished walls, fouled
cistern, and damp magazine. Only several hundred troops could squeeze
within its walls. The fort itself was clearly indefensible. Abercromby
would have to be stopped elsewhere. But where? He called a council of
war among his officers on the night of June 30 and mulled all their reports and perspectives. They swiftly reached the obvious conclusion that
Fort Carillon could only be held by a defense in depth from Lake George
to its ramparts.[39]

At daybreak on July 1, Montcalm sent Bourlamaque with Lieutenant Colonel de Roquemaure's La Reine, Lieutenant Colonel de Fontbonne's Guyenne, and Lieutenant Colonel de Mongay's Bearn battalions to the pontoon bridge. There they entrenched themselves on the west bank. Bourlamaque then sent a picket of a hundred men under Captain François Joseph Germain down the road to Lake George, where they constructed a small redoubt that they called Fort Saint Sacrament, after the French name for the lake. The general sent the other four battalions to the sawmill; he posted the La Sarre and Languedoc Battalions, led respectively by Lieutenant Colonels de Senerzergues and de Privat on the north side, and the Royal Rousillon and 2nd Berry Battalions, led by Lieutenant Colonels de Bernetz and de Trivio, on the south side. Montcalm set up his headquarters marquee on the south bank beside the sawmill. He assigned his engineers, Captain Nicolas Sarrebource de Pontleroy and Captain Jean Nicolas de Desandrouins, to fortify the plateau. Though the engineers paced off and marked where the plateau's fortifications should be erected, inexplicably no work would begin there for another six days, only two days before the British assault. Finally, Lieutenant Colonel de Trecesson's 3rd Berry battalion garrisoned Fort Carillon.

Extending the defense further south up Lake George to reconnoiter and ambush the enemy was essential, but demanded men willing and able to fight in the thick wilderness. With so few Indians or marines, Montcalm had to ask for volunteers from the regular battalions. Enough men stepped forward to fill two companies, one under Captain Bernard of the Bearn and the other under Captain Duprat of the La Sarre. For now he held those men in reserve on the plateau where they prepared for their future wilderness missions. Late that day Indian scouts arrived to report rangers and Mohawks in the area. Montcalm dispatched Langy with thirty troops, filling two bateaux, to scout the southern end of Lake George.

Just as dawn was breaking on July 2 two musket shots and Indian war cries split the calm at the redoubt on Lake George. Germain sent a runner with a warning that the enemy was near to Bourlamaque, who immediately ordered the drummers to beat the call to arms. The troops rushed into their battalion formations.

Bourlamaque soon got the full story. Lieutenant Massdac and six troops had been patrolling not far from the Lake George camp. During a halt Massdac had misplaced his knife and had returned to look for it. He noticed a feather on the ground and bent to grab it just as an Indian fired at him. Massdac raised his musket and fired back. The Indian dropped to the ground then dashed away.

Although that lone Indian scout was hardly a threat in himself, he may well have been the first of Abercromby's expedition. Montcalm ordered the troops at both the pontoon bridge and the sawmill to devote the day to bolstering their fortifications and hauling supplies. Although Fort Carillon was not far away, each camp began constructing its own oven so that the soldiers could enjoy fresh, warm bread each morning.

For now Montcalm found his own Indian allies more troublesome than those of the enemy. Nearly every day some Indians arrived and others disappeared, either on raids or to their distant homes. Only eighteen Indians were then with the army and they were restless. They met with Montcalm and demanded to be released. They relented only after the general held a prolonged talk with them and handed out presents. They agreed to set up camp beside the La Reine Battalion.

The tension in the French army eased somewhat on July 3 when good news and new troops arrived. Langy's two scouting bateaux returned to report that they found no enemy forces on Lake George. At Fort Carillon, Captain Raymond stepped ashore with 80 marines, 30 militia, and Captain François Marc Antoine Le Mercier, the colony's artillery commander. Montcalm ordered Raymond and his troops to join Bourlamaque at the pontoon bridge. Late that day came word that Levis's expedition had been diverted to Fort Carillon. That day's only excitement occurred when a drunken Abenaki Indian murdered his friend and then disappeared into the forest.

The following morning, on July 4, Montcalm sent Duprat and his men to reinforce Germain at the landing and Captain Bernard with 40 men on a scout south nearly ten miles along Lake George's rugged east side; Bernard's patrol crossed no enemy trail and returned to set up a camp atop five-hundred-foot Mont Ange, which rises above Lake George's eastern shore about a half mile from the La Chute River mouth. At seven o'clock that evening, Montcalm dispatched Captain Langy and 104 volunteers, 25 Canadians, and several Indians in bateaux to row southward as far as Lake George's south end if need be, until they either spotted Abercromby's army or were able to capture some British soldiers for interrogation.

VII

MONTCALM'S PATH NOT TAKEN

The most important event in the French army on July 4 was what Montcalm did not do after inspecting Bourlamaque's entrenchments at the pontoon bridge. After tarrying no more than an hour, he pronounced his satisfaction and returned to his camp at the sawmill. Had he instead strolled the other way a half mile further down the road to the redoubt on Lake George he might have recognized that spot's vital importance. Well-placed batteries and entrenchments guarding the quarter mile between Bear Mountain and the La Chute River would have blasted any approaching flotilla of whaleboats, bateaux, and barges to splinters. None of the surviving documents or memoirs explain why Montcalm either did not consider mounting a major defense at the most easily defended place in the region, or rejected this idea.

Had Montcalm taken this action, what might Abercromby have done? If a hasty council of war had decided to mount a waterborne assault, most likely the French troops and batteries massed in the redoubts and breastworks along that stretch of shore would have repelled the British and inflicted heavy losses. Regardless of whether or not Abercromby would have ordered an attack, the only other option was to land his army elsewhere and try to outflank the French at the La Chute River mouth. But where? For miles down the lake nearly all of the heavily forested eastern and western shores rise steeply hundreds of feet. There were a few places where a creek drained into the lake and thus offered a route into the interior, but for a small patrol rather than an army.

The nearest possible landing spot for Abercromby's 17,000 man and thousand-boat flotilla lay on Bald Mountain's south side, where lowlands stretch for several hundred yards. Had Abercromby landed his army there, how would Montcalm have responded after receiving word from scouts posted atop Bald Mountain? Most likely he would have sat tight in his trenches with most of his troops while sending out his marines, army volunteers, and his handful of Indians to harass the British via the trail along Bernetz (Trout) Brook, which flows north to the west of Bald and Bear Mountains and then gently angles northeast to join the La Chute River a half mile north of the pontoon bridge. Abercromby, in turn, would have most likely sent out the rangers and light infantry led by Howe, Gage, and Rogers to do the same. Neither side could have done more. The trail between the two armies was too narrow and ill-marked to accommodate larger bodies of troops.

How then would the campaign have unfolded? It would have taken days at least for Abercromby to land all his supplies and fortify a camp, and weeks to widen the trail leading toward Fort Carillon and gingerly march his army along it. By that time Levis's 3,500 troops and warriors would have reached Montcalm's 4,000. Bloody forest battles would have erupted as French marines and Indians collided with Rogers's rangers, Gage's light infantry, and Johnson's Mohawks. As the British army crept ever closer to his lines, Montcalm would have withdrawn his troops and guns from the landing to fortifications north of the La Chute River. Once Abercromby had secured the La Chute landing, he would have transferred his supply depot there. The first large-scale battle would presumably have taken place as Abercromby sent a large force along the La Chute River's west bank to engage the French entrenchments where the river curves east. But by that time his forces would have outnumbered Montcalm's by only two and a half to one, and the chance of mounting a successful assault would have been even worse than it actually was.

FINAL DISPOSITIONS

But Montcalm chose otherwise. By July 5 the French entrenchments at the pontoon bridge and sawmill were complete and the cannon emplaced. Free now of heavy labor, those not on guard duty could lounge around playing cards, swapping tales, and perhaps dreaming wistfully of their distant homes or pretty girls. That lazy summer day was broken at two o'clock by a musket shot fired by a lookout atop the hill near Fort Saint Sacrament. Officers and troops stopped whatever they were doing and stared toward the flagpole atop the hill. A white flag was run up it and then down. A boat was on the lake. Was it French or British?

It was from Langy's command bearing a message for Bourlamaque. Langy and his volunteers had sailed and rowed south as far as Ganaouske or Northwest Bay where they spied a distant British camp. The British troops the French had spotted were Abercromby's advance guard commanded by Colonel Bradstreet and including Major Rogers and the rangers. Bradstreet ordered his troops, who filled sixty bateaux, to pursue with drums beating. The French easily evaded them. The British rowed back to their camp. Awaiting either further orders or a British advance, Langy and his troops continued to hover three leagues away from the redcoats. Bourlamaque sent orders for Langy to return.

After consulting with Montcalm, Bourlamaque ordered Captain de Trepezec of the Bearn battalion to take three *piquet* (elite) companies of 51 troops each, some volunteer marines and militia, and the Indian guides to hike up Bald Mountain. There they would "observe the enemy's movement and prevent them from disembarking in the area."[40] Should the British row past, Trepezec should return with his troops after counting the British forces. After Langy and his men ground ashore around five o'clock, Bourlamaque hurried them into the forest to catch up with and join Trepezec. That combined scouting force of Trepezec and Langy numbered between 300 and 350 troops.

Montcalm meanwhile issued orders for all troops to be ready to muster at any moment and to send their heavy baggage back to Fort Carillon. That night 150 more Canadians and marines, led by Captains Naudiere, de Saint Ours, and de Gaspe, reached Fort Carillon.

An hour after midnight a flurry of musket shots exploded at the landing on Lake George. Bourlamaque ordered his troops to arms. After a quarter hour of tense waiting in the dark, the troops were ordered to dismiss. It was not the British army after all but merely an enemy scouting party. Rangers had opened fire on some of Germain's sentinels and seized a corporal and a private. The prisoners drew their bayonets, stabbed at their captors, and fled. The rangers dashed after them. Other French pickets opened fire at the shadows stumbling noisily through the pitch-dark woods. The corporal and private breathlessly reached their lines. The rangers slipped away. No one was seriously hurt.

THE BRITISH APPROACH

Just where was Abercromby? On July 4, his army was massed at Lake George's southern end; it included 6,261 regulars, 9,829 provincial troops, and 1,600 boatmen to be conveyed up Lake George by 900 bateaux, 135 whaleboats, and a half dozen or so large barges known as *radeaux* for the artillery.[41] Each man carried thirty-six rounds in his cartridge box and five-days rations in his haversack. Each of the large ponderous bateau carried 22 men with thirty days of rations; the smaller, more maneuverable whaleboats took 10 men without provisions. The troops spent all of July 4 loading supplies and artillery on the boats. They began squeezing themselves into the boats by five o'clock in the morning of July 5; within two hours all were aboard. At eight o'clock that morning the men in the lead boats dipped their oars and began to row.

To his credit, Abercromby organized his flotilla in a way that maximized its speed and security. The army would proceed in four columns, with regulars composing the two center columns and provincials manning the two flank columns. The wings would row two hundred yards from the center columns, which would be fifty yards apart. The heads of each column were ordered to remain abreast. Boats were to remain at least one boat length from those before, behind, and on either side. Each regiment had earlier organized a company of marksmen to lead the way. The size of the company varied according to the size of the regiment; a regiment with 1,000 men formed a company of 100 men, a regiment of 700 men a company of 70 men, and so on. Each regiment's grenadier company would bring up the rear. When all the bateaux, whaleboats, and radeaux were in motion the flotilla extended for six miles.

Leading the way were Rogers's 416 rangers and Gage's 359-man 80th light infantry. The fifteen provincial regiments were split into two divisions or wings. Colonel Phineas Lyman commanded the 3,944-man Left Wing, with 1,949 Connecticut troops split among four regiments and a 75-man ranger company, and 1,995 troops including New Hampshire, New Jersey, and Rhode Island regiments and a company of 90 New Hampshire rangers. Colonel Jedediah Preble commanded the 5,345 man Right Wing, which included six Massachusetts regiments with 4,054 troops and the New York regiment of 1,291 men split among three battalions.

Those provincial wings sandwiched the regulars and artillery. The second column included Lieutenant Colonel John Donaldson's third brigade of Major William Eyre's 888-man 44th and his own 651-man 55th. Lieutenant Colonel Francis Grant commanded the second brigade of Lieutenant Colonel Samuel Bever's 633-man 46th and his own 999-man 42nd (Black Watch). The third column included Colonel William Haviland's first brigade with Major John Tullikens's 560-man 1st battalion and Major John Rutherford's 932-man 4th battalion of the 60th Royal, and Lieutenant Colonel Eyre Massey's 664-man 27th (Inniskilling), along with the 1st artillery battery. The regiments of Whiting and Lyman made up the first echelon of the rear guard, with Oliver Partridge's regiment at the very rear.

Abercromby issued equally explicit instructions for the order of battle once the troops were ashore. Regular regiments would stretch by companies with the troops of each two deep and the grenadier company

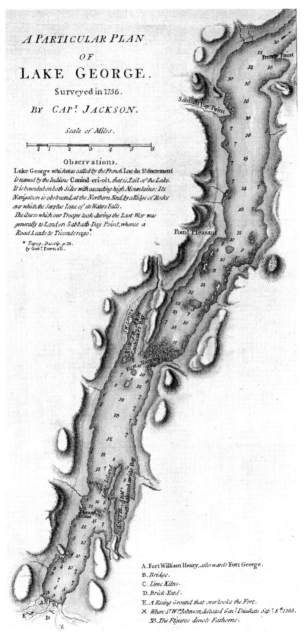

Map 5: Fort William Henry to Sabbath Day Point

Detail taken from "A Survey of Lake Champlain . . ." Drawing by William Brassier. London: Robert Sayer and J. Bennett, 1776 Courtesy of the Massachusetts Historical Society

in reserve directly behind the center. No interval would divide the regular companies. Provincial companies would adopt the same formation with a six-pace interval between them. The light and marksmen companies would be divided into four platoons, with two posted on each flank. Any officer who fired without orders would be cashiered; any soldiers who committed that offense would be executed. When marching in column, a detached platoon would protect each battalion's flank.[42]

The flotilla made good time. By five o'clock that evening it had reached Sabbath Day Point, twenty-four miles up the lake. Those familiar with the previous years' battles around Lake George must have felt a chill as they halted there for a five-hour rest. Sabbath Day Point was the scene of a horrific ambush of Colonel John Parker's New Jersey Blues on July 24, 1757. The Indians had "jumped into the water and speared them like fish," killing or capturing nearly 200 men.[43] A year later one anonymous officer of the 46th wrote that "we beheld there its melancholy remains, both there and on the shore. We made a halt at that Point to wait for the rest of the three brigades and artillery. . . . The whole came up by 11 o'clock at night and we resumed our route."[44] By midnight all the troops had reembarked for the hard row of the remaining twelve miles to the lake's northern tip. They left their campfires burning in the dark to confuse any lurking enemy scouts.

Lake George is shaped roughly like a thirty-two-mile wine bottle, with a narrowing four-mile neck at its northern end. At daybreak on July 6 the flotilla's head reached that neck. Rangers in a score of canoes and whaleboats skimmed up the lake and scanned the steep forested shores for a suitable landing site. But there was no place to land an army except at the lake's north end, where a couple of hundred French troops nervously waited.

A HASTY WITHDRAWAL

As soon as the French guards atop the watch hill spotted the flotilla they fired their muskets and repeatedly raised and lowered their white flag. A scout canoe beached at the landing before Fort St. Sacrement; the men scrambled out shouting that hundreds of enemy boats were approaching. Germain hurried the scouts on to Bourlamaque. About that same time Bernard's troops on the east side of the neck fired at the enemy's lead whaleboats as they skimmed past then hurried back to the pontoon bridge.

The British rangers and light infantry rowed boldly toward the landing. Germain ordered his troops to fire several rounds, set fire to the camp, and then withdrew hastily before the enemy's vastly superior numbers. At seven o'clock he and his troops filed into Bourlamaque's fortifications at the pontoon bridge on the east side of the La Chute River. Bourlamaque hurried a courier to Montcalm to report all that had happened.

The reported strength of the British army so intimidated Montcalm that he refused to consider a battle at the pontoon bridge site that might have delayed Abercromby's advance. Instead he ordered Bourlamaque to withdraw all his troops northeast of the La Chute River, destroy the pontoon bridge behind them, then join the main army at the sawmill camp. He hurried a courier to the engineers Pontleroy and Desandrouins with orders that they march the Berry 3rd Battalion out of Fort Carillon to the heights, where they should begin felling trees and constructing entrenchments.

Why that work on the heights was not begun six days earlier is unclear. Also puzzling is why Montcalm would bother to fortify positions along the La Chute River only to abandon them at word of the enemy's approach. And that was not all that was left behind. Trepezec, Langy, and their men were supposed to withdraw after they spotted the enemy. Montcalm must have hoped they had descended Bald Mountain's west side and taken the trail along the Bernetz Brook and La Chute River that would bring them back safely to the French lines.

The order exasperated Bourlamaque, who was reluctant to abandon an excellent position, as well as Langy and Trepezec. So he ignored the first order and a second before finally obeying the third from Montcalm.[45] Around eight o'clock, Bourlamaque had the bridge destroyed and strode away with his rear guard.

In all, Montcalm committed several errors that morning and in the preceding week. Fortunately for the French those errors were not serious enough to cost them Fort Carillon, although that would not be understood until later. As has been seen, his worst mistake was not to defend his potentially strongest position: the narrow stretch of lake leading to the landing on Lake George's north shore. Batteries on the hills overlooking the landing and entrenchments and breastworks along the shore would have devastated any waterborne assault.

Then there was Montcalm's decision the night before to send over 300 troops through several miles of rugged wilderness to an isolated mountaintop. Those troops were far too many just to watch for the enemy advance and far too few to defend the lowlands at the lake on Bald Mountain's south flank. If the mission was confined to scouting, a handful of experienced woodsmen could have counted the approaching British and hurried back to camp. It made more sense to send that many men if the mission was to ambush an advance British force that had landed on Bald Mountain's south side and was following the trail over the low divide to the Bernetz valley.

Montcalm knew that Rogers was all too well acquainted with that trail, having suffered a disastrous defeat during the Battle on Snowshoes in March. Undoubtedly Rogers had shared that intelligence with Abercromby. Montcalm had good reason to suspect that the British might land part of their army at that trail to outflank the defense at the landing. But no surviving document supports that scenario. Having sent so many troops so far away, Montcalm literally turned his back on them.[46]

Nor is the general's haste to abandon the pontoon bridge entrenchments understandable. It would have taken hours for the British army to secure a beachhead at the landing place, unload the necessary supplies, and send out scouts followed by an advanced guard toward that position. It would have taken at least another day to drag up enough artillery to threaten Bourlamaque with a devastating bombardment. Only then would his withdrawal have made sense. So if Montcalm had played his hand right, he could have delayed Abercromby's advance for at least a day or so.

And delay was essential if the French were serious about defending Fort Carillon. Outnumbered four to one, Montcalm had to fight Abercromby every step of the way from Lake George to Fort Carillon's ramparts. If the French could stymie the British advance long enough, Levis and his 3,500 troops could join them. Then the odds against the French would drop from four to one to five to two. It is a tactical rule of thumb that an attacker needs at least a three to one advantage to carry a heavily defended position, and the arrival of Levis would have tipped the scales in favor of the French. Instead, by neglecting to defend the landing on Lake George and abandoning the pontoon bridge position, Montcalm was unwittingly aiding the enemy. The chance of a British victory increased the closer their massive army got to Fort Carillon.

When Bourlamaque's troops arrived at the sawmill and marched across the bridge, Montcalm posted them on the La Sarre battalion's right flank. He then ordered his own troops entrenched on the river's south side to withdraw. The bridge over the river was broken up as soon as the

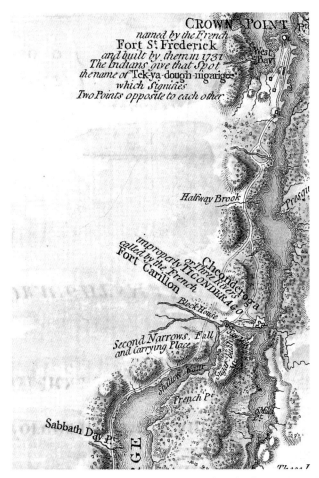

Map 6: Sabbath Day Point to Fort St. Frederick (Crown Point)

Detail taken from "A Survey of Lake Champlain . . ." Drawing by William Brassier. London: Robert Sayer and J. Bennett, 1776 Courtesy of the Massachusetts Historical Society

last soldier tramped across it. A messenger was sent to Fort Carillon with orders to send up to the lowest La Chute River falls bateaux upon which to haul away the cannon, tents, and provisions. Montcalm was preparing for a further retreat. The mood must have been glum. The forest south of the sawmill was now devoid of French troops. At any moment the stillness there might be broken by shadows of rangers slipping through the thick foliage, followed by musket shots and puffs of smoke. Once that happened, Montcalm and his men would know that Abercromby's entire army would not be too far behind.

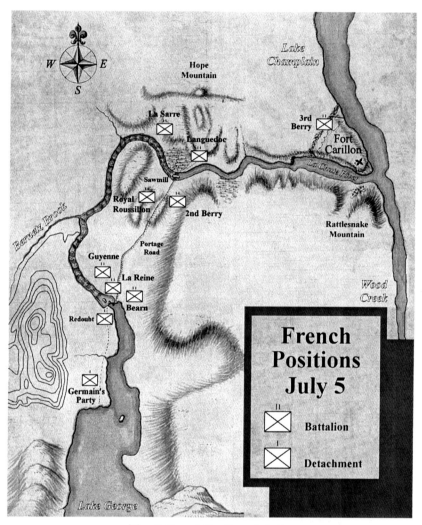

Map 7: French Positions July 5

THE FATE OF TREPEZEC AND HOWE

As the day wore on the anxiety over the fate of Trepezec, Langy, and their men increased. Montcalm would blame Trepezec rather than his own hasty retreat for the fate of that overmanned patrol. In his official report the general claimed that on July 6 "nothing would have been left undesired had a detachment of three hundred men, at whose head I placed an officer of the colony, the most experienced in movements through the forest, as a guide, not gone astray and fallen into a column of English."[47] The sudden sound of scattered shots and then a fusillade of musket shots in the direction of Bernetz Brook would eventually give Montcalm a good idea of Trepezec's location. The general chose not to march his troops to the sound of those guns. Trepezec and his men were on their own.

Upon viewing the British armada rowing down the lake, Trepezec had made a hasty count and then readied his men to return to their

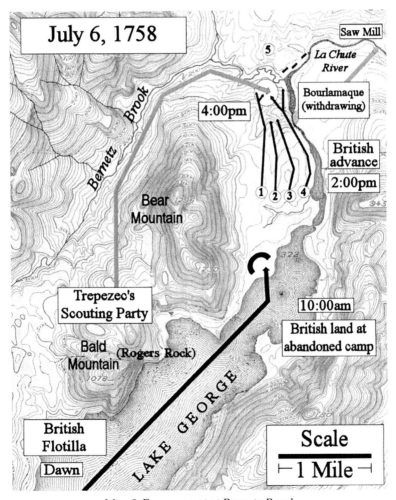

Map 8: Engagement at Bernetz Brook

1. *Colonial provincial column;* 2. *British regular column;* 3. *British regular column;*
4. *Mixed provincial and regular column led by Lord Howe;* 5. *Rangers*

camp at the landing. But somehow he got into an argument with the three Indian guides who angrily stalked off into the forest. Fortunately he still had Ensign Langy, unsurpassed in courage, skill, endurance, and experience in wilderness warfare; only Rogers equaled him on the British side. Langy knew the terrain well. He may have advised Trepezec that if they wanted to rejoin the troops at the landing they should head north down Bald Mountain and then up and over Bear Mountain to the lowland beyond.

That was the most direct route to the landing but the route was strewn with fallen trees, underbrush, and, once they reached the lowlands, boggy ground that exhausted those troops and slowed their hike to a crawl. At certain points during their trek they would have been able to glimpse smoke rising from the fortified camps at the landing and the pontoon bridge, which, coupled with the lack of sustained musket fire, would have been a strong indication that the French army was withdrawing without a fight. Trepezec and Langy's original destination was no longer a viable option. The decision was made to continue north through the tangled forest to Bernetz Brook and then follow it toward the French lines, wherever they now were.

Rogers's rangers, Gage's 80th, and Lyman's Connecticut regiment were the first to jump ashore, followed by the New York and New Jersey regiments. At the abandoned camp at the landing they found a corpse and a straggler, whom they took prisoner. By one account, the French "panic was so great, that they left their camp . . . with all the baggage they had, as also all their provisions, and some hogsheads of wine. Their terror was so very unaccountable, that some of their officers even left their silverhilted swords lying upon their camp tables; all which became a prey to our irregulars."[48] The swords were likely left by Trepezec and his officers who expected to retrieve them after they returned from their scout.

Abercromby intended for his army to advance north in four columns, with the provincials flanking the two columns of regulars in the center; Woolsey's New York regiment would guard the landing. It would take hours to get the army ashore and the regiments assembled into their respective columns. As thousands of troops began to disembark, Rogers and Howe deployed their men in a defensive arc several hundred yards ahead.

From the landing place three passages fanned northward through the forest. The road led due north to the portage and then the sawmill beyond. Shortly before the portage a trail angled slightly northwest

and ran parallel to the La Chute River toward a large hill overlooking
that river and where the Bernetz Brook flowed into it several hundred
yards beyond. Toward the western side of the landing place a path ran
northwest toward Bernetz Brook. Both of those paths joined a path
which ran along the Bernetz Brook.

To screen that eventual advance, Abercromby ordered Rogers and
Howe to lead their men forward. Rogers and his rangers, followed by
the Connecticut regiments of Fitch and Lyman, would secure that hill
about a mile due north of the landing, while Howe would lead the 80th
on the path that angled slightly northwest. As other regiments assembled in their proper column at the chaotic landing, they too moved forward, making room for others to come ashore.

Abercromby undoubtedly gave in to Howe's insistence that he lead
the 80th forward. That was a stupid mistake. As the army's second in
command, Howe should not have led any march, especially one
through such thick forests. Commanders must command, a duty best
fulfilled from a central location of communication and, ideally, obser-
vation; unfortunately, in that forest the former was difficult and the latter was impossible.

At first all went well, but soon after leaving the landing place all four
columns fell into disorder as they thrashed through the undergrowth
and forest. Braddock's ghost perched on the shoulder of every man in
Abercromby's army, especially the redcoats. One soldier recalled that

> we arrived early in the morning at the cove where we were to land; here
> we expected some opposition; but a party of light troops having got on
> shore, and finding all clear, the whole army landed without loss of time,
> formed into columns, and marched immediately; upon our approach, an
> advance guard of the enemy, consisting of several hundred regulars and
> savages, who were posted in a strong intrenched camp, retired very pre-
> cipitately, after setting fire to their camp, and destroying almost every
> thing they had with them; we continued our march through dark woods
> and swamps that were almost impassable, till at length, having lost our
> way, the army being obliged to break their order of march, we were per-
> plexed, thrown into confusion, and fell in with one another, in a most dis-
> orderly manner.[49]

Rogers and his rangers reached the hill about mid-afternoon. Toward
the northeast he could barely make out Montcalm's troops massed
around the sawmill camp. He sent scouts north toward the confluence of
Bernetz Brook with the La Chute River. The Connecticut troops were

beginning to straggle up. Rogers was conversing with the two colonels when firing suddenly broke out toward the rear of their troops.

The forest had not just bewildered the British. Around four o'clock Trepezec's troops were straggling south of Bernetz Brook toward what they hoped would be the safety of the French lines beyond the La Chute River. Unbeknownst to them, Rogers and his troops were ahead, while Howe and his men were approaching their right flank.

Firing broke out when the troops heading Trepezec's column suddenly stumbled into the rear of Lyman's column. When Howe heard the musket shots, he immediately urged his troops toward the battle. As the Connecticut troops blocked the French, Rogers led his rangers in an arc toward Bernetz Brook to cut off the French there. Trepezec and his men were now enveloped on three sides. Spotting the French, Rogers ordered his rangers quickly to fan out, open fire, and charge. Stunned by the rangers' sudden appearance on their northern flank and volleys that tore through their ranks, the French replied with ragged, unaimed shots. The rangers raced among them, bashing in skulls with tomahawks and musket butts.

The firing and yelling in the forest before them panicked the British regulars in the two middle columns, who were stumbling directly toward the French south flank. Some redcoats opened fire without command; others stampeded to the rear. By one account, "the moment the fire was received in front, panic seized our soldiers; entire regiments flung themselves on top of the other, and even the General [Abercromby] narrowly escaped being dragged off in the confusion by the fugitives. In vain did the officers cry out and offer opposition; nothing could stop them; meanwhile our brave rangers defended themselves 200 against the [300] of the enemy, up to the time they were reinforced."[50]

Major Eyre's troops were among those who panicked:

> the firing grew quicker, & it was followed by a loud hidious [sic] yell. Those in the front gave way immediately in the greatest disorder, and . . . ran down for two or three hundred yards . . . no entreaty could prevail with the men for some time; but in about an hour's time after this, we found out, the fire that began this confusion in the front was from ourselves, & by all I could learn since not a single shot was fired against us by the enemy; by this time it was almost dark, we were separated & had some difficulty [regrouping] afterward; but in a very irregular way, the regiments intermixed. . . . I must confess to you, that it's my opinion two or three hundred Indians surrounding us that night, with the apprehensions that some of our people showed, must have ended fatally.

The provincials, however, held steady. Though he was a regular Eyre did not hesitate to give credit where it was due: "I must confess the colony troops behaved extremely well, were in great spirits & [were] willing to do any thing they were desired. However next morning we got some guides to show us the way back to the landing place & there the Army joined in one body."[51]

Massachusetts Private David Perry was one of those provincials who stood when the regulars fled:

> we had proceeded but a short distance into the woods before we were met by the enemy, and a brisk fight ensued. It was the first engagement I had ever seen, and the whistling of balls, and roar of musketry terrified me not a little. At length our regiment formed among the trees, behind which the men kept stepping from their ranks for shelter. Colonel Preble, who I well remember, was a harsh man, swore he would knock the first man down who should step out of his ranks, which greatly surprised me, to think that I must stand still to be shot at. Pretty soon, however, they brought along some wounded Frenchmen, and when I came to see the blood run so freely, it put new life into me.[52]

The fight did not last long. The rush of the rangers, light, and provincial troops on three sides broke the French forces, who were already exhausted and disoriented from hours of thrashing through the forest. The French either pleaded for quarter with arms upraised or fled blindly through the woods. In all the British killed 45 French and captured 148, while suffering only 10 dead and 6 wounded.[53] Even after the fighting ended the firing sporadically continued, as edgy pickets shot at imagined Indians and French slipping through the brush. This often sparked equally edgy officers into ordering their men to volley.

The British victory, the war's first large-scale defeat and capture of French troops since William Johnson's 1755 victory at Lake George, proved to be demoralizing. It was marred by a tragedy that would haunt and perhaps doom the entire British campaign. Howe had charged into the midst of the battle, "notwithstanding all the remonstrances made him."[54] A musket ball shattered Howe's life, and with it the morale of the British army. Captain Moneypenny was near Howe when he was killed: "Never a ball had a more deadly effect. It entered his breast on the left side, and (as the surgeons say) pierced his lungs and heart, and shattered his back bone. I was about six yards from him. He fell on his back and never moved, only his hands quivered an instant."[55]

Howe's death inspired adoring eulogies from friends and foes alike. No one was more troubled by Howe's death than Abercromby, who now would have to lead rather than preside over his army. He wrote that his second in command "was very deservedly universally beloved and respected throughout the whole army, it is easy to conceive the grief and consternation his untimely fall occasioned; for my part, I cannot help owning that I felt it most heavily and lament him as sincerely."[56]

Howe embodied the army's spirit. Major Thomas Mante wrote that with Howe's loss "the soul of General Abercromby's army seemed to expire. His enterprising spirit infused a noble ardour into every rank, and his activity was such as created an emulation amongst the soldiers. . . . From the unhappy moment the General was deprived of his advice, neither order nor discipline was observed, and a strange kind of infatuation usurped the place of resolution."[57] Bougainville acknowledges that the "disheartened English gave us twenty-four hours delay, and this precious time was the saving of us and of the colony."[58] Colonel James Wolfe deemed Howe's death "irreparable, because there is not another soldier [like him] in his Majesty's service, and I do not at all doubt that, in two campaigns, he would have driven the French out of North America."[59] But no one summed up the tragedy better than Francis Parkman: "The death of one man was the ruin of fifteen thousand."[60]

Abercromby ordered Howe's body taken to Albany where it was supposed to be embalmed and sent to his family in England. The hot, humid weather quickly began to rot the corpse, however. General John Stanwix had Howe's remnants buried at St. Peter's Church in Albany.[61]

That was the only decisive choice Abercromby was capable of making that evening. The victory of his rangers, provincials, and light infantry in the forest coupled with Howe's death bewildered him. His troops were scattered between the landing place and Bernetz Brook. Imagining that Montcalm's troops and a horde of screaming savages might attack at any moment, Abercromby called a council of war where he raised those fears. More seasoned hands dismissed them. The officers urged a march toward Fort Carillon the next day. Abercromby tepidly agreed and ordered his army to lay down on their arms while pickets ringed the encampments.

Trepezec, Langy, and eventually 60 remnants of his command straggled out of the forest into the French camp. Trepezec was shot in the gut and would die an agonizing death the next morning at Fort Carillon. Langy himself suffered a slight bullet wound in his leg. Around the same time Captain Duprat arrived with his volunteer company to report that rangers were skulking where Bernetz Brook joined La Chute River, threatening to outflank the French at the sawmill.

Upon hearing those reports, Montcalm convened a council of war.[62] His officers were split over what to do. Bougainville insisted that they stand and fight, and even advocated a sortie to surprise the disorganized British front. Chevalier de Bernetz and Jean-Joseph de Montgay, commanding the Rousillon and Bearn battalions respectively, were just as adamant that the British could outflank their position and thus the only sensible option was to withdraw to the plateau. A few did not want to stop there. The Canadian commanders and de Trivio of the 3rd Berry called for blowing up Fort Carillon and retreating north. Others were undecided.

Montcalm ordered another retreat. He would take his stand atop the plateau west of Fort Carillon. With Raymond's marines and the militia covering their flanks, the regular battalions were underway by five o'clock and reached the plateau two hours later. They would be joined that night by 183 Canadians and marines led by Captain M. de Gannes. Montcalm set the army to work strengthening the breastworks and abatis already begun earlier that day.

Eleven years earlier, on July 19, 1747, Montcalm was among 5,300 casualties the French suffered when they attacked the fortified hilltop of Assieta, Italy, defended by Austrian and Piedmontese troops. After he recovered, Montcalm would later carefully study that battle, especially the enemy fortifications. He may well have had that distant battle in mind when he chose to defend his present position. Regardless, he was taking an enormous risk.[63]

CHAPTER 6

The Battle of Fort Carillon

The whole conduct after Lord Howe's death was madman-like.
—Anonymous provincial officer

*The ground was strewn with the dead and dying . . . I could hear the men
screaming. . . . A man could not stand erect without being hit . . . for the balls
came by handsfull.*
—Private David Perry

*We have not had the success we flattered ourselves with, and have lost a
number of brave men, which I grieve and lament.*
—Major General James Abercromby

 THE ADVANCE AND DECISION

Howe's death spooked Abercromby more than anyone else in his army. On the morning of July 7 he ordered his regiments scattered in the forest between the landing and Bernetz Brook, to concentrate back toward the lake. He later explained that "the troops being greatly fatigued, by having been one whole night on the water, the following day constantly on foot, and the next night under arms, added to their being in want of provision, having dropped what they had brought with them in order to lighten themselves, it was thought most advisable to return to their landing place, which we accordingly did about eight that morning."[1] It was rather strange for the general to later relate such solicitude for the same troops that he would hurl against the French breastworks the following day.

Abercromby spent the morning at the landing supervising the untangling of regiments and unloading of supplies. He issued orders to reduce indiscriminate firing, noise on the march, and confusion in transmitting messages. Good news arrived that may have stiffened his sagging backbone. Amherst's army had landed near Louisbourg and was preparing to besiege that citadel. Johnson and his Indians were on their way.

Meanwhile he pondered a vital question: with Howe dead, who would lead the army? Brigadier General Thomas Gage was next in line but, like Abercromby, hesitated to leave the landing's safety. Three years earlier he had commanded General Edward Braddock's advanced guard when it blundered into a force of French and Indians that overwhelmed the British in a murderous crossfire. Gage survived, but Braddock and nearly 456 troops did not; 412 wounded managed to escape. That trauma was burned deeply into Gage's psyche.

Contrasting with Gage's timidity was Lieutenant Colonel John Bradstreet, the army's most vigorous high-ranking officer and wilderness fighter after Howe. Bradstreet heatedly advocated a brisk march forward. Abercromby agreed and asked Bradstreet to lead the advance. It was a wise decision but characteristically Abercromby would soon revoke it.

Bradstreet was one of the French and Indian War's flawed heroes.[2] He excelled as an administrator, leader, strategist, and warrior. He was born in Nova Scotia and as a young man joined the 40th regiment based there. He was baptized by fire during the 1745 siege of Louisbourg, where his exceptional courage was noted. Then, for the next decade, history took little note of him until war again broke out with France. He was tapped to head the bateaux corps in 1756. It was an inspired choice. Keeping troops supplied is a Herculean task in any war, especially in the wilderness. He fulfilled his missions brilliantly, supervising the building of thousands of boats, massing, moving, and guarding supplies, and heading numerous convoys to Oswego and Fort Edward. He turned an ambush by French, Canadians, and Indians on the Onondaga River in 1756 into a victory by leading a flank attack that routed the enemy. Yet, much like Robert Rogers, controversy dogged his life. Accusations of corruption, hotheadedness, and intrigue tarnished his reputation. Throughout his career, he embroiled himself in disputes with nearly all of his superiors, including eventually Abercromby.

At eleven o'clock, Abercromby ordered Bradstreet to lead 5,000 troops, including the 44th, six companies of the 60th's 1st Battalion, two Massachusetts regiments, John Stark's ranger company, 1,000 boatmen, and two cannon, to advance as far as the sawmill a mile north of the landing and a mile and a half from Fort Carillon. Arriving at that position, Bradstreet waded his troops across, posted most in a defensive position, and set the rest to work building a new bridge. He sent rangers forward to scout the enemy's position and impatiently awaited Abercromby and the rest of the army. At three o'clock, with each of his flanks screened by Rogers's rangers and the 80th Light Infantry, Abercromby set off from the landing with nearly all the rest of his army. Only Melancthon Woolsey's 2nd Battalion of DeLancey's New York regiment remained behind to guard the landing, supplies, and flotilla.[3]

The army's morale began to rise after its plunge of the previous day and night. New Jersey Chaplain John Brainard wrote that "at that time our affairs appeared very encouraging notwithstanding the great loss we had sustained on the death of Lord Howe."[4] A British officer remarked that "we were one and all infatuated with a notion of carrying every obstacle, with so great a force we had."[5]

That elation began to fade as word of what lay before them began to filter through the ranks from returning scouts. All day ranger patrols slipped through the forests to creep as near the French lines as they dared. They furtively watched as the French chopped down all the trees within a long musket shot of their breastworks, stripped away the leaves, and sharpened the branches. Any attacking troops would not only face withering musket fire from Montcalm's breastworks but a bewildering maze of abatis that broke up and slowed their advance. The rangers must have been astonished as they watched: the French "officers . . . planted their colors on the work and, axe in hand, were the first to set the soldiers an example, and each strove with the greatest ardor to surpass the other."[6] In the British army only rare officers, like Rogers or Howe, treated the soldiers as men rather than beasts of burden or slaughter, and strove to lead by example. The rangers captured several stragglers and brought them before Abercromby. Questioned separately they all declared that Montcalm had 6,000 troops around Fort Carillon and soon expected the arrival of Levis with 3,000 more.

Clearly, if unhindered the French would complete their horseshoe barricade across the plateau before the next morning. At a council of war Bradstreet urged Abercromby to continue the advance and attack before the French finished their fortifications. Abercromby demurred. He would rest his army and order an attack the following morning. Bradstreet heatedly protested that by then it would be too late. Bradstreet's opposition and tone irritated Abercromby, who reacted to the dissent by dismissing him from the council. He would later deny him the honor of commanding the assault on July 8.

Abercromby wanted information that confirmed his decision. He ordered two of his aides, engineer Captain Matthew Clerk and Captain James Abercrombie, to thoroughly examine the enemy lines. Accompanied

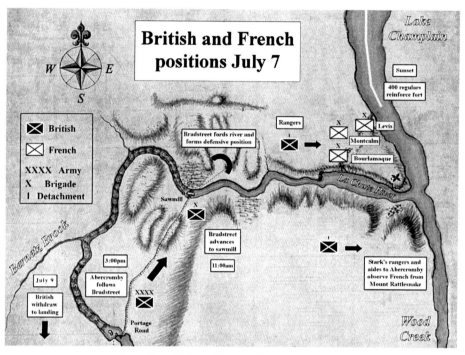

Map 9: British and French Positions July 7

by Stark's rangers, the two officers climbed Mount Rattlesnake. From atop the mountain they enjoyed a spectacular view of Fort Carillon more than a mile away, across the waters where the La Chute River flows into Lake Champlain. They then hurried back to Abercromby's headquarters with a vivid image to justify the attack. According to the 44th's Captain William Hervey, "Abercrombie and Clerke went to reconnoiter the enemy and brought word that they were making a breastwork which we might easily get to and push down with our shoulders."[7] That was just what Abercromby wanted to hear.

That sanguine view of the enemy swiftly spread through the army, at once raising the morale of the troops and utterly deluding them as to the horrors that awaited them the following day. Lieutenant William Grant of the 42nd Regiment recalled that Clerk and Abercrombie had spent July 7 "reconnoitering the French lines before Ticonderoga and finding out the easiest approaches to them. The engineers who had been sent to take a view of the lines this day, reported to the general that they could be easily forced, even without cannon, if they were attacked with spirit."[8] The general and his officers agreed to assault the French lines the following morning and spent the evening of July 7 working out the details.

THE FRENCH PREPARATIONS

Montcalm knew he had taken an enormous risk in withdrawing his army to the plateau a half mile before Fort Carillon. His army was facing northwest while its back was to Lake Champlain.[9] Under abler leadership the British army could have simply cut off the French army's land and lake escape routes, and then bombarded and starved their enemy into submission.

His worries lightened a bit around sunset on July 7 when 400 detached regulars arrived with word that other troops were on their way; Levis himself would appear late that night. He was also cheered by how rapidly and efficiently the fortifications across the plateau had risen. His engineer captains, Desandrouins and Pontleroy, could not have supervised the construction of a better defense given their limited time, troops, and equipment. Behind that forest of abatis was an arc of breastworks eight to ten feet tall, constructed of squared logs with dovetailed ends fitted together. These were backed by a firing platform and cut by loopholes.

To man those defenses, Montcalm split his army into three brigades and a reserve. He took personal charge of the 480-man Royal Rousillon and 450-man 2nd Berry battalion in the center, while Bourlamaque commanded the 460-man La Sarre and 426-man Languedoc battalions on his left, and Levis the 410-man Bearn, 470-man Guyenne, and 365-man La Reine battalions on his right. Each battalion had roughly a hundred yards of entrenchment to defend. A battery of six cannons in a redoubt anchored the breastworks' left. A four-cannon battery was started on the breastwork's right, but it would not be completed until the day after the battle. The volunteer companies of Bernard and Duprat guarded the low ground between the plateau and the La Chute River on the left while Captain Raymond's marines and militia stretched along the broader ground sloping gently from the plateau down to Lake Champlain. Those troops guarding the flanks constructed their own breastworks and abatis from felled trees. While its grenadier company would join the reserve within the horseshoe, the rest of the 3rd Berry battalion commanded by Lieutenant Colonel Trecesson would guard Fort Carillon and convey

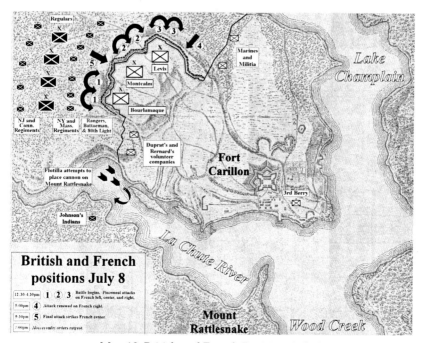

Map 10: British and French Positions July 8

ammunition to the front. Colonel Mercier commanded Fort Carillon's artillery. Altogether Montcalm would have 3,858 troops, including 3,370 regulars, 472 marines and militia, and 16 Indians stretched along the horseshoe, the flanks, or in reserve.[10]

Montcalm's line had two potential weaknesses. First of all, it was a very thin grey-white line that stood ready to receive those masses of redcoats. That problem would be alleviated somewhat by the felled trees with sharpened branches, which, like an aroused porcupine, would slow and break up an assault, This would allow French troops to shift along the breastwork to mass their muskets against the fragmented attackers. The general boosted the flexibility of his defense by posting the grenadier and *piquet* companies of each battalion in reserve so that they could be rushed to join the defenders at any hard-pressed point. Abercromby would unwittingly aid the French by failing to coordinate his four separate forces to charge simultaneously rather than piecemeal against the breastwork.

The other potential weakness lay on the low ground on the horseshoe's flanks, which fell away sharply down to the La Chute River on the left and gradually to Lake Champlain on the right. If the British could break through on one or both flanks they would be in a position to march to the arc's rear and open fire. To attack those thinly defended flanks, however, the British would have to march across an enfilade of fire from the ends of the breastwork, along with cannon shots from Fort Carillon. Here again Abercromby would aid the French by never attempting to outflank them.

By the evening of July 7 the work was almost done. The exhausted troops were withdrawn behind the barricades where tents had mushroomed. The soldiers stretched around smoky fires over which kettles of soup bubbled. The two volunteer companies spent the night in the woods firing sporadically at lurking rangers. Canadians under Ensigns Langy and Daillebout scouted the enemy lines. Fires were fed all night along the edge of the woods to keep the rangers well back from the French lines.

Montcalm issued several pages of regulations that covered virtually any contingency during the coming battle. Most important were his instructions on shooting: "the great fault of the regulars lies in hasty firing without aim; the result is ammunition speedily exhausted and that the enemy continuing to fire, the soldiers become discouraged. The officers . . . will see to it that the soldiers fire slowly and they must urge him to take good aim."[11] Considering the carnage they would inflict on the British, the regulars seem to have taken Montcalm's shooting tips to heart.

On the eve of battle, the sutlers made a killing of their own by charging the nervous and exhausted soldiers an exorbitant nine livres for a six-quart keg of brandy. An incensed Montcalm later complained to Vaudreuil that such outrageous gouging by the sutlers sapped the soldiers' morale as well as their meager savings. He would have put a stop to it but felt he lacked the authority to regulate their prices and practices. Doubtless he also feared that any crackdown would fray the already strained ties between the French and Canadians. Finally, the general may well have worried that preventing the sales could damage his relations with his own troops; those soldiers might have protested the sky-high prices, but they still laid down their money. The governor later wrote that the general had full power to expel them under a 1757 ordinance Vaudreuil had signed.[12]

The French drummers beat the generale at five o'clock on the morning of July 8. The companies were assigned work details. Some dug earth or hauled logs into place to strengthen the barricade and its firing platform. Others chopped down more trees further from the lines and sharpened them into abatis. Guards were posted 150 paces beyond the furthest woodcutters. Companies patrolled the forest. Aside from glimpses of rangers snaking through the brush there was no sign of Abercromby's army.

Montcalm placed himself in the breastwork's center. With him were his aides Captain Louis Antoine de Bougainville, Captain de la Roche-beaucourt, Lieutenant Marcel, Colonel de Montreuil, and the engineers Desandrouins and Pontleroy. He repeatedly questioned whether his decision to stand and fight was right. Captain Pierre Pouchot observed that the general "was rather irresolute all that morning. He did not know whether to resist the enemy attack or to withdraw toward St. Frederic. It is certain that if we had been obliged to adopt the latter course, all his army would have been killed or captured, lacking a line of retreat."[13]

Around noon, about sixty bateaux appeared on Lake Champlain. They ground ashore not far from the fort. The bateaux were crammed with supplies and 80 marines led by Captain Plessix. The troops were immediately marched to Raymond's command on the right flank. The arrival of those supplies meant one less worry to plague Montcalm. Until then, the army would have exhausted its food within eight days. Now they might hold on a few days more if need be. But if Abercromby settled in for a long siege, Fort Carillon was doomed. Their only salvation lay in a highly improbable enemy act. Would Abercromby be so foolish as to forgo a siege and instead shatter his army against their fortifications?

THE FINISHING TOUCHES

As Montcalm and his army nervously awaited their enemy's next move, Abercromby and his officers put the finishing touches on their battle plan. The assault would consist of three phases. In phase one the rangers, provincials, and light infantry would lead the army's advance opposite the breastworks and then open fire to wear down the defenders. Meanwhile, four six-pounder cannons and a howitzer would be floated down the La Chute River aboard rafts with an escort of twenty bateaux filled with troops; those guns would be emplaced at the foot of Mount Rattlesnake. The second phase involved that battery enfilading the French breastworks with a bombardment. The final phase would be an all-out attack by the army at four different points of the French line.

That plan was certainly questionable under the circumstances. If Abercromby truly believed that Montcalm had 6,000 troops entrenched and would soon be reinforced by 3,000 more, then risking his army in an assault supported by only four cannons and a howitzer was unwise to say the least. The wisdom of conducting a formal siege rather than attack should have been obvious even to a military novice.

That siege should logically have involved splitting the formidable firepower of over forty mortars, cannons, and howitzers into three batteries, one dragged atop Mount Rattlesnake, another emplaced opposite the breastwork, and the third set on Lake Champlain's shore to cut off Montcalm's retreat. As those guns were hauled into place, the general should have hurried most of Rogers's rangers and Johnson's Indians a dozen miles north to Fort St. Frederic to gather intelligence and harass that understrength garrison. The rangers and Indians would have thus provided ample warning of any reinforcements and would have been in a position to resist their advance.

So why then did such an experienced if not gifted general and his officers do what they did? Clerk and Abercrombie had assured them the day before that the French lines could be carried by a mass assault. To Abercromby's credit, he "wanted that the engineers should be certain for what they told him with regard to the lines; so . . . he sent them out again to take as near a view of the lines as possible, early in the morning of the eight with a proper escort."[14]

Several ranger companies escorted Clerk and another engineer, Charles Rivez, down the La Chute River's south shore.[15] As the engineers scanned with spyglasses the French lines, the rangers opened fire. Most of the musket balls fell short; one broke the arm of Lieutenant d'Arenes of Bernard's volunteers. The French returned an ineffective fire.

What Clerk and Rivez saw reinforced the previous day's assessment. In his report to Abercromby, Clerk asserted that an assault could succeed if the entrenchments were "attacked before they were finished."[16] But before that happened, he suggested that the French lines be softened up by artillery barrages from two batteries, one at the base and the other atop Mount Rattlesnake. Bradstreet had made his own reconnaissance of the French lines and echoed the conclusions of the engineers.

Abercromby promptly agreed to two of Clerk's three suggestions—a bombardment by a battery emplaced at the foot of Mount Rattlesnake followed by a massive assault; there was not enough time to hack a trail to the top of that mountain and drag cannons and munitions to the summit. The general later justified his decision as being supported by a consensus among his officers: "Before I undertook the attack we had the reports and opinions of two very expert engineers, who had been on that ground at different times before, and had seen the ground and works the preceding night and that morning. And, upon their report, all the principal officers were unanimously of opinion that the attack should be forthwith made on the entrenchment."[17]

Although the council of war was unanimous before the battle, afterwards the manner in which the reconnaissance was conducted and who conducted it was widely condemned. Charles Lee of the 44th Regiment sharply criticized Abercromby's choice of Clerk as "his favorite engineer (but I should here inform you that this favorite engineer is quite a stripling, who had never seen the least service & of scarcely any rank on the establishment), thro' partiality to whom he had removed all the other engineers who were his superiors on the most trifling errands, in order to give him chief command."[18] That image was widespread. Of the criticism heaped on Abercromby after the battle, much was "for heakening to Boys who never saw a fight and neglecting to ask Counsel of knowing of any one experienced Officer in the Army."[19]

Much of that dissent was unfair. Abercromby had good reasons to thrust that vital mission on Clerk's young shoulders—that "stripling" was the highest-ranking and most experienced engineer available. Illness had laid low Abercromby's chief engineer, Major James Montressor. The second-ranking engineer, Major William Eyre, had squabbled with Abercromby over various issues and rejoined his regiment, the 44th, as its senior ranking officer. Thus did circumstances more than a decision elevate Clerk to such a lofty position. But Clerk was no novice in engineering or the field. Although he had spent little more than a year in North America, he had gained valuable field experiences, most importantly in a November scout of Fort Carillon followed by extensive planning for a winter campaign to capture it.

Yet Clerk's advice was contradictory. He at once called for bombardment of the French fortifications by two batteries, of which the one atop Mount Rattlesnake would take days to emplace, and an immediate assault before the French finished their defenses. How could such a bright young man offer such conflicting advice? Did he feel pressured as Abercromby's "favorite" to give in to the general's own inclination to attack? What else could have led him to assert that the breastwork was so frail that the troops could shove it over? Whatever animated his thinking, Clerk would carry it to his grave. Ironically, his advice sealed his own fate. He rejoined his 27th Regiment for the attack on the barricade before Fort Carillon. There a bullet would mortally wound him.

In any event, it was Abercromby who was ultimately responsible for acting on Clerk's report. Rather than send a surrogate, the general himself should have observed and analyzed the French lines from the vantage point, and not from the low ground along the La Chute River but atop Mount Rattlesnake. One anonymous officer spoke for the army when he asserted that "the grounds had never been properly reconnoitered which proved to be a fatal circumstance to the army & will ever be a reproach to the general."[20] A cursory glance at the French lines would have revealed the futility of a mass bayonet charge across ground littered with felled trees and backed by a log breastwork—which was manned by several thousand troops waiting with leveled muskets. And Abercromby neglected to fulfill an essential part of Clerk's proposal— the artillery bombardment. The general would order his men into those killing fields without benefit of either his own reconnaissance or an artillery barrage to soften up the enemy.

After the campaign, Abercromby would try to scapegoat Clerk for his own failings. But at least one Whitehall official would exonerate Clerk, arguing:

> he was not to blame in that unsuccessful attack at Ticonderoga. The view he had of the French works was from a hill on the Opposite Side of the River within Musket Shot of the French Lines and on their Flanks there he proposed to have erected a Battery and had actually four Cannon at the Foot of that hill ready to draw up . . . Clerk intended to have erected a Battery upon that hill which would so have raked the French Lines (and unattacked by them because on the opposite Side of the river) that they Could not have stood to their posts. . . . Nay such was the advantageous Situation of that Hill that a Battery upon it with a small alternation in the Direction of the Cannon would have answered for Battering the Fort.[21]

Although the aborted decision to mount a battery atop Mount Rattlesnake would not be widely known during or even well after the battle, many in Abercromby's army clearly recognized that peak's importance. Captain Charles Lee of the 44th observed that Mount Rattlesnake "seemed to offer itself as an ally to us, it immediately commanded the lines from hence two small pieces of cannon well planted must have drove the French in a very short time from their breast work, the consequence of which wou'd have been that the greatest part of 'em must either have surrendered or drown'd themselves in the lake . . . this never was thought of, which (one would imagine) must have occurred to any blockhead who was not absolutely so far sunk in Idiotism as to be obliged to wear a bib and bells."[22] This colorful view of the commander became ubiquitous in the British army.

That view, however, was not entirely fair. As has been seen, Abercromby agreed to Clerk's suggestion to plant cannons at the base if not atop Mount Rattlesnake and wanted them to open fire on the French lines before the assault. But when French cannon fire forced the flotilla carrying those cannon to turn back, Abercromby allowed attack after attack to proceed anyway.[23]

Abercromby's urgency was hardly justified. After all, time was on the British side. True, the exaggerations of French prisoners and deserters had nearly doubled the number of Fort Carillon's defenders, while warning of 3,000 additional troops fast approaching Fort St. Frederic just twelve miles north. Yet if the enemy in the breastwork before him really did number 6,000 men, then that was all the more reason not to attack but to besiege. Furthermore, a competent commander would have sent his rangers and Indians toward Fort St. Frederic to confirm the reports of those reinforcements. Even if the combined forces of Montcalm and Levis numbered 9,000 troops, the British army's 17,500 men would have still outnumbered them by 8,500. Abercromby had more than enough men to cut off and besiege Montcalm while blocking Levis's advance. Those same prisoners and deserters that inflated French numbers also revealed Fort Carillon's dwindling supplies. A siege would have forced Montcalm to strike his colors within a week.

Around nine o'clock William Johnson and 435 warriors strode into Abercromby's army. It had taken them more than a week of swift marches and rows to catch up. Johnson had led them from his mansion on June 29 while Deputy Superintendent George Croghan stayed behind to collect the stragglers. As usual, it was difficult to keep the Indians under control. On July 5 they arrived ten miles from Fort Edward. To Abercromby, Johnson wrote that the Indians "have been out of provisions these 2 days which will greatly add to their natural voracious appetites, therefore hope you will order your commissary to issue their officers the provisions on their arrival." He then added in a postscript, "It must be you will forbid sutlers or any others selling or giving them any liquor without my orders & knowledge. The consequences may be very bad if they get any liquor."[24] On July 6, Croghan and 55 warriors caught up with Johnson's 370, which included 173 Mohawks, 68 Oneidas, 30 Onondagas, 22 Tuscaroras, and 12 Senecas from the Iroquois League, along with 18 Scoharys and 47 Mohicans.[25]

After all the time, energy, and money Johnson had spent recruiting those Indian allies, and the speed with which he had led them to the British camp, his reward was to have Abercromby fail to utilize them in any meaningful way. The general ordered Johnson to deploy his Indians atop Mount Rattlesnake. The only positive thing that can be said about that decision was that at least they were out of harm's way. As Montcalm put it in his official dispatch, they "opened a considerable fire which did not interrupt the work. We did not amuse ourselves by answering them."[26] Those accounts that had Johnson's Indians peppering the French lines with musket fire are curious. The mountaintop is far beyond musket range of the breastworks or fort. Whatever shots the Indians squeezed off most likely plopped into the waters where the La Chute River flows into Lake Champlain. Probably some of those Indians descended to skulk along the La Chute River mouth and fire across it toward the French lines.

The Crown had spent a small fortune recruiting those Indians and all Abercromby could think to do was to give them a grandstand view of what became one of the more humiliating and senseless debacles in British military history. Those Indians would carry word of the French slaughter of the redcoats back to their councils, making it all the more difficult and expensive to recruit them the next year. Ideally, most of those Indians should have been deployed with the rangers against the marines and militia on the French right flank, the most vulnerable along their line. Others should have been sent north to Fort St. Frederic to take scalps, prisoners, and information.

What explains Abercromby's decision? The official reason penned by Captain Hugh Arnot was to stir "a mock fight with a great deal of whooping and Noise (Indian fashion) in order as it was suppos'd to let the Enemy know we had Indians."[27] But that same "mock fight" would have been more effective within musket range of the French right flank. Psychology rather than strategy may offer a better explanation. Like most British commanders, Abercromby found Indians exasperating with their incessant demands and barbarous warfare. Most likely the general merely wanted to get the "savages" out of his way. Yet another possible reason why the Indians were not committed to battle was that many were still not committed to alliance with the British. They would take advantage of whatever happened. The French believed that the Iroquois in particular had come "to witness our defeat and to act, afterward, openly against us."[28] Regardless, the presence of the Iroquois on Mount Rattlesnake did startle the French. After all, the

French considered all the Iroquois except the Mohawks either allies or at the very least neutral during the war.

By late morning Abercromby had devised his order of battle. The rangers, 80th Light Infantry, and provincials would lead the way and post themselves beyond musket shot from the La Chute River across to Lake Champlain. From left to right, DeLancey's New York regiment and the Massachusetts regiments of Bagley, William, Partridge, Doty, Ruggles, and Prebles slowly marched through the forest toward the clearing. The New Jersey and Connecticut regiments followed but would remain in reserve. The regular troops would approach last and pass then through the provincials, light infantry, and rangers to lead the attack. Each regiment's light infantry company would attack first, followed by the grenadiers, and then the line companies. The 27th and 60th's 1st and 4th battalions would attack the British right, the 44th and 55th the center, and the 42nd Highlanders and 46th the left. They were ordered to "march up briskly, rush upon the enemy's fire, and not to give theirs until they were within the enemy's breastworks."[29] Alas for the British, the only redcoats to make it over the barricade would be prisoners.

The main assault would begin at one o'clock.[30] Controversy arose among the officers when they received the order to attack in line rather than columns. Columns are less unwieldy and easier to maneuver through broken terrain than lines. By concentrating the attacking troops at a critical point they are more likely to break through the enemy's line. Major William Eyre of the 44th argued that had the regiments attacked in column "we could more easily force our way thro' the felled tress than by making so large a front three deep. But it was said this would cause confusion. In short, it was said we must attack any way, and not be losing time in talking or consulting how."[31] That haste would make for an enormous and tragic waste.

Could regiments attacking in column rather than line have overrun those breastworks? Historian John Shy believed so: "if Abercromby had attacked with regiments in column formation, he would surely have broken Montcalm's position and probably would have decisively defeated the numerically inferior French."[32] But nothing is certain in war. Those columns would have been subjected to the same withering fire as they struggled through the fallen trees and tried to climb the towering breastworks.

This debate of column versus line is obscured by the French reports, which all describe the British as attacking in column rather than line.[33] What explains that discrepancy? The regiments of each of the four separate attacks marched onto the plateau in column. At the clearing's edge the regiments deployed from columns into lines two ranks deep. But the integrity of those neat parade-ground lines was impossible to keep once the regiment marched forward. The troops undoubtedly bunched up as they squeezed through gaps in the abatis. Then, after each repulsed attack, the surviving regimental officers, fearing their men would scatter or desert in the thick woods, may well have rallied them en masse around their flags and drummers before marching them out again. Thus the French defenders mostly saw what appeared to be enemy columns rather than lines.

Another controversy was the order to charge with the bayonet: "No Officer on pain of being Cashiered with Infamy, to fire without Orders—No Soldier, to fire without Orders, on pain of Death."[34] Thus did Abercromby hobble his troops with one more handicap by forbidding them to return the enemy's fire. As their initial bayonet charges were bloodily thrown back, the officers would disobey that order, allowing their troops to load and fire at first by platoon, but later at will as the losses mounted and unit coherence dissolved.

Abercromby has been flayed for the key fateful decisions made on July 8. Yet those choices were not Abercromby's alone to make. Eighteenth-century strategy and tactics were decided by councils of war in which the highest-ranking officers debated and forged a consensus under the army commander's guidance. Aside from Bradstreet, Abercromby's officers were in unanimous agreement with every course of action decided upon. Their relative enthusiasm or reluctance for those decisions, however, cannot be precisely determined. Yet at least one of his aides implored Abercromby to besiege rather than assault the enemy. Captain James Abercrombie "was for bringing up our Artillery next Day & attacking it in form but others who had not seen half the Service & whose nerves are not quite braced for war, advised the contrary, which by my Soul I am heartily sorry was preferr'd to mine."[35] But the decision for a grand assault prevailed.

THE GRAND ASSAULT

The battle of Fort Carillon began a half hour past noon. Firing broke out between the French sentries and the rangers and advanced guards of provincial regiments who crashed through the woods toward Montcalm's left front. Bursts of firing rippled elsewhere beyond the clearing as other provincial regiments, followed by the regulars, marched toward the plateau and encountered the French pickets. The French guards and workmen dashed back to the barricades. French drummers beat the command for the battalions to form. The line companies massed three deep behind the barricades while the grenadier and *piquet* company of each battalion stood in reserve.[36]

Abercromby had initially planned for the provincials and light infantry to pin down the enemy, with the regulars held in reserve and sent forward only after the battery at Mount Rattlesnake's foot had opened fire. According to Captain Arnot, Abercromby believed that the heavy fire of the provincials and light infantry followed by huzzahs signaled that his troops had breached the French lines; he then immediately ordered the rest of his army to attack without an artillery barrage. In Arnot's words, the mass "attack would have stop'd there until our Cannon came up if it had not been from a very heavy fire from the irregulars and Provincials gave with a huzaa at the same time, which made our Gen believe & was so told (for He could not see what was a doing) that some part of the Army had enter'd their Lines, then the whole Army was order'd to March up and attack (quite out of Breath from their Distance)."[37]

The general's aide, Captain Abercrombie, gives a different version:

> The New York Reg by Accident fell upon an Advanced Guard of the Enemy, the Picquets who were supported by the Grenadiers & they by the Whole Line, rushed on to the attack before any of the Army were formed, as the place was invested by our Irregulars the whole Army marched in One Column, & as the Reg came up they joined piecemeal in the attack. All this time the General imagined it was only our Irregulars but to his great surprise, when he came up with the Highlanders he found all the rest of the Regulars attacking the Intrenchment.[38]

Another account has the troops attacking on their own initiative rather than the general's orders: "When Major [Thomas] Proby [leading the 55th] in too great a hurry advanced to the attack with small arms, and was followed in a hurry by the rest: The Troops advanced most Courageously but all went to Confusion."[39]

Did the regulars attack on Abercromby's orders or their colonel's initiative? Given the conflicting evidence that is impossible to say. Regardless, shortly after those first volleys were fired on July 8, the fog of war once again engulfed Abercromby. The general lost control of the battle and blindly ordered yet more attacks. Wishful thinking rather than a rational assessment determined that decision. After all, it was Abercromby who only a hour or so earlier had instructed the provincials and light infantry to advance to the clearing and pepper the breastwork with musket fire, thus pinning down its defenders while the rest of the army marched into position.

When Abercromby sent word to the four columns to attack, many of those regiments were widely separated and still struggling through the woods into position. Those groups of British regiments, supplemented by provincial sharpshooters, were supposed to charge at once. Instead they advanced piecemeal as soon as they entered the clearing, which meant those on the British right flank with the shortest march from the sawmill camp charged first, followed by the center and finally the left.

To worsen matters the abatis broke up each column of regiments into knots of men desperately trying to push forward into the hail of musket balls that slaughtered them. Captain Pierre Andre Gohin, Comte de Montreuil, was behind the barricade as "the enemy opened their attack by a most brisk fire of musketry and immediately advanced to fight with the cold steel, but our fire was so well sustained and directed that it was impossible for them to approach nearer than 15 or 20 paces."[40] Even when the British managed to level their muskets and fire there was little to aim at. As one British soldier wrote, behind the breastworks the "French were invisible; nothing was to be seen of them but a small bit of their caps, whilst they were keeping up a terrible and continual fire. Every man who wished to approach nearer than 15 paces was irreparably dead."[41] "Friendly fire" apparently inflicted some British casualties: "we received considerable damage from our friends in the rear who fired at random."[42]

The grand assault began as the effort continued to emplace an artillery battery at the foot of Mount Rattlesnake. Two barges, each mounting two six-pounder cannons, and one with a howitzer, accompanied by about twenty bateaux had been laboriously hauled down the portage road and floated below the falls at the sawmill.

When the French spotted that flotilla, Montcalm marched Poularie's grenadier company and the Royal Rousillon's *piquet* company to leaven the volunteer companies of Bernard and Duprat anchoring the left flank. The French infantry opened fire as did three cannons mounted on Fort Carillon's nearest wall commanded by Captain Louvicourt. Of the seven or eight cannon shots fired, most hit the river with huge plumes of spray or tore into the trees beyond. Several cannon balls smashed through a barge and a bateau, spilling the screaming men into the dark water. The French troops marched up to the riverbank and fired volleys at the boats. Faced with that deadly barrage of cannon and musket shots, the flotilla commander ordered a hasty withdrawal upstream out of range.

After the first blood-soaked repulse, Abercromby might still have taken Fort Carillon. It should have been clear enough, even to him, that none of his troops had breached the enemy line and that the position was too powerful to carry by storm. The general could then have ordered a proper siege whereby the troops were withdrawn beyond musket shot and entrenched while artillery and ample munitions were dragged to the front line, on Lake Champlain, and atop Mount Rattlesnake. In a few days those batteries could have begun pounding the French breastworks to splinters.

But Abercromby justified his orders to continue the attack with two arguments. First he dismissed the assertions by some that bringing up the artillery could have been accomplished in "several days." As evidence he cited reports that the French had taken three weeks to bring artillery over the portage before Montcalm's campaign against Fort William Henry in 1757. Whether or not that was true, Abercromby had five times more manpower than Montcalm did the previous year. Some of the provincial regiments could have been deployed to haul the guns and munitions into place. The New York regiment alone may have numbered as many as 1,700 troops. One of Abercromby's officers spoke for the army's dismay when he wondered, "Why our Cannon was not suffered to Come up for it Might easily have been Landed out of the reach of the Fort Guns."[43]

Abercromby had another excuse for not mounting a siege. He feared that the French would disrupt that process by sending the Canadians and Indians against his rear. But Montcalm's forces, including his Canadians and handful of Indians, were bottled up in the French fortifications. Patrols by rangers, light infantry, and Indians, and provincial forces posted at strategic places would have secured the road from the landing to the siege lines.

Finally Abercromby was obsessed with prisoner reports that reinforcements would swell the French to "10 or 12000 strong before we could have brought up a small part of our Artillery against their lines." That should have been all the more reason to bring up the guns rather than launch yet other attacks. He ultimately justified his decision by citing his engineers' reports on the evening of July 7 and morning of July 8 that a determined assault would overrun the breastwork.[44] But that notion was disproved by the bloody result of the first attack. And yet despite that reality, Abercromby ordered his regulars to charge again and again.

The 42nd Black Watch was initially kept in reserve. As the other regiments marched forward into that storm of lead, the Highlanders demanded that they also be unleashed against the French. The command was given and they marched bravely forward, broadswords in hand and bagpipes wailing. Lieutenant William Grant recalled that

> the oldest soldiers present never saw so furious and so incessant a fire. The affair of Fontenoy was nothing to it; I saw both. We laboured under insurmountable difficulties; the enemy's breastwork was about nine or ten feet high, upon the top of which they had plenty of wallpieces fixed, and well lined on the inside with small arms. But the difficult access to their lines was what gave them a fatal advantage over us; they took care to cut down monstrous large fir and oak trees . . . which covered all the ground from the foot of their breastwork about the distance of a cannon shot every way in their front. This not only broke up our ranks, and made it impossible to for us to keep our order; but it put it entirely out of our power to advance briskly, which gave the enemy abundance of time to mow us down like a field of corn, with their wall pieces and small arms, before we fired a single shot, being ordered to receive the enemy's fire, and marched with shouldered arms until we came up close to their breastwork.[45]

By the day's end 315 of the Black Watch lay dead and another 333 were wounded, including Colonel Grant.[46]

Compounding the debacle, Abercromby neglected to hurl any of his troops against the weak French right flank. Twice that day Levis would order Raymond to send his marines and militia forward to enfilade the British regiments marching against his stretch of the barricade. The first sortie was led by Captain d'Hery and the second by Captain Denau, both officers detached from the La Reine battalion. Each crossfire cut heaps of dead and thrashing, screaming wounded through the British ranks.

Throughout the battle Montcalm either sent his aides, engineer Captains Desandrouins or Montreuil, with orders to his subordinates, or rushed himself to a threatened position. Supervised by Adjutant General Montreuil, several companies of the Berry Regiment's 3rd battalion conveyed ammunition and water barrels to the front. Thirty to forty of those troops were killed or wounded as they laboriously crossed and recrossed the open ground between the fort and entrenchments. That water moistened more than several thousand parched throats. Fires broke out along parts of the breastwork and had to be quickly doused before they spread.

After the regulars retreated, the provincials advanced. Massachusetts Private David Perry, was among those ordered

"to run to the breastwork and get in if we could." But their lines were full, and they killed our men so fast, that we could not gain it. We got behind trees, logs, and stumps, and covered ourselves as we could from the enemy's fire. The ground was strewed with the dead and dying. . . . I got behind a white oak stump, which was so small that I had to lay on my side, and stretch myself; the balls striking the ground within a hands breadth of me every moment, and I could hear the men screaming, and see them dying all around me. . . . A man could not stand erect without being hit . . . for the balls came by handsfull. It was a clear day—little air stirring. Once in a while the enemy would cease firing a minute or two, to have the smoke clear away, so that they might take better aim. . . . One of the men raised his head a little above the log, and a ball struck him in the centre of his forehead, and tore up his scalp clear back to his crown. He darted back, and the blood ran merrily.[47]

From the French lines Captain Pierre Pouchot recalled how the "enemy behaved with the greatest bravery in this attack, bearing the brunt of terrible musket fire without flinching. Several of them were killed only 10 or 12 feet from the entrenchment. Our soldiers also behaved admirably, with great cheerfulness and sang froid."[48]

Even more tragically, a misunderstanding during a lull in the fighting led to more heaps of dead and wounded. Around midafternoon, Captain Jean d'Anglars de Bassignac of the Royal Rousillon battalion tied a red handkerchief to his sword, mounted the breastwork, and defiantly waved it. Since displaying the enemy's colors signaled an intention to surrender, the British colonel opposite him believed that was what the French intended to do. He ordered his regiment forward with clubbed muskets to take the French into captivity. Since clubbed muskets also signal surrender, the French then believed that it was the British who had given up. The French troops scrambled atop their breastwork to watch the event. Though briefly confused like the others, Captain Pouchot suddenly realized that the British were advancing rather than surrendering. He ordered his troops to open fire. The volley tore through the British ranks and they hastily retreated. The British would later cite this incident as an example of French perfidy.[49]

Pouchot insisted that it had been a misunderstanding. A British soldier gave a very different account of what happened. The French "hoisted English colors, clubed their firelocks & beckoned to us appearing in that manner very thick on the breastwork on which Major Moneypenny ordered the whole to advance ceasefiring which was done by several platoons on the left. But coming within 15 or 20 yards of the enemy they struck their colors and threw in upon us a most terrible and heavy fire such as we had never yet experienced which killed multitudes and obliged us to retire to recover the disorder we were thrown in."[50]

Throughout the afternoon the British regiments shattered against the French abatis and musket fire, retreated, regrouped, and marched forward again. In between attacks, the British and French exchanged distant volleys between the woods and entrenchments. Around five o'clock the remnants of the two left columns joined to charge the angle between the Guyenne and Bearn battalions. Montcalm and Levis rushed their grenadiers to join the other companies firing desperately against the redcoats. Their combined firepower broke the British column. During that attack a musket ball crushed Bourlamaque's collarbone and shoulder blade while another tore into his groin; he would survive to live the rest of his life in pain. Lieutenant Colonels Etienne Guillaume de la Senezergues de La Rodde and Privat, of the La Sarre and Languedoc battalions, took over command of that wing, assisted by Montcalm, who joined them several times during the next couple of hours of fighting.

By late afternoon the firing slackened. Montcalm ordered his commanders to have volunteers bring in wounded or dazed British in their fronts as prisoners. An hour later the British made one last attack—their sixth! This one by two columns against the center where the Royal Rousillon and Berry stood waiting. It was shredded like all the previous charges.

None of those attacks ever had a chance of success, a reality obvious to all on the field after the first attack's bloody failure. Yet the officers and their troops obeyed each order to march forward into that storm of lead and forest of abatis whose ground was cluttered with their comrades' shattered bodies. The carrot and stick of British military discipline partly explains their obedience in the face of certain defeat and likely maiming or death. That training combined the harshest penalties for disobeying orders with constant appeals to the troops to uphold regimental and national pride. But if asked why they did it, like most soldiers they probably would have replied that they fought rather than ran so they would not let their comrades down.

And where was Abercromby while French musket fire was decimating his army? It was widely reported that Abercromby never left the sawmill's safety where a provincial regiment guarded him.[51] But according to his aide, Captain Abercrombie, the general accompanied the 42nd to a forested knoll on the La Chute River's northern shore on the British right flank and remained there through much of the battle.[52] A French map of the battle, titled "Plan du Fort de Carillon et de ses Environs avec L'attaque des Retrenchments de 1758," corroborates that account, although how the French could have known where Abercromby was during the battle is unclear. If Abercromby was where his aide and the French locate him, he was close enough to the battle to hear the rattle of musketry and the screams of his troops as they were being slaughtered. But the forest obscured that gruesome sight and, more importantly, blinded him from understanding the battle's dynamics and thus prevented him from making tactical adjustments. Given Abercromby's rigid mentality, it is unlikely that he would have altered his tactics. After all, he received a succession of runners bringing word of the slaughter, yet he ordered more attacks.

THE BRITISH RETREAT

Around seven o'clock Abercromby finally sent word for his army to retreat. With the rangers covering their withdrawal, first the regulars and then the provincials fell back up the La Chute valley. The troops could drag away only a portion of their wounded comrades. Perry recalled, "We got away the wounded of our company, but left a great many crying for help . . . as soon as we left the ground, the enemy let loose his Indians upon them: for none of those that we left behind were ever heard of afterwards."[53]

The British losses were staggering: 1,967 in all, including 464 regulars killed, 1,117 wounded, and 29 missing, along with 87 provincials killed, 239 wounded, and 8 missing. It was about 11 percent of their total force. The French losses were, not surprisingly, far fewer: 104 killed and 375 wounded. At 479 altogether, this was about 10 percent of their total force. Among the French commanding officers, along with the two balls that plowed into Bourlamaque, a musket ball grazed Bougainville's head and two cut through Levis's hat without touching him. The intrepid Canadian Lieutenant Langy suffered three slight wounds.[54]

Montcalm did not order his troops to pursue. He felt his ammunition and numbers were too few, the exhaustion of his troops too great, the enemy still far too numerous, and the woods too thick with foliage and hundreds of Indians. He expected the British to resume their attack the next morning and did not want to risk his troops in any reckless ventures. Less understandably, he did not send out troops to bring in all the British wounded who were moaning, pleading, and cursing among the abatis.[55]

Instead the general ordered wine and beer barrels rolled up to each battalion and tapped. He and Levis then circulated among the troops, who were flushed with alcohol and pride, to congratulate them on their valor and victory. The general reminded his officers to ensure that the troops properly cleaned their muskets and replenished their cartridge boxes. As night fell, with their ears still ringing from a half dozen hours of gunfire, half the troops were allowed to fall into an exhausted sleep behind the barricade while the other half worked to strengthen it. They changed roles midway through the night.

That evening, Abercromby ordered the wounded carried down to the bateaux and dispatched up Lake George; the wounded filled 80 bateaux. The rest of his army camped around the sawmill. He sent word to his regimental commanders to prepare their men to withdraw to the landing the following day. Those troops not too dazed or wounded may well have muttered bitter denunciations of the general who had ordered them to the slaughter.

What explains Abercromby's decision to withdraw? Why did he not instead entrench his army and bring up his cannon for a proper siege? His troops still outnumbered the French. Patrols up to Fort St. Frederic would have found no reinforcements waiting to relieve Fort Carillon. Reason cannot justify his decision. The general simply panicked. He made a decision that was condemned by his contemporaries and has been discussed by historians ever since.

Abercromby predictably concocted plenty of excuses to justify his behavior. In a letter to Pitt dated July 12, he laconically explained that "we sustained such a considerable loss, without any prospect of better success, that it was no longer prudent to remain . . . [and] was therefore judged necessary for the preservation of the remainder of so many brave men, and to prevent a total defeat, that we should make the best retreat possible."[56] His excuses only inflated with time. In another letter, dated August 19, he presented the ludicrous claim that his withdrawal prevented the loss of his entire army: "if the Body of men that was with me had been cut off or made Prisoners, the Enemy might have done what they pleased in the Northern Provinces."[57] But that was never a possibility. His army was not faced with destruction. Montcalm would not dare to attack an army four times larger than his own if it were entrenched or even massed before him.

These were merely the excuses for retreating to the landing on July 9. Then there was the matter the very next day of hastily packing up his army and fleeing thirty-two miles up Lake George to the fortified camp on its southern shore. The general maintained that when "we could make no Impression, after receiving so great a Loss, Would it not have been Madness to the highest Degree to have attempted it a second Time?"[58] Indeed so. But the options were not confined to retreat or attack. Again Abercromby could have conducted a proper siege of Fort Carillon. Had he done so he most likely would have eventually triumphed. Abercromby then shifts his blame to that ever-convenient scapegoat for the British, the Americans: "tho the provincials could scarcely be said to be engaged that Day . . . the Losses which they take Credit for, having happened chiefly on the 6th, yet upwards of two thirds of them retired upon the 8th with great Precipitation to our Landing Place—And after the Attack was over, I returned to the Sawmill, so as to post a Guard at the Bridge to stop the Remainder of them—I was told at the same time that more of the Regulars than was necessary took the same Route."[59] Once again the general utters an irrelevance. Even if the retreat of most provincials and many regulars had been hasty, nothing prevented Abercromby from ordering those same troops to march back up the road the next morning.

That command to retreat astonished many. One anonymous officer wondered

> what could have occasioned the panic at headquarters the Lord knows. The provincial troops are still in [good] spirits and had not lost 500 men. Its true the regulars had sustained considerable losses but not equal to what we expected to lose on landing, if the enemy opposed us there. Had we entrenched at the mills and the next day made our approaches regularly we might have beat down their breastworks and in three or four days been master of the fort as they had not three or four thousand men there . . . to oppose us. But the whole conduct of the army after Lord Howe's death was equally madman-like.[60]

But some shared Abercromby's terror that Montcalm would launch a counterattack: "'Twas very fortunate that we had not been pursued in our retreat; we should have certainly lost 2,000 men more."[61] Outspoken John Bradstreet did not hold his fire. He blasted Abercromby, or "Nabbercromby" as he called him. He reportedly bellowed loudly to all that could hear, "if our Booby in Chief had only acted with the spirit and prudence of an old woman, their whole country must inevitably have this year been reduced."[62]

Bradstreet could do more than just express moral indignation. He again proved his mettle after the Fort Carillon battle. Demoralization and confusion prevailed at the landing as nearly 14,000 troops milled about and tried to force themselves into the boats. He untangled the troops back into their regiments, deployed them in a defensive perimeter around the landing, and embarked them one by one, a difficult task made much easier when the French declined to pursue.

With the wind at their backs, the flotilla made good time. They reached the southern end of Lake George on July 10 and all were disembarked by the end of that day.

ASSESSMENTS

The French generale was drummed an hour before daybreak on July 9. The troops quickly mustered and then marched into line behind the barricade. Beyond the abatis strewn with hundreds of British dead and wounded the forest was silent. Troops were dispatched among the abatis to drag back the wounded and kill those who resisted. Of the 70 severely wounded British soldiers brought in, only 34 would survive.[63] The few Indians with Montcalm disappeared into the woods to search for plunder and fresh scalps.

About this time thick pillars of smoke were seen to arise from the falls and landing. Montcalm sent Bernard's volunteers to learn what had happened. They found that Abercromby had ordered burned all those supplies and the bateaux below the falls that in his haste to flee he had abandoned.

Around eight o'clock Montcalm received two independent reports of what the British were doing. Bernard's company returned to report that the British had retreated. Then, of all people, Lieutenant Wolff and his escort appeared. Abercromby had detained that diplomatic mission throughout the campaign, allowing him to witness the confidence with which those 17,500 troops had set forth toward Fort Carillon and their demoralizing defeat.

Montcalm sent Levis at the head of the grenadiers, volunteers, and Canadians to investigate. Levis and his men gingerly stepped around the bloated bodies and flotsam of a routed army: Doreil reported that "his [Abercromby's] retreat has been a flight in terror and utmost disorder, abandoning wounded, provisions, ammunition, implements, . . . and nearly 500 dead bodies junked on one side and another."[64] At the landing the French were later able to retrieve two hundred barrels of flour that the British had not taken the time either to burn or dump in the lake.

The stench of hundreds of corpses rotting in the humid summer air was becoming unbearable. The French spent the day scouring the battlefield, burying the dead from both armies and shoring up the weaker stretches of the barricade. Montcalm sent the prisoners and his report of the battle with an escort commanded by Captain de La Roche to Montreal.

The governor's brother, Captain François-Pierre Rigaud de Vaudreuil, arrived on July 11 with a small escort. He was followed the next day by about 2,400 marines and over 450 Iroquois, Abenaki, Hurons, Ottawas, Nipissings, Mississaugas, and warriors from other tribes. Those Indians scattered through the forest to rip scalps from any dead they could find scattered in the woods and most likely digging up those who had been hastily buried. On July 12, Montcalm paraded his 6,669-man army, which included 3,528 regulars, 2,671 marines and militia, and 470 Indians, and had the victorious troops sing a Te Deum. Moved by the service, the general remarked "that never was a victory more especially due to the finger of providence."[65]

How might Rigaud's troops and Indians have affected the battle had they been present? Ironically, they might have actually tipped the battle against the French! To Abercromby, the sooner his troops attacked the better. He sought to overwhelm the French before they finished their barricade and 3,500 more troops and Indians arrived. Would Abercromby have been more cautious had those reinforcements already been in line? Certainly the justification for hurling his regiments against the enemy as quickly as possible would have disappeared. With the entire French army before them, perhaps his officers would have convinced their commander to bring up his cannon and conduct a proper siege. If so, Montcalm would have had to retreat or, if Abercromby had taken the initiative to plant batteries on the shore of Lake Champlain that could cut off that retreat, surrender.

And if Abercromby had gone ahead and attacked anyway, would the presence of several thousand extra troops have prompted Montcalm to follow up his victory with a vigorous counterattack? Probably not. Throughout his three years in North America, Montcalm tossed away several chances to turn limited into decisive victories. In 1756, he could have followed up Oswego's capitulation by marching at least to the British forts at the Great Carrying Place and perhaps beyond, but instead he abandoned Oswego and withdrew to Montreal. In 1757, he could have followed up Fort William Henry's capitulation with a march on Fort Edward, as Vaudreuil had ordered him to do. He declined, citing various weak excuses. At Quebec in 1759, Montcalm mostly kept his troops in their defenses despite several chances to destroy parts of the British army—most notably after Wolfe's assault on the Beauport line on July 29 left several thousand redcoats with soaked cartridges stranded on mudflats with their backs to the St. Lawrence.

Montcalm found those reinforcements a burden rather than asset. He complained that Vaudreuil had sent him "a great many men . . . whom I have neither desired nor demanded. They will consume my provisions, and I doubt not but it has been done in order to write that I have been placed in a position to make the most of my victory, and three hundred Indians were refused me at my departure, who would have annihilated the English on their retreat."[66]

The general was certainly correct about all those extra mouths to feed, the advantage to the French cause those Indians could have rendered had they arrived with Montcalm at Fort Carillon on June 30, and how Vaudreuil would use their presence to criticize the general for not advancing on the British. But he is being disingenuous about the rest. Montcalm had repeatedly called for those reinforcements; they had simply arrived after they were no longer immediately needed.

Though unleashing 300 howling warriors on the retreating enemy on the evening of July 8 would have been ideal, nothing but his own caution prevented Montcalm from sending his marines and militia against the British rear, backed by his regulars. Had he done so, Montcalm most likely would have routed and quite possibly could have taken the British army. It all depended on whether the marines and militia punched through the rangers covering the British rear. Given how devastated in numbers and morale the British regiments were, along with their earlier panic in the woods on July 6, a vigorous attack by the Canadians and French might well have stampeded them in terror. The road was narrow. The three entrenchments the French had dug along the portage road, at the sawmill, pontoon bridge, and landing, all faced the wrong direction. With his regiments scattered through the forest and those who had found the landing scrambling aboard the bateaux, Abercromby might have escaped with only a fraction of his huge army. If Abercromby can be condemned for his recklessness, Montcalm can at least be criticized for his timidity.

In that pursuit the French would most likely have had little to fear from the 450 British Indians. Most of those Indians remained all day on Mount Rattlesnake, where they had watched in disbelief the slaughter of the redcoats before the French entrenchments. Victories embolden and defeats dispirit Indian warriors. By that day's end few would have been willing to lift a hatchet to defend a redcoat against the French. Any accompanying the British retreat from the plateau would most likely have fled with the rest had Montcalm chosen to attack. After dark, undoubtedly more than a few Indians descended from the mountain to skulk along the plateau's fringe to loot and scalp the dead British.

If Montcalm can be criticized for failing to convert a limited into a decisive victory, how has history treated Abercromby? The general has rightfully been castigated for his debacle from his own day through ours. The war's first history appeared a half dozen years after the war. In his *The General History of the Late War,* John Entick asks "who can exculpate a general for commanding his men to attack such a fortified camp without cannon . . .? Who can command his care of himself . . . not advancing . . . further than two miles from the seat of action? Who can give a solid reason for his flying. . .?"[67] Who indeed? Those damning questions will forever echo through history. Thomas Mante was no less blistering in his book, which appeared nine years later. Abercromby's campaign was "ill-formed and ill-guided;" the general was rightfully dismissed as a result.[68] In his near-perfect marriage of scholarship and literature, Francis Parkman asserts that the "English general answered the utmost wishes of his enemy . . . The rashness of Abercromby before the fight was matched by his poltroonery after it."[69] In this century, Lawrence Gipson wrote that "no military campaign was ever launched on American soil that involved a greater number of errors of judgement on the part of those in positions of responsibility."[70]

Despite this seemingly withering barrage of condemnation, Abercromby does have at least two defenders. The better of these defenses is offered by John Cardwell, who argues that Pitt's micromanagement rather than Abercromby's tactics caused the defeat.[71] In making that claim, Cardwell distorts an otherwise sound analysis. No doubt Pitt tended to call up more provincial troops than strategy demanded or the colonial assemblies could afford. But the provincial colonels delayed their march or halted at Albany not just to await the shipment of enough muskets and other equipment for their men. The longer they hesitated to join the army, the longer they put off having to serve under often arrogant regular officers and harsh discipline. It is not certain that the campaign would have begun sooner had Abercromby not awaited the provincial contingents. After all, he awaited William Johnson's Indians as well. Most importantly, Abercromby alone was responsible for his decisions in the field. It was not Pitt who ordered the murderous assault on the French lines. If Abercromby had besieged rather than attacked Fort Carillon, he would have won the war's decisive battle and would be remembered as a prudent general rather than an inept butcher.

Leslie Buell's defense is even weaker.[72] She argues that Abercromby had to attack before those reported 3,000 reinforcements arrived. But even with that swollen French army, the British would have still fielded twice the number of troops. Sending a ranger company along Lake Champlain north to Fort St. Frederic would have alerted the British of the arrival of those reinforcements. If they had arrived, part of Abercromby's army could have besieged Fort Carillon while the rest blocked the advance of those reinforcements by land or lake. William Johnson would find himself in a similar situation when he commanded the British army besieging Fort Niagara in 1759. He managed to defeat the French rescue force and capture Fort Niagara. Abercromby could have done no less at Fort Carillon.

John Shy offers an alternative to both the blistering condemnations and the strained defenses of Abercromby. Was Abercromby really incompetent? Shy answers yes, with qualifications: "James Abercromby was a conscientious officer of moderate ability who, when confronted with a crucial situation, made decisions which seemed logical at the time but were ultimately disastrous."[73] While Abercromby may indeed have been conscientious and moderately able, the "logic" of his decisions is debatable. Many of his officers heatedly objected to all of Abercromby's crucial decisions and offered far more "logical" alternatives for each tactical challenge. Shy is on firmer ground when he argues that the general was indeed incompetent, "judged by the only standard which gives meaning to the word, for he failed in battle. Moreover, that failure obviously impaired his subsequent actions. But one is tempted to speculate that, granted a victory at Ticonderoga,

Abercromby would have probably been able to carry the war on to its conclusion at least as well as Amherst accomplished that task."[74]

That is a sensible conclusion. Victories embolden while defeats demoralize; each makes another more likely. Abercromby and Amherst shared similar temperaments and plodding, limited abilities. One failed and the other succeeded in similar circumstances. Had Amherst commanded in 1758, would he have also hurled his army against Montcalm's breastworks? Perhaps, perhaps not. One thing is certain— he learned from Abercromby's mistakes. In 1759, he besieged rather than assaulted those same fortifications.

How does Abercromby assess his own performance? Although he had no one to blame but himself, he did what he could to downplay the tragedy. To Governor DeLancey he offered his classic understatement: "we have not had the success we flattered ourselves with, and have lost a number of brave men, which I grieve and lament."[75] "With a heartful of grief & concern," Abercromby details to Lord Barrington how formidable the French defenses were to justify why his troops did not take them.[76]

His justifications backfire. If that field clogged with felled trees with sharpened branches, the ten-foot breastwork, and over 3,500 massed French muskets was so daunting, why would Abercromby ever think of ordering an assault, let alone actually doing so? Being engulfed in the "fog of war" is inevitable for participants. Deliberately losing oneself in it, as Abercromby did, is not. Abercromby would have a lot of embarrassing questions and anger to confront when he returned to London.

During the three-day Fort Carillon campaign, Abercromby and Montcalm faced asymmetrical strategic and tactical challenges. Abercromby succeeded strategically and failed tactically while Montcalm did the opposite. Strategically the French should have fought a defense in depth from Lake George to Fort Carillon, with the most important battle at the water's edge, while the British should have tried to push quickly up the trail to bottle up the French in Fort Carillon. The wilderness neutralized the British advantage in numbers while the two and a half miles on the portage road from Lake George to Fort Carillon allowed the French a series of strong defenses. Inexplicably, Montcalm spurned these advantages for a reckless gamble before Fort Carillon. Thus did Abercromby succeed and Montcalm fail strategically. But it was tactics rather than strategy that decided the campaign.

The British should have conducted a methodical siege while the French, having made the decision to retreat to the plateau, should have held tight in case the British were foolish enough to attack, or retreat under the cover of night if the siege threatened to succeed. Tactically Montcalm succeeded and Abercromby failed tragically. The British general then compounded his disastrous tactics with the strategic blunder of ordering his army to retreat all the way back up Lake George. Thus ended the greatest battle for Fort Carillon. But dozens more, on and off the field, remained to be fought that blood-soaked year of 1758.

166

CHAPTER 7

Pursuits

If our Booby in Chief had only acted with the spirit and prudence of an old woman, their whole country must inevitably have this year been reduced.
—John Bradstreet

Will he return to attack us?
—Montcalm

TURMOIL WITHIN THE BRITISH CAMP

Safely back at Fort Edward, where he established his headquarters, General Abercromby leisurely pondered what to do next. On July 13, after consulting with his officers, his momentous decision was for most of his army to sit tight at the Lake George Camp and lick its wounds. Virtually none of his colonels were keen on the notion of reembarking the army for another go at Fort Carillon and most were utterly opposed. Yet something had to be done. After all there was a war on. And one of his colonels was eager to square off with the French as soon as possible. So the general allowed himself to be talked into ordering an attack elsewhere.

For a couple of years now, Lieutenant Colonel John Bradstreet had urged the commanders in chief—first Loudoun and then Abercromby—to authorize a raid against Fort Frontenac on Lake Ontario's faraway northeast shore. Having just returned from the disastrous campaign did not deter Bradstreet. Indeed, avenging that debacle was all the more reason to act decisively. Bradstreet unleashed his formidable persuasive powers on Abercromby. The question was debated at that July 13 council of war.

Bradstreet had few friends among his less aggressive brother colonels. While no one could possibly question his daring and prowess, those virtues were part of the problem: he made the rest of them seem timid and fumbling in comparison. And then there was the style of his substance. Deeply rankling was his tendency to loudly bang his own drum and barely conceal his scorn for less competent and courageous officers, even—and especially—the commanding general himself.

So although Abercromby and the colonels argued the mission's pros and cons on strategic grounds, more than a few did so with very mixed feelings. They were happy to see Bradstreet go perhaps to his likely demise, yet they wished to deny him any possible glory should he succeed. Abercromby was among that crowd. He finally signed off on the scheme, reasoning that Bradstreet might just pull it off, which would repair at least some of the devastation that Abercromby had inflicted on his own reputation and that of his army. And if he did not succeed, Abercromby would at least rid himself of the disruptive presence of Bradstreet and several provincial regiments for a while—and perhaps permanently.

An elated Bradstreet met with the provincial colonels whom Abercromby had tapped to accompany him. The expedition would include the Massachusetts regiments of Joseph Williams and Thomas Doty, Oliver DeLancey's New Yorkers, John Johnson's New Jersey Blues, and Henry Babcock's Rhode Islanders, all of whom would be conveyed by Bradstreet's own boatmen battalion. Starting the next day, those regiments one by one drew provisions and headed south. Within ten days they were massed at Schenectady waiting to embark on bateaux west to Lake Ontario. With reinforcements Bradstreet's army would eventually number 3,100 men.[1]

Bradstreet's enthusiasm for carrying on the fight and the humiliation of the Fort Carillon campaign shamed Abercromby and most of the colonels. Suddenly they had second thoughts about squandering several months of fine campaign weather. At a council of war on July 18, Abercromby agreed to a second campaign against Fort Carillon. Yet there was a convenient catch that would delay that offensive for months and probably indefinitely. Having just sent off three thousand of his troops with Bradstreet, Abercromby insisted that he would need more men. But where would they come from?

After dismissing his colonels, Abercromby wrote General Amherst at Louisbourg, asking him if after his campaign was successfully concluded he would "send the remainder [of his regiments] here by the way of New York; as, if that should be possible before the harvest when the Canadians and Indians always go home, we should then be able to make a second, and, I flatter myself, successful attempt."[2] Apparently he sent that letter to Governor Thomas Pownall of Massachusetts and asked him to forward it. A minor controversy would later erupt when it was learned that although Pownall did as he was asked, somehow the letter never reached Amherst.

If Abercromby was proving himself ever more inept at fulfilling his military duties, he was at least decisive in pursuing humanitarian concerns. One issue had troubled him ever since he had reached North America—the fate of British prisoners of war. Now that he had some prisoners of his own he could bargain more effectively with the French. On July 21 he wrote General Montcalm to assure him that the British were treating the 7 French officers and 144 troops captured on July 6 "with all possible care and humanity" and feigned confidence that the French were doing likewise for British prisoners. He complained that Governor Vaudreuil had earlier rejected his offer for a prisoner exchange. He then asked Montcalm to consider doing so and to pressure Vaudreuil to agree.

Two goodwill gestures accompanied his letters and the escort north to the French lines. He returned Canadian militia Captain Coriveau, who had pleaded to be allowed a six-month leave to take care of his family; and two paroled British officers, Colonel Philip Schuyler and Captain Martin, who were both captured at Oswego and whom the French had given leave to visit their families earlier that spring. Abercromby authorized Schuyler to negotiate for a prisoner exchange. His letter ended with the none-too-subtle warning that "however good the treatment prisoners receive in the place of their captivity, they always have much to suffer."[3]

Montcalm's reply was prompt. He thanked the general for the humane care for the French prisoners and assured him that the British in his charge were enjoying the same. He forwarded letters from his prisoners to their families. Though he assured Abercromby that "no person would desire the exchange more than I," the general stood firm with the governor that none was possible until the British complied with the Fort William Henry capitulation, which required those paroled regiments to sit out the war. Montcalm then asserted, "as there is question of my proper act, I can say nothing except that I have nothing to reproach myself with on that occasion."[4] Regardless, as Montcalm was under Vaudreuil's command, only the governor could make the final decision. Thus he would forward Abercromby's letter to Montreal.

Abercromby soon received a puzzling reply. Vaudreuil started out by dismissing the notion of any exchange, arguing that the issue was really one only their respective sovereigns could decide. The governor then performed an astonishing backflip. He accepted the negotiating power Abercromby had granted Schuyler but pointed out that it applied only to officers. He was, however, open to the idea that all prisoners could be exchanged. Responding to his constituents' entreaties, he insisted that in any trade priority go to Canadians, then made a special plea that if marine ensign François Marie Picote de Belestre, "who was taken in the neighborhood of Fort Cumberland in Virginia, be actually at your Excellency's disposal, I request that he may be included in these exchanges."[5]

Abercromby penned a cordial letter to Montcalm on August 12 in which he again promised to provide good care for the officer prisoners and expressed his wish that the French would reciprocate. His letter to Vaudreuil that same day reconfirmed his revocation of the Fort William Henry agreement, but lauded the governor's treatment of British prisoners; he promised the same for those French in British hands. Two days later he repeated his request in yet another letter to Montcalm.[6]

The correspondence between the enemy leaders would continue through the autumn. Pleasantries cloaked the hard line each took. Abercromby insisted on a man-for-man exchange. Probably with a measure of glee, Vaudreuil replied that as soon as Abercromby abided by the Fort William Henry capitulation, he would be happy to do so since "the scarcity of provisions induces me to get rid of them."[7] The negotiations ended when Abercromby would not yield on Fort William Henry. Nonetheless, on November 11, Vaudreuil released Schuyler, five officers, forty-five civilian men, twenty-six women, and twelve children, some of whom he had ransomed from the Indians.[8]

Meanwhile, in the month after the battle of Fort Carillon Abercromby shook up his staff. It is not clear who the general fired as scapegoats for his own gross mismanagement or who resigned in disgust. The half dozen officers that formed his headquarters included chief of staff Brigadier General Thomas Gage, aides de camp Captains James Abercrombie and James DeLancey, brigade Majors (the chief of staff for a brigade) Captains Alexander Monypenny and John Gates, adjutant quartermasters Captains Gabriel Christie and Allan McLean and Lieutenant George Coventry, and engineer Ensign Charles Rivez.[9]

While Abercromby's priorities were launching the Bradstreet raid, prisoner exchange, and staff shakeup, he did not lose track of his other duties. Always a stickler for details, he immersed himself in military affairs great and small. He was involved, to some degree, in everything from other campaigns, contracts, court-martials, Indian negotiations, and the like—everything but moving again against Fort Carillon.

With Abercromby's defeat vultures circled over more than the dead before Fort Carillon. The general was mired in indecision and self-pity. Once word of his debacle reached London he would most likely be recalled in disgrace. With Abercromby unwilling to lead in a manner befitting a commander in chief, ambitious senior officers jousted to take that role.

Among those who tried to insert themselves into that leadership void was Colonel James Prevost, who led the 60th Royal American's 4th Battalion. He was a newcomer to the British army, having been born in Switzerland and having previously served in the Sardinian and Dutch armies before receiving a lieutenant colonel's commission for the newly formed 60th in 1756.

Prevost and Abercromby despised each other. To avoid conflict, Abercromby had sidelined Prevost before the Fort Carillon campaign by forcing him to take leave until further notice; Major John Rutherford took Prevost's place at the battalion's head. Prevost was not just disliked by Abercromby. The colonel's arrogance and aggression made him among the most reviled officers in British service. Major James Robertson scathingly described Prevost as "the most abandon'd Imposter that ever Gull'd a Nation . . . who without a Single Quality of a Soldier and . . . even without having ever seen or learned Service has lyed himself into rank of a General."[10] Colonel James Wolfe charged Prevost as "the most universally detested by all rank. . . . He is fit for no part of command and does not know how to obey."[11]

After Abercromby's army limped home, Prevost tried to reassert his authority. He was at New York City on July 12 when he learned of Abercromby's defeat. He immediately headed north to join the army and arrived at the Lake George camp on July 18. With a severe shortage of officers, Abercromby promptly promoted Prevost to brigadier general. Abercromby would soon regret that decision.

Prevost quickly deepened his unpopularity. He imposed a tax on sutlers, who passed it on to the soldiers as a price hike. He objected to Bradstreet's command of the Fort Frontenac campaign and pestered Abercromby to recall him. Most importantly, appalled by the army's collapse of morale and discipline, he talked Brigadier General Thomas Gage into jointly penning a detailed proposal on July 20 for reestablishing order and spirit among the troops, and proposing that "the army must maintain some flexibility to go over on the offensive if the Southern and Eastern expeditions favor our arms or the Lake Ontario diversion meets with success."[12]

When Abercromby did not even acknowledge receipt of the proposals, a furious Prevost sent a letter on July 29 that blasted him for his silence. He criticized Abercromby for his indecision and fear to lead the army against "an enemy inferior in numbers & which is truly less worthy than us. . . . We know, Sir, that one can supply you with numerous specious pretexts to justify inactivity & our lack of success. . . . We plea with you to seriously consider" our plan.[13] Perhaps fearing that to push matters further might jeopardize his career, Gage refused to sign that letter.

Abercromby again ignored Prevost's attempt to shame him back into the field. Instead, on August 1, he named him to command all the troops guarding the communication line from Albany to Fort Edward. If he thought the post would pacify Prevost, he was mistaken. Prevost wrote a third letter on August 20, citing reports that Montcalm's Canadians and Indians had departed, leaving only the regulars. He proposed leading an expedition that might pin down Montcalm and prevent him from sending his regulars to Canada should Amherst attempt to invest Quebec. He would secure the landing place at Lake George's north end by sending Major Robert Rogers with a large body of troops to Sabbath Day Point and Major Herbert Munster with the 60th down Wood Creek. When the enemy chased or maneuvered to block those two forces, Prevost would lead the bulk of the British army to occupy the landing place. The French would then withdraw to Fort Carillon, which would be besieged and eventually taken. To increase the pressure on Abercromby, Prevost circulated his proposal to the colonels and other leading officers. Major William Eyre openly backed the plan.[14]

If nothing else Prevost's plan would at least send part—and ideally all—of the army forward, but it depended on the highly unlikely event of the ever-cautious Montcalm snapping at one or both of the dangled baits. It was an embarrassing nuisance to Abercromby since he was looking for an excuse to sit tight rather than head north again. Yet he could not ignore such a pointed and widely circulated proposal from one of his key officers.

So Abercromby finally called in Prevost and Eyre, not to let them elaborate their proposal but to try to talk them out of it. Abercromby assured them that he would implement their plan if ample reinforcements arrived from Amherst. He did so knowing full well that either

Amherst could not spare those regiments, or he could not send them before the snow flew on Lake George. Thus he "agreed on the importance of making the approach, but judged it to be useless." Instead he ordered Prevost to march south "with 3,000 men (including 500 regulars) to secure a sixty-mile line of communications with eight outposts in the woods."[15]

At this point, with not one but three of his direct attacks having failed, Prevost backed off and tried to hit Abercromby from the rear. He wrote an impassioned letter to William Augustus, the Duke of Cumberland, the army's captain-general and King George II's second son. Prevost explained that he was "loathe to inflict any more Sorrow on [Abercromby] we let the matter rest. . . . In the future, unless I receive a direct order to do so, I am determined not to write to anyone anymore. I will suffer in silence. I will do my best wherever I am employed and will wait with patience. . . . Far from believing that I have the necessary talents to cure these evils, as God is my witness, there is nothing more in this world that I would fear than a command, because I feel I do not have the requisite qualifications to carry it out."[16] Of course, Prevost hoped that Cumberland would wield his authority either to force Abercromby to act or replace him with someone who would. Yet any assertion by Cumberland could not be implemented until the campaign season was long past.

Meanwhile Prevost and anyone else who wanted another campaign against Ticonderoga faced a terrible quandary—the army was melting away. Diseases festering in the offal and waste littering the army camps killed or debilitated ever more troops. Private David Perry recalled that "while lying in camp, our water and provisions were very bad, the men grew sickly, and a great many died of dysentery. But the same Almighty Power that warded off the balls in the day of battle, preserved me from the desolating scourge of disease."[17] Desertion produced even more losses. General John Stanwix's army in the Mohawk valley was the worst afflicted; 994 provincial troops had deserted by mid-August. Under Abercromby's nose a mass desertion by troops of Colonel Henry Babcock's Rhode Island regiment almost turned into a mutiny when an officer tried to stop them. The largest mass desertion for a single regiment afflicted Colonel Thomas Doty's Massachusetts troops shortly after it returned to Fort Edward. Abercromby sent troops after them and dispatched an express to Thomas Pownall to intercept the deserters when they reached Massachusetts. The governor sent Lieutenant Governor Thomas Hutchinson at the head of militia to apprehend then.

Hutchinson and his troops captured fifty-three deserters at Worcester and sent them back under an armed guard to their regiment at Fort Edward. There Abercromby promised to pardon them if they returned to duty.[18] Other than that, the general and his officers could do little in the face of mass provincial desertions. They drew the line, however, with deserters from regular regiments. For those who were caught, the general simply ordered his officers "to execute them without delay."[19]

Abercromby bolstered his claim that he lacked enough troops to attack Fort Carillon by citing every intelligence report that indicated the position was all but impregnable. In one of his letters to New York Governor James DeLancey, for example, he relayed a report by two French deserters that Montcalm had felled more trees, raised the barricade before Fort Carillon, and now commanded as many as 13,000 troops. Yet in that he found justification in keeping most of his army encamped at Lake George's southern shore. That forced the French to concentrate most of their troops at Ticonderoga which meant that Bradstreet's expedition would have an easier time taking Fort Frontenac.[20]

TURMOIL WITHIN THE FRENCH CAMP

The British army was not the only one plagued by bitter feuds among its officers. The victory at Fort Carillon hardly ended the private war between Vaudreuil and Montcalm. Indeed, it appears to have exacerbated it. The pride Montcalm naturally felt for his victory turned into an unseemly gloating—directed at the Canadians rather than the British. To a certain extent that was understandable. Two years of interservice rivalry worsened by his constant struggle with Vaudreuil had clearly frazzled Montcalm. To War Minister Belle Isle he boasted, "what affords me the most gratification in this affair is that the regulars do not share, so to speak, its glory."[21] He and his officers boasted that the natives played no role in the battle, "perhaps the first that has been fought in Canada without Indians," while the Canadians had only a minor part.[22]

Montcalm and his officers were adamant about getting off their versions of the battle to the War Ministry before Vaudreuil got his into the hands of the Marine Ministry. During Montcalm's sojourn in North America, Vaudreuil had continually and notoriously stolen credit for Montcalm's victories and heaped upon the general blame for his failures. Doreil, the army's chief commissary officer in Canada who returned to France in late 1758, said as much in a letter to Belle Isle:

As we have reason to suspect that the bureaux of the Marine will endeavor to vaunt the glory of four hundred men belonging to the troops and militia of the Colony, who were in this action, and to diminish those of the troops of the line, I must inform you . . . of what the Marquis de Montcalm has written me . . . on this subject: "I must say that the Colonial troops and the Canadians have behaved very indifferently. M. de Trecesson, the Commandant, has been obliged to fire on some of them who were abandoning their post, in the two sorties. . . . Nevertheless as a good servant of the King I have considered it for the good of the service to praise them in a narrative which was to be published . . . Captain de Raymond of the Colonial troops . . . and the Canadians . . . has personally acted very well; I greatly fear that M. de Vaudreuil will not do anything for him because he does not like him. I have been obliged to deceive both the French officer and soldier who say openly, M. de Vaudreuil was desirous of having us strangled by giving us so small a force to face a real danger, whilst he was uselessly retaining a corps of two or three thousand men for the purpose of making experiments in the country of the Five Nations, where three hundred men would have sufficed.[23]

Predictably, once Vaudreuil learned that Montcalm had attributed his victory largely to his regulars he protested vehemently to Versailles. The governor asserted that the marines, militia, and Indians had valiantly performed all their orders, especially in the two flank attacks against the British assault on July 8. Some of Vaudreuil's criticism was quite valid. He asserted that Montcalm had failed "to dispute the ground with them inch by inch," from the British landing at Lake George's north end to the march on Fort Carillon—an inaction that was "humiliating to the nation."[24]

As Montcalm and Vaudreuil battled behind the scenes, the general and everyone else pondered a more pressing question: "Will [Abercromby] return to attack us?"[25] If so, it appeared Montcalm was no more eager than previously to contest any renewed British offensive at the landing. On July 17, he sent Captain Rigaud, the governor's brother, with half the marines and militia to the sawmill, and on July 19 Captain Luc de la Corne with the rest to the pontoon bridge site. They were instructed to rebuild the defenses at both positions. It was only midsummer. Expecting Abercromby to regroup and try one last assault against Fort Carillon before the snow flew, Montcalm was determined to render his already formidable defenses more so. Yet, paradoxically, the general seems to have been ready once again to abandon those positions before the British. He posted Rigaud and his militia at the sawmill with orders to fall back to the entrenchments before Fort Carillon if the British army returned. Montcalm lacked confidence in the militia, perhaps with good reason—on July 28 he remarked sarcastically that there was "much panicked terror in the advanced camps" from false alarms of the enemy advance. Yet Vaudreuil was correct in pointing out that entrenching the Canadians rather than sending them against the British caused "our light troops [to lose] the advantage they possess of fighting the English in the woods."[26]

It would not be long before Montcalm lost whatever advantage the newly arrived militia and Indians gave his army. No sooner did they arrive on July 12 when they demanded to be allowed to return home on August 15, the militia for the harvest and the Indians for the hunt. This gave Montcalm less than a month to deploy them on the offensive Vaudreuil demanded. The number of troops under his command peaked around July 31, when the army numbered 6,748 troops, including 3,528 regulars, 1,112 marines, and 2,108 militia.[27]

The stress of warring in North America continued to grind Montcalm down. The constant challenge of staving off attacks by an enemy superior in numbers and supplies was wearying enough. That strain, as we've discussed, was compounded by his rear-echelon battles with Vaudreuil over strategy and ego, the interservice rivalry between the army and marines, the animosities between the French and Canadians, and the constant efforts necessary to keep the Indians in camp. And finally, there was the exorbitant financial cost of being the ranking general and hosting all manner of events through the long winter months in a land where prices were three times that of France.

Given all this, not surprisingly, Montcalm ended a July 12 report to Belle Isle with the plea: "For myself, I do not ask you any other than to procure me the King's leave to return. My health suffers, my purse is exhausted. At the end of the year I shall owe the treasurer of the Colony ten thousand ecus. And more than all, the trouble and contradictions I experience; the impossibility in which I am placed of doing good and preventing evil, determine me earnestly to pray his Majesty to grant me this favor, the only one for which I have ambition."[28]

Here the general and governor enjoyed complete accord. Vaudreuil too begged that Montcalm be recalled as "he desires it himself and has requested me to demand it of you. So far from thinking of injuring him, I consider, my Lord, that he deserves to be promoted to the rank of lieutenant-general: he will be able to serve very usefully in Europe. No person renders more justice than I do to his excellent qualities, but he does not possess those which are required for war in this country; tis necessary to have a great deal of suavity and patience to command the Canadians and the Indians."[29]

Vaudreuil was swift to retaliate for the slight to Canadian pride. In letters on July 12, 16, and 17, he conveyed no congratulations for Montcalm's victory. Instead, the governor ordered the general to hound the defeated British with "detachments both on the lake and at the head of the bay. They could not be too numerous, so as to harass our enemies vigorously, cut off their communication between Fort Lydius [Edward] and old Fort George [on Lake George], and intercept their convoys; we have no better manoeuvre to force them to abandon their position, bateaux, artillery, campaign train, provisions, &c. to oblige them to retire, and thereby deprive them forever of all hope of renewing their attempt."[30] It was essential, Vaudreuil insisted, for Montcalm to act before Abercromby shifted troops to the Louisbourg campaign, French provisions were exhausted, and the Canadians had to return to the harvest. To that end, he would send the general "all the militia belonging to the government that are fit for duty."

The governor's attitude was insulting and condescending to the proud veteran of three decades of warfare. Montcalm accused Vaudreuil of setting a trap. Vaudreuil would blame him if he did not march "with all his forces" or for any defeat if he did:

> The Marquis de Vaudreuil's letter appears to have been written only with a view to make the Marquis de Montcalm responsible for all the events that may arise, so as to say: I have sent him all the forces of the Colony; he has had them for a month, and did not know how to profit by them, in order to prevent the enemy from establishing himself at Fort George. If, on the contrary, the Marquis de Montcalm was marching with all his forces and did not succeed, the Marquis de Vaudreuil would not fail to write: He has marched with all his forces without orders and has compromised the Colony.[31]

The general found it "always astonishing that the Marquis de Vaudreuil considers himself qualified at a distance of fifty leagues to determine on the operations of war in a country he has never seen, and where the best Generals, after having seen it, would have been embarrassed." He reminded the governor that the British army still numbered about 14,000 men, twice that of the French army. The reinforcements that Vaudreuil sent would not strengthen the French to the point where they could march against the British. Instead, those extra troops burdened the army with extra mouths to feed and bodies to shelter. He informed the governor that only a superior force that cut off the enemy's supply line would force its retreat. Smaller forces could make life difficult for the enemy but not defeat it. He concluded with barely concealed sarcasm: "Were I so fortunate, Sir, as that your important occupations would permit you to be at the head of the army, you would see everything yourself, and I should have the satisfaction to receive clearer and less embarrassing orders, and you would have judged that I have combined boldness, prudence, and some activity." Montcalm dismissed Vaudreuil's orders as "the work of a thoughtless Secretary, and not that of a warrior," words that must have especially stung the equally proud governor.[32]

The general's reply did not humble the governor. Vaudreuil simply repeated his orders. To that, Montcalm's short reply simply echoed his counterarguments, adding that if the governor were on the spot he would agree with the general, another dig at Vaudreuil's inexperience and failure even to visit the war he was directing. To Versailles Montcalm accused Vaudreuil of lacking the "experience in war and knowledge of a frontier he has never seen."[33]

In a third letter, Vaudreuil was just as forceful as in his previous two in spurring the general to action. Once again Montcalm repeated his arguments but added a promise to maintain the public facade of goodwill between them and a plea that they bury their differences: "The Marquis de Vaudreuil will find in my observations some distrust of him; this will never prevent me applying myself to the good of the service and of the Colony . . . on all occasions . . . the Marquis de Vaudreuil's tokens of respect and affection, it were desirable that, forgetful of the past, we should labor without delay on a new path, and that I should not have to complain of or dread the obscurities and doubts of his instructions and letters."[34]

Though opposed to marching against Fort George, the general promised to obey a direct order from the governor to do so: "I am ready to march thither with the entire army. Such will not be my advice, but a distinct order from you will be sufficient for me." He made one final request: "The same love of truth prompts me to inform you that I demand my recall from both ministers. . . . If you will be so good, Sir, as to write with them in obtaining that favor for me, it will make me forget all the annoyances I may have had. I shall preserve, in return, a gratitude which will equal the respect" for the Marquis de Vaudreuil. With his scheme exposed, Vaudreuil never sent Montcalm that order. Had he done so, the governor rather than the general would have been responsible for any disaster. In a letter date August 2, Montcalm tried to soften the harsh feelings by assuring Vaudreuil that their dispute "will never diminish either my zeal for the public good, nor my affection for you."[35]

To undermine Montcalm, Vaudreuil needed allies among the French officers. He wooed Levis, the second in command, by pouring flatteries upon him in letters that often waxed sycophantic. Upon getting news of the Fort Carillon battle, Vaudreuil heaped upon Levis the praise that should rightfully have gone to the commander. He then defended himself against accusations that he had shortchanged Montcalm: "I am not losing an instant to augment Montcalm's forces and despite the scarcity of provisions I hope that within a few days he will have about 6,000 men under his orders." The governor then added: "I am counting that he will be in a state to profit from all the happy circumstances for making his campaign decisive for this colony."[36] The next day Vaudreuil sent another letter to Levis, writing, "I am convinced that . . . you will neglect nothing to contribute to executing my views because you sense better than anyone the consequences."[37] The governor further pressed his position on July 22 when he wrote to Levis, "you have seen how I have stiffened Montcalm by augmenting his troops and well provisioning him. My object in doing so . . . is to ease his ability to send the grand detachments to harass our enemies, interrupt their communications with Fort Edward, and to eliminate several convoys. I don't doubt at all my dear lord that you concur with all possibility the execution of my views."[38]

Vaudreuil's entreaties put Levis in an awkward, delicate position. After all, he was Montcalm's second in command and Vaudreuil's subordinate. In his replies to both men he diplomatically offered his sympathies while relentlessly pursuing his own interests. When Montcalm petitioned Versailles for permission to return to France, Levis wrote that as second in command he was ready and eager to take charge: "Montcalm had asked his recall to the court because of several frustrations which he has had with Vaudreuil and who since this time seems pacified . . . I count well that the command will devolve on me and that I will not be sent a superior officer."[39] But two days later he wrote King Louis XV requesting permission to take the last vessel from Canada and return to France. Apparently the endless frustrations of warring in North American had gotten to Levis as well. Versailles would deny the requests of both generals.[40]

The feud between Montcalm and Vaudreuil disturbed everyone. One of Vaudreuil's closest advisors, Marine Captain Michel Jean Hugues

Pean, wrote to Levis, "I see painfully that Montcalm greatly mistrusts Vaudreuil. I fear that they will fall out and that will be a very great evil. I will neglect nothing to reunite them. It's absolutely necessary under the circumstances."[41] Not surprisingly, Pean sided with the governor and believed that Montcalm was responsible for the feud, that he was imagining slights from the governor. Pean "tried to persuade him that Vaudreuil is not trying to embarrass him, and tried to make him envision all the evils that a rupture [would] . . . cause."

As if all the bickering over strategy was not wearisome and petty enough, a new and much more serious quarrel broke out. Montcalm's status among the Indians had soared ever higher on the wings of his victories in 1756 and 1757—and with the aid of sensitive diplomacy and numerous gifts. Then, in the summer of 1758, despite his great victory before Fort Carillon, Montcalm's status plummeted.

The horde of Indians who arrived on or after July 13 became an irritating headache for the general. Montcalm complained that as soon as the "savages" arrived they skulked about to loot, murder some wounded prisoners, and devour provisions, making "a cruel war against our sheep, chickens, wine, and anything else in sight." Especially notorious "were the Abenakis who of all the savage nations . . . have young men the least submissive to their elders and the chiefs for advice and war." Montcalm "counciled with the chiefs to reproach them for the disorders. [But it was] enormously difficult, nearly impossible to stop them." The general condemned the "savages" for "their vile, mercenary, cruel souls."[42]

He also denounced them for taking so long to arrive. Their tardy appearance was hardly their fault: Vaudreuil had earmarked them for the ill-conceived and eventually aborted campaign by Levis into the Mohawk valley. The chiefs and their warriors "were heartbroken" to have missed the battle of Fort Carillon. Montcalm, however, was anything but understanding. When the Indians revealed that "we were greatly mortified in not having shared his victory," he replied not with understanding but with frustration. He "answered us curtly: You are come at a time when I have no more need of you. Are you come only to behold dead bodies? Go behind the fort, you will find some. I have no more need of you to kill any English."[43]

While Montcalm's anger was partly provoked by frustration with Vaudreuil's machinations, the Indians infuriated him as well. As soon as they reached Fort Carillon, the chiefs demanded more gifts and supplies. To the general, it seemed the Indians were trying to shake him down after having already greatly benefited from Vaudreuil's generosity—and with no guarantee that they would war effectively against the British. The incessant thefts, murders, and demands of these hundreds of Indians, with their bellies and hands to fill, enraged Montcalm.[44]

Greatly insulted, the chiefs withdrew from their council with Montcalm to debate what should be done. Some insisted they immediately return home. But a consensus was hammered out that they council with Montcalm again the next day with hope that by then his anger would have abated. It had not. When the chiefs asked Montcalm to send them against the British, he exploded again, this time cursing them in the most insulting terms. Apparently they had demanded a higher than usual price in gifts for their proposed raid to bury their indignation at how Montcalm had treated them the previous day. Their price would rise with each insult from Montcalm.

The deadlock festered for another week. A few warriors disappeared south into the forests to ambush British supply caravans and patrols between forts George and Edward. Disgusted with their treatment, others departed for their distant homes. By the end of July, the number of Indians had dropped from its height of 470 two weeks earlier to about 300. Yet those who remained had to be fed and continued to try to steal everything they could. Over the next few weeks other war parties would arrive, but the total number of Indians would steadily decline as boredom and animosities provoked even more to leave.[45]

Montcalm faced a dilemma. The price the Indians demanded for their service was soaring, yet the indirect cost of dismissing them could be greater still. Their complaints to Vaudreuil would give the governor ample ammunition for his personal feud against Montcalm. Further, at some point Montcalm and the other commanders would desperately need Indian allies. What would be the French fate if the warriors folded arms in defiant neutrality, or even raised their scalping knives with the enemy? While Montcalm dithered, the Indians devoured his diminishing food. The chiefs broke the impasse when they announced that they would all abandon the French.

Montcalm agreed to a series of councils on July 22, at which he presented them with a wampum belt. He tried "to induce them to remain" by assuring "them that he has nothing on his mind against them as they suppose; that he will be very glad to keep them."[46] Ganetagon, a chief, "flung the Belt into the middle of the ring" and declared he was leaving for Montreal with his men. Other chiefs did the same. A worried Montcalm demanded to know why they were leaving. The chiefs detailed

the insults they had suffered since their arrival and concluded that
Montcalm's "head was turned since he had beaten the English without
us; that he may need of us but should not find us." The general pleaded
with the chiefs that they at least leave some men as scouts. "We answered that the ill humor of the warriors did not permit us to leave him
a single one. Finally he altered his tone; he got M. de Levis to speak to
Ganetagon, who is much attached to that gentleman. We held a third
meeting and, out of respect to [Vaudreuil], and in consequence of M. de
Levis' behavior, we left him with some warriors, after which we departed" for Montreal.[47]

There the chiefs vented their heated feelings at a council with Vaudreuil on July 30; "We come for comfort to you, Father, and to warn
you that our men are so disgusted that they will never consent to go
where M. de Montcalm will command." With over four decades of experience in negotiating with Indians, Vaudreuil knew just how to
sooth their indignation:

> You cannot fail to anticipate the grief I feel in hearing your words. I can-
> not credit what you have told me of the Marquis de Montcalm. I render
> more justice to his sentiments in your favor; you must have misunder-
> stood him or have exhausted his patience. However that be, forget the
> past, and you, Chiefs, endeavor to remove the dislike of your warriors to
> serve under the Marquis de Montcalm. I am persuaded that eventually
> they will be glad to do so, and acknowledge that so far from despising
> them, he loves them and is very glad to have them with him.[48]

Having assuaged some of their anger by opening his heart to them, he
then eased all ill-feelings by opening his supply room and handing out
the appropriate number and types of gifts.

Vaudreuil was surprisingly mild in his criticism of Montcalm. On
August 1, the day after the council broke up, he implored the general
"to entertain for these Nations all the regard they deserve. Such is the
King's intention. They have for a long time contributed to the honor of
his arms, and the defense of the Colony."[49]

Montcalm replied that only a group of malcontents had gone home
when he had scolded them for committing "disorders . . . in the camp,
killing and pillaging the provisions of the hospital and of private persons, and that I had adhered to your injunctions in sometimes refusing
them brandy . . . Indians, you are aware, only do what they like." Many
Indians not only remained but were currently among three expeditions sent to harass the English. The general then turned the tables on

Vaudreuil, relating that the Indians had "in full council, complained of you having detained them whilst wishing to fly to our succor."[50]

As usual in their rivalry, Montcalm and Vaudreuil appealed for allies at Versailles. Montcalm sent copies of his correspondence with Vaudreuil over the Indian dispute to Marine Minister Claude Louis d'Espinchal, Marquis de Massiac, along with a cover letter, which explained: "I send you a piece of mischief which issued . . . by some domiciliated Indians . . . I write to you on the subject in order that you may not give yourself the least uneasiness nor feel any on account of the pain an ill-concocted intrigue may afford me."[51] Here, Montcalm saw a conspiracy where none existed. He was solely responsible for provoking the Indian dispute by his own inability to suppress his frustrations. Vaudreuil had nothing to do with it. Yet, considering Vaudreuil's previous "intrigues," Montcalm's suspicions if not his actions are understandable.

Intendant François Bigot waded into the dispute with an August 13 letter to Massiac in which he dismissed "the little reproaches they believe themselves justified in making against one another." Though silly in themselves, those "picques" were potentially disastrous to New France. Bigot worried that "a report of a rupture would be as dangerous to the Colony as the entrance of an English army." He pronounced Montcalm and Vaudreuil

> both necessary parties for the preservation and defense of Canada. The former has made himself known as a good General and a man of vast detail, smart and active, zealous for the service. The latter does what he pleases with the Indian Nations and the Canadians, and he is thoroughly conversant with the nature of the fighting in this country; he also knows how to turn to advantage the terror the English have of the Indians. As I am equally attached to both, I should live on the best terms with them but I doubt that they will do the same; their hauteur is too much opposed the one to the other, and for a long time they have appeared to me to associate only politically.[52]

It is not easy to reconcile the Bigot of this letter—a model of reason, moderation, and patriotism, with the corrupt, greedy, cynical character whose machinations were bleeding New France white. His ability to cloak himself in such praiseworthy attributes is a vital reason why he was so successful at the latter.

Montcalm's ranking officers penned their own missives to Versailles lauding the general, criticizing the governor, and pleading for more troops and supplies. Deputy Commissary General Doreil was the most prolific letter writer and Montcalm supporter:

> I must not observe silence on what the General, through modesty, does not express. All that he has performed since his arrival in America, without forces and without means . . . is admirable and even incredible under all the circumstances. . . . What he has done in saving Canada at the moment it was most in danger is so much above all eulogium. . . . Three years passed in this cruel situation, at last weary their patience. The measure is full. The Marquis de Montcalm has only to reproach himself with too much goodness and deference. He asks you for his recall, my Lord; I am astonished that he has not demanded it sooner.

Having defended his chief, Doreil then expressed his own unhappiness: "On my knees I beg you to grant me [a recall], which I am long soliciting in vain. I have abandoned children in the cradle, and all my affairs in France. They are endangered for more than three years; occasion me considerable losses, and are completing my ruin there." But if Versailles did nothing else, it must "confide the general government . . . to the Marquis de Montcalm. He possesses political science as well as military talent; a statesman and a man of detail, a great worker, just, disinterested even to scruple, clearsighted, active, and having nothing in view but the public good; in a word, a virtuous and universal man." As for Vaudreuil, "he will always have one original drawback—he is a Canadian. That qualification is of a more serious consequence than I could express."[53]

Doreil expressed his confidence in Montcalm over Vaudreuil even more in a letter on August 31 to War Minister Belle Isle. Doreil flatly asserted that "Canada is lost if peace be not made this winter. The English have at this moment over sixty thousand regulars or provincials in America; we have not five thousand to oppose them, including land and Marine troops, near one thousand of which are dispersed in different posts and garrisons." He dismissed the power of reinforcements to save Canada:

> The Minister of the Marine has been always too much flattered, and perhaps people will dare flatter him still. Ten or twelve thousand troops may be called for; a considerable fleet of ships of war to convoy them and the necessary provisions and stores; all this might, indeed, enable us to hold out a little longer, and postpone our utter ruin, but the King would not be indemnified for the enormous expense this new reinforcement would occasion. War continuing, Canada would always finish by being taken

sooner or later . . . the continuation of war in this hemisphere is ruinous to the King, more in consequence of bad administration and great cupidity than of indispensable expenses.[54]

Vaudreuil also pleaded with Versailles to make peace with Whitehall. He shuddered at Montcalm's idea of leaving regular troops in New France like the soldier settlers of the Roman Empire: "Nothing would appear to me of more advantage to this Colony than to withdraw all the battalions from it as soon as peace is concluded; besides costing a great deal, they will always foster a spirit of division."[55] He did, however, call for assimilating any soldiers who wished to remain behind into the marines or settlements.

Contrary to Vaudreuil's claims, Montcalm did follow up his victory of early July with attacks that Montcalm himself described as combining "boldness, prudence, and some action."[56] Those attacks were really large-scale raids. They were designed to reap as much carnage and destruction on Abercromby's army as possible in order to intimidate its timid general from once again marching on Fort Carillon. Montcalm had no illusion that the raids would force the British to retreat from Lake George, a reality he made clear to Vaudreuil. In the governor's reply, he, of course, criticized the general, but then he added a surprising twist to his orders. Vaudreuil expressed his "fear that those detachments have not been sufficiently strong; therefore I doubt not but you will augment the first that you will organize . . . my intention is not that you should march with your army to drive the English forces from old Fort George, but only that you should send out large detachments."[57]

A triumphant smile must have spread across Montcalm's face as he read the last line. Finally he had in writing an unambiguous statement regarding the governor's expectations. But if Vaudreuil's object was to harass rather than take old Fort George, what was the point of sending larger detachments? Though Montcalm undoubtedly had enough provisions and bateaux to send a larger force including regulars, he was correct to maintain that to do so would have been folly. The British had at least twice as many regulars and total number of men at arms.

What could be gained from sending regulars stumbling through the wilderness? The French regulars performed brilliantly at Fort Carillon's entrenchments but were no more able to embark on Indian-style raids than their British counterparts. Montcalm's predecessor had tried to send them out three years earlier. General Dieskau's combined force of regulars, marines, militia, and Indians was defeated by an inexperienced provincial force led by Colonel William Johnson in three separate battles on September 9, 1755, at Lake George's south end. Since then the British regulars and provincials alike had grown more skilled in wilderness warfare and they were screened by ranger companies as adept as any Canadians and Indians. The larger the French force that Montcalm sent south, and the more regulars it included, the more likely it would be detected. What happened then would of course depend on an array of factors, such as leadership, tactics, setting, and so on. But the larger the French force defeated in the face of all those British troops and rangers, the more unwieldy and vulnerable would be its retreat.

SUMMER RAIDS

The first bloodshed after the battle of Fort Carillon occurred little more than a week later. On July 16 Captain Jacque François Legardeur de Courtemache led 300 marines, militia, and Indians south down Lake George. Shortly after landing near the Fort George Camp, Courtemache's Indians discovered a patrol of 8 men and immediately attacked. That prompted 300 British to emerge from nearby entrenchments. Both sides opened fire. The British quickly scurried back into their fortifications. The Indians took 35 scalps or prisoners at a loss of 3 dead and 3 wounded.[58] On July 20 Canadian and Indian raiders laid an ambush near Halfway Brook and "scalped about 9 of Colonel Nichols' regiment thro their own negligence having contrary to orders set out from [Lake George Camp] early in the morning without waiting for the escort."[59] On July 21 another raiding party returned to Fort Carillon with 10 prisoners and 24 scalps. That raid could have been even bloodier except "the impatience of the Indians prevented this detachment from destroying a party of 300 English which had taken refuge in a stockaded . . . depot on the Fort Edward Road."[60]

The largest raid yet was launched on July 24 when Captain Luc de la Corne set off with 200 Canadians and 400 Indians to the Fort Edward road. La Corne had hoped to depart two days earlier but was delayed by one of the whims of Indian warfare: the Abenaki and Iroquois joined in a massive lacrosse game that involved hundreds of warriors and thousands of livres worth of wages. Though it is not clear who won the match, La Corne's raid would be a success.[61]

On July 28, La Corne and his men secreted themselves in the forest along the road between Halfway Brook and Fort Edward to await an approaching supply train of 44 wagons and 240 oxen accompanied by 150 drovers, sutlers, and even 12 women and children; it was escorted by 50 soldiers. Suddenly La Corne's raiding party split the air with musket fire and war cries. La Corne's several hundred screaming men rushed forward swinging war clubs and hatchets. The terror must have petrified the British, for they offered little resistance. The Indians and Canadians ripped 111 scalps from the dead, took 80 prisoners, and burned what loot they could not haul away. Only 1 Iroquois was killed and 2 slightly wounded in the attack. With contemptuous irony one French report noted that the "English, tis known, feel this loss very sensibly. Some baggage and effects belonging to General Abercrombie, as well as his music, were among the plunder."[62]

The British reaction to these raids was mixed. With their regiments decimated at Fort Carillon and ever more of their soldiers being picked off in the surrounding forests, the regular colonels—with the exception of General Gage—preferred to hunker down in camp. Gage, along with ranger leader Rogers, provincial colonels Lyman and Williams, and Major Israel Putnam, begged Abercromby to retaliate.

The general reluctantly relented. On July 29, he dispatched Rogers and Putnam with 650 men, including 400 rangers, 150 troops of the 80th Light, and 100 regular volunteers in bateaux up Lake George to the narrows, where they were to land and try to intercept one of the returning raiding parties. He then reinforced Rogers with Colonel William Haviland's 27th Regiment. The following day he ordered Lieutenant Colonel Eyre Massey of the 46th to lead his men and two ranger companies to Halfway Brook to search out and destroy any lurking enemy raiders. All of those reinforcements amounted to about 1,000 troops.

Some of the hunters became the hunted. A detachment of the 27th led by Captain John Wrighton was nearly ambushed near Fort Anne by about 50 or 60 Indians, but they managed to flee without losses. Somewhere between Fort Edward and Halfway Brook, Colonel John Hart was leading 200 troops of the New Hampshire regiment when they actually "fell in with the rear of the enemy, who having made free with liquor were so drunk that it would have been an easy matter to have cut them off."[63] But Hart hesitated to attack and the Indians staggered off into the forest.

Abercromby allowed Rogers and Putnam, and their 650 troops only a short breather after they returned to the Lake George camp. He dispatched them on a long scout over to Lake Champlain's South Bay. On

August 6 those troops set up an ambush. Rogers's men deployed where Wood Creek flows into South Bay while Putnam's were further along South Bay. That day a canoe with 6 Indians appeared offshore near Putnam's troops. A soldier inexplicably called out, "Pray what boat may you be?"[64] The Indians swiftly paddled off. The trap was exposed, and Rogers and Putnam wisely decided to withdraw along Wood Creek south toward Fort Edward.

Their instincts were good. A large French force was coming their way. On August 4, Captain Joseph Marin de la Malque had embarked on Lake Champlain with 50 regulars, 100 Canadians, and 150 Indians with the mission to scout along Wood Creek toward Fort Anne's ruins. Marin's force caught up to Putnam's rear guard near the ruins on August 8.

As usual the accounts vary. Albert Spicer recalled that the French and Indians learned of their position when Rogers and several of "our officers shot at a mark thinking there was no danger." Doreil recorded that

> Marin made his arrangements to fight the enemy. He forced them to waver in two volleys, which killed a great many; but having been supported by the regulars, they rallied and the firing was brisk on both sides for nearly an hour. M. Marin, perceiving that they were receiving reinforcements, and the Indians, who feared that they would not be able to carry off the wounded, demanded to retire, he was obliged . . . which he did in good order and without being pursued, after having for an hour longer kept up a fire with such picked men as he had, who performed prodigies of valor. The Indians, in general, have also performed well; but of 100 Canadians, more than 60 deserted. . . . This somewhat astonished the Indians and prevented [Marin] . . . from deriving all the advantage he could from the circumstance. . . . Meanwhile our loss is but trifling in comparison with that the enemy must have suffered, which is estimated at more than 200 men. Scouts, sent on their trail, have seen a great many wounded, whom they were carrying on litters, and a great many dead on the field of action. M. Marin took some prisoners, 2 of them officers. . . . On our side we have had 3 soldiers, 3 Canadians, and 4 Indians killed; two Cadets, one soldier, 5 Canadians, and 4 Indians wounded—the majority of them very slightly.[65]

Another account has Marin following the withdrawal of Putnam and Rogers. Marin spread his 225 Canadians and 219 Indians in an ambush across the trail leading north from Fort Anne's ruins along Wood Creek and may have lured Putnam to turn his troops around and head back. Putnam and his men walked right into the trap. Hearing the gunfire, Rogers hurried his troops north to the rescue and after a sharp fight chased off the enemy. The British suffered 49 dead, 40 wounded, and 5 captured, and the French 12 dead and 10 wounded. Putnam himself, a lieutenant, and 3 soldiers were dragged away as prisoners.[66]

Abercromby's version made the fight a British victory rather than defeat: "after a dispute of two hours, the enemy gave way with a loss of about 150, two of which were brought in prisoners, the remainder killed or scalped; of the latter they reckon 56, and at least 15 of them Indian scalps. Our loss is trifling, a few scalped or killed, which our people buried . . . Rogers . . . merits much to be commended, he having . . . acted the whole time with great calmness and officer-like."[67]

Whoever won, the heavy casualties apparently did not faze Rogers and his men. That night French Indian scouts that crept close to their camp found them "drinking and singing."[68] Nonetheless, the French and Indians inflicted far more losses on Rogers and Putnam, and their men than they suffered.

Following that battle most ranger patrols kept hidden and held their fire as enemy forces passed through the forest or on Lake George. An exception occurred on September 5, when rangers slipped through the enemy patrols and ambushed some Indians hunting not far from Fort Carillon; the Indians fled with one slightly wounded.[69]

The French scoured Lake George's forested shores and islands for the British. The indefatigable Marin led yet another party out on August 20, this time with 3 French, 30 Mississaugas, and 20 Iroquois and Hurons in canoes on Lake George. A few days later the Iroquois and Hurons deserted him. Nonplused, Marin pushed on to the forests around southern Lake George and set up an ambush along a frequently used trail. For three days they waited but no enemy passed within range of their muskets and hatchets. So Marin led his men back to Fort Carillon. Marine Lieutenant Jean Clement Sabrevoix de Bleury led out a small patrol in late August but he also returned empty-handed. The largest effort was a 300-man raid led by Captain Repentigny down Lake George on September 13. They spent four days scouring the waters and islands for the enemy but they found none. Repentigny brought his men back on September 17. Ensign Langy led 22 marines and 18 Indians to Lake George's southern end on October 7. It took him six days to convince the Indians to join him. Having done that it cost Langy nearly as much patience to strike the enemy. He and his men returned on October 17 with 1 scalp and 1 prisoner.[70]

For Montcalm, obtaining information about Abercromby's intentions was as important as harassing him. What he learned reassured him.

British captives and deserters who reached Fort Carillon confessed a similar message: Abercromby had no immediate plans to head toward Fort Carillon. A British deserter who appeared on August 1 revealed that Abercromby had wanted to reembark his army eight days after it reached the south shore of Lake George, but most of his colonels had refused to go along. Abercromby decided to await reinforcements from Amherst, should he capture Louisbourg. Other prisoners and deserters corroborated that report.

FRENCH DEFEATS AND BRITISH INDECISION

The elation among the French at their string of victories subsided on August 3 when an express courier brought disastrous news—General Jeffrey Amherst's expedition had taken Louisbourg on July 27, capturing 5,637 soldiers and sailors and destroying a half dozen warships. The question then was how Amherst would follow up that victory. Would he sail his expedition on to Quebec or reinforce Abercromby's army for another thrust toward Fort Carillon?[71]

The threat of another British campaign lingered. Montcalm wrote that "the obstinacy of the enemy in remaining in force in his camp will oblige us to wait for the ice before entering into cantonments."[72] Yet the number of armed men under his command steadily diminished. By mid-August over 500 militia and hundreds of Indians had returned home; only 76 warriors, including 42 Mississaugas, 19 Abenakis, 9 Iroquois, 4 Nipissings, and 2 Micmacs remained. Hundreds more militia would embark north over the next few weeks for the fall harvest until none remained. Even the regulars were diminishing—of 3,193 on the rolls 652 were either sick or detached back in small detachments to posts all the way to Montreal. Meanwhile, Abercromby's army would swell if Amherst sent reinforcementst.[73]

Then news arrived from Vaudreuil on September 6 of yet another disaster, this one more immediately threatening than Louisbourg's capture: Bradstreet and his army had captured and burned Fort Frontenac on August 24 after a two-day siege. Bradstreet had paroled the fort's commander, Captain Pierre Jacque Payen de Noyan et de Chavoy, and his 110 troops, who descended to Montreal with the disastrous news. Where was Bradstreet now? Using captured supplies, would they rebuild the forts at Oswego on Lake Ontario's south shore that Montcalm had taken in 1756? Would those victorious troops row on to Fort Niagara and take that undermanned, crumbling post? Even more catastrophic, what if that British expedition headed down the St. Lawrence to Montreal itself?

Leaving Levis in command, Montcalm embarked the next day for Montreal to consult with Vaudreuil. The general and governor concluded that Bradstreet lacked enough troops to venture an attack on Montreal. However, the French were powerless for now to prevent him from besieging Fort Niagara or fortifying Oswego. All they could do was sit tight and await word of Bradstreet's next move. Only then would they decide how to react. Given their antagonistic relationship, Vaudreuil may well have replied that Bradstreet's capture of Frontenac would have been impossible had Levis's expedition to the Mohawk valley taken place.

On September 13, Montcalm headed back to Fort Carillon and arrived in three days. A week later, on September 26, a deserter brought in news that chilled Montcalm and his men: Amherst and 6,000 troops were on their way to Albany. If this were true then the British surely intended to make another assault on Fort Carillon that year.[74]

Or would they? It was not until August 28, three weeks after Montcalm had gotten the same news, that Abercromby, wallowing in inactivity at the Lake George camp, received a courier with Amherst's July 27 letter announcing that his expedition had taken Louisbourg. This was the news that Abercromby had awaited and, given his timidity, secretly dreaded. On July 18 he had written Amherst to send him troops after he took Louisbourg. Only then would Abercromby feel confident enough to have another go at Fort Carillon. It would be tough to find an excuse not to do so if those troops actually arrived. But Amherst's letter made no mention of Abercromby's request for reinforcements. Abercromby began to suspect that his July 18 letter had not reached its destination.

The following day the general fired off a letter of congratulations to Amherst and another request for "the reinforcement of some regiments of regular troops to be able to make a second attempt."[75] He entrusted the delivery of that letter to his aide, Captain James Abercrombie. The general also wrote Thomas Pownall and James DeLancey, the respective governors of Massachusetts and New York, asking them to assist with the troop transfer. To DeLancey he explained that he "was desirous to seize the first fair opportunity to make a second attempt & am preparing matters accordingly. I am just to hint to you that our present strength is not sufficient for such an undertaking. It would be necessary that we should have a couple of thousand of your militia to be disposed of in the communication, to guard the different forts between Albany and

[Lake George]."[76] To Pitt, Abercromby gave this equivocal promise: "if they arrive in time, which I hope they may, and from the intelligence we can get, it be found practicable to make a second attempt upon Ticonderoga, I shall not fail to improve the advantage of this reinforcement, and with their assistance and that of Divine Providence, I hope we shall prove more successful."[77]

That was an extraordinary statement. Abercromby was stringing together some mighty big "ifs" and "hopes." If one failed they all would, thus aborting a second campaign. Was Abercromby serious? Or was this just an attempt to make it look like he might do what he had no intention of doing?

Abercromby's call for reinforcements and promise to return to Fort Carillon if they arrived on time seems like nothing more than a very elaborate facade to hide his inaction. No evidence exists to suggest that he truly intended to march again against Fort Carillon. If troops were all that he needed for a second attempt, then why had Abercromby recently agreed to Bradstreet's plan to take Fort Frontenac on Lake Ontario and earmarked 3,100 troops for that campaign? Even then he had plenty of troops on hand. True, when he wrote Pitt he had dispersed much of his army between Lake George and Albany. Yet those troops could be swiftly concentrated for another campaign. Although desertion and sickness would steadily thin its ranks, the army remained formidable. As late as October 6, the official count was 10,945 troops. In camps near Lake George there were 8,269 troops, including 3,757 regulars, 4,113 provincials, and 399 rangers. From there to Albany were scattered camps of 848 regulars, 1,678 provincials, and 76 rangers—or 2,602 total.[78]

What Abercromby needed was not more troops but the backbone to get his existing army once again before Fort Carillon, this time for an elaborate siege rather than mindless slaughter. There was no reason why Amherst would send troops to Lake George. After all, Amherst's victory opened up a chance for one even more important: his armada could sail on to besiege lightly defended Quebec.

One big problem made that unlikely, however: Amherst was as much a diddler as his commander. Victory mired Amherst in indecision as much as defeat bogged down Abercromby. To Abercromby, Amherst wrote, "I can't yet judge in what manner we shall be able to pursue the future operations of the campaign. I hope it will be found practicable to get to Quebec, which is what I wish the most to do."[79] But, like Abercromby, Amherst's actions differed from his claims. Within days after accepting Louisbourg's surrender, he broke up his army in scattered raids around the Gaspe peninsula, Cape Breton, and the Bay of Fundy. He then dumped any responsibility for his next move in Abercromby's lap: "I would be glad to receive any commands you may have for me which I shall try to execute to the best of my power."[80] With a letter advancing no faster than sail or horse could carry it, Amherst was guaranteed at least a month, and, if he were lucky, five or six weeks before he received a reply.

The practicality of Amherst sailing to Quebec or Abercromby heading back to Fort Carillon diminished each day. Both men delayed any decisive action until it was no longer possible. Each could then claim that the late season or other circumstances kept him from pressing the matter. How deliberate was such deception? Most likely it was more subconscious than conscious. But the impact was no less tragic. The war might have ended a year or so earlier if vigorous and skilled rather than timid and incompetent generals led Britain's armies. Both sides would have been spared enormous losses in blood and treasury.

Amherst did not receive news of Abercromby's disaster until the evening of July 31. Without Abercromby's orders to send him reinforcements, Amherst and his officers carried on their debate over what to do next. It was not until August 6 that Amherst and the fleet commander, Admiral Edward Boscawen, "concluded we could not go to Quebec, so that I offered a large sum of money for pilots to go there, and took care it should be believed that we were resolved to attempt it, which may have some small effect in . . . Abercromby's favour."[81] So Amherst was thinking of a diversion rather than reinforcement to help Abercromby. It would be another five weeks before he got word that Abercromby wanted most of his army.

On September 3, Amherst wrote Abercromby a report on his operations over the previous five weeks. He was considering sending six battalions to Boston but had not yet done so. He did not acknowledge receipt of Abercromby's July 18 order for him to send reinforcements as swiftly as possible to Fort Edward. There was a reason for that omission, which Abercromby had long suspected but could not confirm for another month. Amherst never received those orders.[82]

That same day Governor DeLancey also wrote Abercromby. He does not seem to have taken the general's plan for a second attempt on Fort Carillon very seriously since he does not even address that issue until the second page. DeLancey promised to "tell you my present sentiments very freely." First he dismissed the possibility of mobilizing the militia to protect the communication lines. He then offered what assistance he could without specifying just what that might be.[83]

Letters continued to cross in the mail. On September 4, Abercromby wrote Governor Pownall a vague request that he forward the 60th Royal Americans from Boston if possible. But he did not specifically express his hope for a second try at Fort Carillon. In his reply Pownall mentions nothing about another campaign.[84] If Abercromby were serious surely he would have told his closest confidant about his plan. These omissions are also significant because Abercromby would later blame Pownall for not forwarding to Amherst his order for reinforcements.

Five days later Abercromby asked DeLancey to send him any troops that could be gathered at New York. Apparently DeLancey interpreted this to mean provincial troops. The irritated governor chided Abercromby for requesting "a thing which it is not in my power to comply with; you know I cannot raise money without the Assembly and law without money."[85] He again promised to assist any reinforcements that passed through New York on the way to Albany. In subsequent letters Amherst, Pownall, and DeLancey do not mention the second try. By this time it had long been quietly forgotten.[86]

Captain Abercrombie, meanwhile, had done his duty as best he could. Upon reaching Boston on September 11 he presumably briefed Pownall on the second campaign and asked him to forward the general's order to Amherst for reinforcements. As for those troops then in Boston, he found they lacked "some essential necessary articles which I had ordered and are now too late to send back for."[87] He asked Pownall to "make a proper example" of those who did not send the equipment. All along he enjoyed Pownall's lavish hospitality.

But where was Amherst? The general was then approaching Boston with five regiments. The captain, of course, could not know that. Growing impatient, he requisitioned from Pownall the sloop *Province* to sail in search of Amherst. The captain and general met at sea on September 12 and returned to Boston together. Having done all he could to expedite the reinforcements, the captain headed back to Lake George, which he reached on September 21. Amherst dispatched four regiments, the 17th, 47th, 48th, and 63th, for Albany; some went by ship while he led the others overland on the 225-mile trek from Boston. Meanwhile, on September 30, Abercromby wrote Amherst urging him to hurry on the troops as soon as possible. He still spoke of a second effort against Fort Carillon, but this was more insincere than ever given the late season. Less than a week later Abercromby would receive word that the reinforcements had arrived at Albany and were awaiting further orders. Amherst joined Abercromby at the Lake George camp on October 5.[88]

Those two men so similar in temperament came to a quick and unsurprising conclusion: autumn was too advanced for a second campaign against Fort Carillon. The four regiments waiting impatiently at Albany for word to head north received orders to sit tight, since it was not "judged advisable or practicable to employ them this season this way, by reason of it's being too far advanced and the enemy from repeated intelligence too well prepared for our reception."[89] It was probably during their talks that Amherst revealed he had never received Abercromby's July 18 order for reinforcements. They then discussed scenarios for 1759.

Politics and the paranoia it can breed are omnipresent in human affairs. Apparently the commander of British troops in the Mohawk valley, General John Stanwix, was concerned that Amherst was coming to replace him. Upon Amherst's departure on the morning of October 7, Abercromby reassured Stanwix that this would "remove all the difficulties you foresaw; but had he staid here it would no ways have interfered with your command . . . I shall make any observations on his conduct which from first to last is calculated with no other view than to embroil matters."[90]

The last sentence is intriguing. Did Amherst, the conqueror of Louisbourg, swagger into his meeting with Abercromby, the butcher of Fort Carillon? Did he act more the commander than commanded? Did he poorly conceal his desire for Abercromby's job? Just what was said in two days of meetings between them was undocumented. Abercromby would shortly thereafter speak warmly of Amherst. But Amherst may well have been overbearing and Abercromby naturally resentful.

As ever Abercromby would look everywhere for blame but in the mirror. Typically he indirectly accused Pownall of not forwarding that last letter properly, which he called "a great disappointment to the service."[91] Pownall was apologetic, insisting "that nothing could give me more uneasiness than the idea of an implication that the service or yourself suffered by any inattention of mine." He assured Abercromby that he had forwarded the letter directly to Amherst as soon as he had received it. Both letters were cloaked in niceties, gratitude, and friendship.[92]

Then there was the announcement that a second campaign was canceled. Although few if any who knew Abercromby had ever taken his claims seriously, the general offered elaborate justifications for abandoning the plan. To General John Forbes, he wrote that

the reinforcements . . . not arriving at Albany till the 3rd or 4th [October] . . . without any artillery or artillery people, which we stood in great need of, and our reiterated intelligence of the great strength & defensible state of the works at Ticonderoga upon which the enemy have constantly been busy ever since our visit, made it impractical to attempt any thing but with the greatest regularity of form, which from the advanced season and the weather coming on bad there was by no means sufficient time for, and left no other prospect than that of risking the lives or health of the troops without any visible likelihood of annoying them the least effectually, and therefore with the advice of Major General Amherst, and the other principal officers with me, I came to a resolution of laying aside that attempt for this campaign.[93]

He then claimed that camping his army at Lake George's south end somehow deprived "the enemy of the least opportunity of acting offensively." To Pownall he later admitted that

to reattempt the reduction of Ticonderoga which from its present strength and the numbers in and around it would require a much longer time to make any impression on it, than it would have been possible in these inhospitable forests for our troops to hold the field, accordingly, not to endanger the health and lives of so many brave men, without even a probability of annoying the enemy any thing effectually, I have been obliged to lay aside any first resolution, and to content myself with remaining here until I hear of the enemy's removing into winter quarters, or that from severity . . . of the weather, they cannot altho they should be inclined attempt anything against us.[94]

As the distractions of raids and the campaign season dwindled, Abercromby could focus on what really seemed to matter to him: administration. A flurry of letters from Abercromby's pen to his far-flung subordinates addressed all the problems of feeding, quartering, clothing, warming, and disciplining soldiers through the fierce North American winter that lurked just around the corner. That difficult task the general performed quite well. But he would not be in America when winter struck.[95]

At the Lake George camp, Abercromby ordered the guns, powder, and bateaux sent back to Fort Edward, and had other equipment buried ashore or sunk in Lake George, including the sloop *Halifax*. Between October 16 and 22 around 260 boats were sunk and 30 hidden in the woods. The rigging and guns were buried. As for his troops, Abercromby ordered 1,600 troops, including 1,000 of the 4th Battalion of the 60th and six ranger companies numbering 600, to winter at Fort Edward. At Albany and surrounding camps 2,850 troops were billeted: 1,000 from the 42nd, 700 from the 55th, 600 from the 1st Battalion of the

60th, 150 royal artillerymen, 100 New York Independents, and 300 in hospitals. Posted at Schenectady and posts up the Mohawk valley to the Oneida Carrying Place were 700 troops of the 46th, 1,300 of the 63rd, 300 New York Independents, and 100 men from a ranger company; there were 500 troops at Fort Oneida, 150 at Fort Herkimer 150, 70 at Canajoharie, 100 at Fort Hunter and Johnson Hall, 500 at Schoharie and Stone Arabia. Further afield, 700 troops of the 17th were quartered at Philadelphia, 700 of the 27th and 1,000 of the 47th in New Jersey, 1,000 of the 42nd at New York, 1,000 of the 44th on Long Island, 1,000 of 48th in Connecticut, and 525 of the 80th at Kingston.[96]

Having done all he thought necessary, Abercromby left his Lake George camp on October 26 for Albany. An unwelcome but not completely unexpected message awaited him there, as we shall see.

FINISHING TOUCHES

Winter was approaching. The first snow flurries swirled on October 4. That same day a courier arrived from Vaudreuil with news that Bradstreet had not only failed to attack Fort Niagara but had not even refortified Oswego; he and his men were now back in Albany. At least the threat from Lake Ontario had disappeared. But what about the British army around Fort Edward?

As the days grew steadily colder and the winds stripped the brightly colored leaves from the trees, another British campaign against Fort Carillon seemed ever more remote. Scouts and prisoners revealed that Abercromby was dispersing his army into winter quarters. Montcalm began to relax his own vigilance. By October 18, he had sent home most of the militia and nearly all the Indians. But he kept his regulars at Fort Carillon until he was certain that Abercromby had decamped.

To determine that, Montcalm dispatched two parties of about 30 Canadians and Indians each, one commanded by Florimond to scout around Fort Edward and the other by Charly around Lake George's southern end. The final word that Montcalm eagerly awaited arrived from two sources on October 31: a deserter and Charly confirmed that the British army had disappeared except for Fort Edward's garrison, which included a battalion of Royal Americans and Robert Rogers's ranger companies; the next day Florimond returned with the same news.[97]

It was only then that Montcalm had the remaining Canadians, and the La Reine and the two Berry battalions depart in stages from November 1 to 3 for Quebec. The general himself, accompanied by the Lanquedoc Battalion, left on November 4. Then over the next week the La Sarre, Royal Rousillon, Guyenne, and Bearn battalions packed up and embarked for Montreal. Captain d'Hebecourt of the La Reine Battalion would once again command Fort Carillon's winter garrison of 400 troops, while Captain Lusignan and 200 marines guarded Fort St. Frederic.[98]

The troops who returned to Canada suffered severely on their journey as they rowed slowly day after day through freezing temperatures and fierce winds. It was a miserable, ignominious end to a triumphant year. They and their general had won the 1758 battles for Ticonderoga, but the war was far from over, and time was not on their side.

CHAPTER 8

Parting Shots

I am now to acquaint you that the king has judged proper that you should return to England.
—William Pitt to James Abercromby

Canada is lost if peace be not made this winter. The English have at this moment over sixty thousand Regulars or Provincials in America; we have not five thousand to oppose them . . ."
—Doreil to Belle Isle

THE FATE OF NEW FRANCE

The Battle of Fort Carillon in July 1758 was the only important French victory that year. Three other campaigns at Louisbourg, Frontenac, and Duquesne ended with British triumphs. The fortress of Louisbourg was besieged by Amherst and capitulated in late July. Fort Frontenac was captured and destroyed by Bradstreet in August. Fort Duquesne was blown up and abandoned by the French at the approach of Forbes in November.

Each of those defeats might well have been a French victory had the fates been kinder and the decisions of key participants different, just as Fort Carillon might have been a French defeat. Those defeats and the ever-tighter British blockade made it increasingly clear to the defenders and inhabitants of New France that their colony was suffocating and was at the brink of collapse. By late 1758, Montcalm despaired that the end was near: "The war is entirely changed in this part of the world according to the manner the English are attacking us; nothing less is at stake than the utter and impending loss of the Colony or its salvation, that is to say, the postponement of its fall. It is with this view that we must act; tis this truth which must be unceasingly before our eyes."[1]

The question was increasingly not whether New France would endure, but what would run out first: food or munitions. On November 1, 1758, Governor Vaudreuil sent to Versailles a request for a huge amount of artillery munitions and related equipment, including 31,200 cannon balls of six different grades from one to eighteen pounders; 14,500 shells of five grades; half million pounds of lead; 700 pounds of cartridge papers; 6,000 grenadier muskets and 6,000 tulle muskets with bayonets; 2,000 tulle muskets without bayonets for the Indians; 8,000 priming horns for the militia; 15,000 hand grenades of three sizes; 10,000 gunnery matches; a half million pounds of gunpowder; and 24 twelve-pounder cannons. He made a special plea for more gunpowder. Anticipating surprise at the amount requested, the governor explained that "without the gunpowder captured at Monongahela, Oswego, and Fort William Henry, New France would have run out long ago."[2]

Death by starvation rather than battle was the greater danger, especially for the peasants. In a report to Versailles, Marine Captain Pean explained that "the farmers, after having furnished the last bushel of their wheat for the subsistence of the troops which were marching against the enemy, were supporting themselves only by the aid of some vegetables and wild herbs; eighteen months ago the people, without excepting a single officer, had to be reduced to four ounces of bread a day; they have been reduced to two ounces only." He went on to say that "the provisions brought by several ships during the year have been immediately forwarded to the armies. . . . The harvest is reported very bad. . . . Tis therefore to be presumed that this Colony is about to be exposed to much more serious suffering than it has experienced in preceding years, during which people have been under the necessity of consuming all their cattle. Many people have died of hunger."[3]

While the masses weakened with malnutrition and despair, the rich continued to flourish. Corruption permeated virtually every official transaction in Canada. Doreil, the king's deputy commissary general, did not mince his words in detailing that reality when he returned to Versailles that winter:

The chiefs, the proteges, the proteges of the proteges, all these must make on a profit on everything the state buys. . . . Under the agreement of the King with the Commissary of the Stores, [the King] is obliged to furnish him everything necessary for the conveyance of provisions. . . . When the troops are not in a fort, when in camp or marching, then the Commissary of Stores no longer furnishes the rations; it is up to the King to feed them. Since the Commissary of Stores alone has the provisions, he sells to the King at his own price and the conveyance is contracted for. . . . This land will perish after having ruined France through the monstrous abuses of these privileged select.[4]

As if a lack of munitions, starvation, and corruption were not debilitating enough, the French faced the loss of their native allies. Word of the French defeats and Montcalm's insults spread through the Indian grapevine, and that news, along with the ever-diminishing supply of French gifts, would cause most warriors to remain in their villages in 1759 and thereafter. Montcalm voiced his fear to War Minister Belle Isle that "the Indians, who usually side with the strongest or most fortunate, will all abandon us to ranger themselves alongside the English."[5] As if French defeats did not shake the Indian confidence enough, the scarcity of goods caused by the blockade and corruption strained relations to the breaking point. He was especially worried that the Iroquois, who "are always assuring us of their attachments are receiving presents from" the British, so that "their hearts are with the latter and their fears with us. . . . The [French] King has given and expends a great deal for the Upper Indians; were everything distributed they would all be on our side."[6]

Even the weather seemed to conspire against the French. Canada's winters are always long and bitterly cold, but that year of 1758–1759 was especially severe: "an early frost, unexcelled within the last fifty years, has occasioned much suffering to the troops. . . . On Lake Champlain a real tempest . . . scattered our fleet of bateaux . . . and the ice made us shudder on entering the river. But luckily we . . . lost only some bateaux and baggage and only four soldiers."[7]

All that New France's defenders could do was to fight on. But that year's defeats and British advances demanded a new strategy for the new year. That strategy had to rest on no more than 3,200 regulars and, at most, 15,000 marines and militia against British forces numbering three or four times as many. Significant reinforcements or even supplies could not be expected. Versailles' ministers had continually warned Vaudreuil and Montcalm that they had to make do with what little they had. The governor and general were locked in a fierce tug-of-war over what strategy could best stave off defeat a little longer.

Montcalm argued that desperate times demanded desperate measures. He dismissed the old raiding strategy as irrelevant and self-defeating with such massive British armies battering at New France's gates: "It is no longer the time when a few scalps or the burning of a few houses is any advantage or even an object. Petty means, petty ideas, petty Councils about details are now dangerous and waste material and time." The general advocated a hedgehog defense whereby all troops were concentrated at Isle aux Noix, La Presentation, and Quebec to take advantage of interior lines and their small number of troops: "Tis the trunk of the tree that's attacked; whatever concerns the branches is of the greatest indifference." That meant abandoning Lakes Ontario, Erie, and Champlain. Montcalm argued that ties with upper Canada and Louisiana could be maintained via the old Ottawa River route. Regardless, New France did not have enough troops to defend its steadily shrinking boundaries.[8]

Vaudreuil, not surprisingly for a native-born Canadian, insisted on pushing forward New France's defenses to their furthest extent and then fighting with delaying actions and staged withdrawals, if necessary, against the British offensives: "I essentially adhere to contesting the ground on our frontiers inch by inch with the enemy."[9] After all, the British were attacking New France through its branches—thus the branches must be defended to save the trunk. He adamantly rejected Montcalm's notion of withdrawing from Lakes Erie, Ontario, and Champlain: "As for the abandonment of the lakes, I shall never adopt that step, and should circumstances reduce me to guard the head of the rapids and defend its passage which will never be the case except in the last extremity, I shall require for that only a very small force, the major part of which will only be Canadians and Indians."[10] The difficulties the British faced in North America, marching and rowing their armies and defending their thin supply lines, was an important ally of New France. A hedgehog defense would surrender those advantages and simply allow the British to conquer New France sooner and easier.

Vaudreuil pointed out that after the raid on Frontenac, Bradstreet had withdrawn all the way back to the Mohawk valley. The governor proposed rebuilding that fort, reestablishing the navy on Lake Ontario, and reinforcing Forts Niagara and La Presentation. Curiously for a forward-defense advocate, Vaudreuil did not call for fortifying Oswego, which would plug the only British invasion route leading directly on to Lake Ontario. Had Montcalm fortified Oswego after he captured it in 1756 and also erected an advanced post at the Great Carrying Place, the French would have enjoyed a perfect jumping-off point for raiding or invading the Mohawk valley, as well as a defense in depth for Lake Ontario. They would also have been in position to block Bradstreet's raid.[11]

Vaudreuil also noted that the British had abandoned their Lake George camp and concentrated their troops at Fort Edward on the Hudson River. He sent a report to Montcalm arguing that if they abandoned Forts Carillon and St. Frederic, it was possible that "the enemy, by taking possession of them, would immediately construct a navy there that would soon be superior to ours, and even be enabled to throw all his strength into that quarter, whence it would follow that the fate of this Colony would depend on only one battle won or lost; that indubitably the Indians nations, believing our defeat inevitable, would pounce from all points on the heart of the Colony and total ruin would be the result in a short time."[12]

The tug-of-war resulted in compromise. By late autumn 1758, Montcalm had grudgingly conceded that Vaudreuil possessed the authority to make decisions for the defense of the colony and by doing so accepted in principle his strategy for defending New France. He then submitted an elaborate plan for Lake Ontario's defense, which involved establishing a fort at the head of the St. Lawrence River. That fort would defend the valley and serve as an advanced post from which they could attack the British if they reestablished themselves at Oswego. Like Vaudreuil, he called for rebuilding the flotilla, but he promised that "I shall build on the lakes better vessels for war than the sloops and drawing less water."[13] He also warned Vaudreuil that he had better establish a flotilla on Lake Champlain as well, or "it will be impossible to maintain ourselves there."[14]

Though split on nearly everything else, the French and Canadian leaders were unanimous in urging Versailles to make peace with the British before they conquered New France. The situation may have been bleak but it was not hopeless. Campaigns lay ahead whose winner was by no means inevitable. Indeed the French could well have subsequently won both the vital Quebec and important Niagara campaigns had the opposing commanders made different choices. A greater infusion of troops and supplies by Versailles could have further lessened the odds against France. A thousand more whitecoats at the Plains of Abraham or Belle Isle might have overwhelmed the British on those battlefields.

On November 13, three small ships set sail from Quebec for France, with two envoys, Bougainville and Doriel, on separate ships taking pleas and reports back to Versailles. Bougainville was to report and return. Doriel was released to deal with his business and family affairs, but would echo his colleague's account of the administrative, logistical, military, and moral crisis steadily destroying New France.

The essential question before the king and his ministers at Versailles was whether Canada was worth defending. Once again the ministers reviewed the litany of New France's weaknesses: too few inhabitants and troops, inadequate munitions, powder, cannon, food, and Indian gifts, weak fortifications, fickle Indian allies, incessant bickering between Vaudreuil and Montcalm, appalling corruption by Intendant Bigot and his "Great Society," and, worst of all, overwhelming British land and sea forces poised to conquer. Indeed the odds were so bad that for Versailles to send more troops and supplies would merely mean throwing them into Britain's ever-tightening net. Even if Versailles had chosen to massively reinforce Canada, it lacked the naval and financial power to do so.[15]

In the end, Versailles would send only the bare minimum of supplies, munitions, Indian gifts, and a couple hundred recruits to flesh out the battalions. It approved Montcalm's hedgehog strategy, in which the troops were split among three commands, but "kept concentrated in a sort of center, with bateaux, warlike stores, and provisions all ready on the three routes, in order to repair rapidly and in force to the first point attacked; or, if many be attacked at the same time, to that one the defense of which will offer us the most advantages, and there combine stratagem with the most determined boldness."[16] Finally it agreed with Montcalm's plan of retreating to Louisiana if Canada fell.

New France, seemingly against all odds, would survive another two years, the result of its defenders' élan and its attackers' sluggishness. Montcalm would not live to see the final surrender. He was killed leading his army against the British on the Plains of Abraham before Quebec on September 4, 1759.

ABERCROMBY'S FATE

Bad news, like good, traveled across the Atlantic only as fast as winds and currents allowed. Word of Abercromby's disaster reached Whitehall when his aide, Captain James Cunningham, appeared with the general's official report on August 20. That was actually sooner than would have been the case had not Abercromby delayed the monthly packet boat to London so that his assumed victory could be reported as soon as possible.

It would take the government nearly a month to debate and decide what to do. It was not until September 18 that Prime Minister Pitt conveyed the government's decision to Abercromby. He first explained that when the general's "letters of the 29th June and 12th July" arrived, they "were immediately laid before the King. I am now to acquaint you that the King has judged proper that you should return to England. . . . His Majesty having been pleased to appoint Major General Amherst . . . as commander in chief of the King's forces in North America." Abercromby was to hand over all documents to Amherst. A ship would await the general in New York to carry him, his servants, and baggage back to London.[17]

In an accompanying letter, Pitt conveyed more of George II's mind:

> the King saw with much concern that an enterprise of the greatest importance had unhappily miscarried, with so considerable a loss of brave officers and soldiers. At the same time, the great spirit which the troops shewed in their unfortunate attempt gives the King just room to hope for future success. And I am ordered by His Majesty to direct you to express to the officers and soldiers His perfect satisfaction in their behavior. I have the pleasure to acquaint you that the King particularly approves your care and diligence in making the best and speediest provision for the wounded men.[18]

Of course, there would have been far fewer wounded and "loss of brave officers and soldiers" had Abercromby been the least bit competent.

With Pitt's letters aboard, the HMS *Harriot* left Falmouth on September 22 and reached Albany on November 1. Abercromby himself had arrived at Albany only a few days earlier, having left the Lake George camp on October 25. The day after receiving his recall Abercromby wrote Amherst a perfunctory letter announcing the change in command and his intention to forward his papers to him as soon as possible.

Abercromby would later claim to be unconcerned about his recall to England. Indeed he was relieved that "the anxiety of mind & fatigue of which I have suffered this campaign & the variety of tempers & characters I had to deal with, & look forward to a return . . . with the greatest composure of mind retire from the busy world & spend my time with infinitely greater satisfaction with my family and friends." He did, however, graciously acknowledge that he was "succeeded by such a worthy man as Mr. Amherst," which gave him "particular pleasure. I have known him long and . . . love and esteem him, & I'm persuaded that both the army & the colonies will be extremely happy in him."[19]

Those were kind words indeed for his successor. Any tension at their Lake George meeting must have quickly dissipated. Abercromby was magnanimous in defeat, a consolation for Amherst if not for the two thousand dead and wounded inflicted on his army with the attack he had ordered against Fort Carillon. The letter abruptly ends there. A note scrawled at the bottom of the page announced that he would embark immediately for New York. That was on November 16.

Abercromby arrived at New York on November 20. It would be another three weeks before the formal transfer of power took place on December 12, shortly after Amherst joined Abercromby. Abercromby would then embark on the HMS *Kennington* for the long sail to London. With a very few notable exceptions, the British have traditionally tolerated the failures of their generals. The letters Abercromby had received from Pitt were gentle. Still, Abercromby must have wondered whether he would receive an icily correct or warm greeting in London. Astonishingly, he would be promoted rather than cashiered, to lieutenant general in 1759 and full general in 1772. However, he would never again lead an army on campaign. Until his death in 1781, he would spend most of his remaining years in parliament, where he would most notably take a hard line against the American protests against every tax imposed upon them from 1765 to 1775, and against their independence struggle thereafter.[20]

LAST SHOT

Henceforth the British would enjoy the initiative and the French could only delay their inevitable defeat. Yet the British might well have conquered Canada in 1758 rather than 1760 had Abercromby besieged rather than assaulted Fort Carillon in July 1758. Even in the unlikely event that Montcalm would have escaped, he would have had to retreat not just from Carillon but from the equally indefensible Fort St. Frederic all the way back to Isle aux Noix, where Lake Champlain empties into the Richelieu River.

It would have taken Abercromby several weeks to transfer all his boats and supplies from Lake George to Lake Champlain. But sometime in August, his army would have been ready to row north, down Lake Champlain. The news of Abercromby's victory and northern advance might have spurred Amherst to sail on to Quebec after taking Louisbourg. The French would most likely have defended Isle aux

Noix, but might well have chosen to retreat before Abercromby's superior numbers all the way back to Montreal—much as Bourlamaque did before Haviland two years later. Abercromby and Amherst could have besieged Montreal and Quebec, respectively, by September at the latest, and, given the weakened state of New France, both cities most likely would have fallen. If so, that year's epic battles for Ticonderoga would have been decisive indeed.

NOTES

In citing works in these notes, short titles have generally been used. Works frequently cited have been identified with the following abbreviations.

BFTM	*The Bulletin of the Fort Ticonderoga Museum*
Bougainville Journal	*Adventures in the Wilderness: The American Journals of Louis Antoine de Bougainville, 1756–1760*
Bourlamaque et Levis	*Lettres de M. de Bourlamaque au marechal de Levis*
Colden Papers	*The Letters and Papers of Cadwallader Colden*
Collections des Manuscrit	*Collections des Manuscrit Contenant Lettres, Memoires, et autres Documents Historique Relatifs a l'Histoire de la Nouvelle France*
Cumberland Papers	*Military Affairs in North America, 1748–1765: Selected Documents from the Cumberland Papers in Windsor Castle*
Forbes Papers	*Writings of General John Forbes Relating to His Service in North America*
Guerre du Canada	*Guerre du Canada: Relations et Journaux de Differentes Expeditions faites durant les annees 1755, 1756, 1757, 1758, 1759, 1760*
HL	Huntington Library
Johnson Papers	*The Papers of William Johnson*, 14 volumes
Knox Journal	*The Siege of Quebec and the Campaigns in North America, 1757–1760*, by Captain John Knox
Lettres Militaires	*Lettres et Pièces Militaires: Instructions, Ordrers, Memoires, Plans de Campagne et de Defense*
Levis Journal	*Journal des Campagnes du Chevalier de Levis en Canada, de 1756 a 1760*
Levis Lettres	*Lettres du Chevalier de Levis concernant la guerre du Canada, 1756–1760*
Montcalm Journal	*Journal du Marquis de Montcalm durant ses campagnes au Canada de 1756 a 1760*
Montcalm et Levis	*Guerres du Canada, 1756–1760, Montcalm et Levis*

NYCD	Documents Relative to the Colonial History of the State of New York
Pitt Correspondence	The Correspondence of William Pitt, 2 volumes
Pitt Secretary of State Correspondence	The Correspondence of William Pitt, when Secretary of State with Colonial Governors and Military and Naval Commissioners in America
Pouchot Memoirs	Memoirs on the Late War in North America Between France and England, by Pierre Pouchot
Rogers Journal	The Annotated and Illustrated Journals of Major Robert Rogers
Vaudreuil et Levis	Lettres du marquis de Vaudreuil au Chevalier de Levis
Wilderness Chronicles	Wilderness Chronicles of Northwestern Pennsylvania
Wolfe Letters	The Life and Letters of James Wolfe

INTRODUCTION: "LIKE CHAFF BEFORE THE WIND"

1. The most comprehensive although dated study of Ticonderoga's history remains Edward P. Hamilton, *Fort Ticonderoga: Key to a Continent* (Ticonderoga, New York: Ticonderoga Press, 1995); it was first published in 1964 and the 1995 edition was not updated. For scholarly studies on virtually all aspects of the history of the fort and the surrounding region, see the many editions of the BFTM.

2. *Journal du Marquis de Montcalm durant ses campagnes au Canada de 1756 a 1759*, vol. 7, H. R. Casgrain, ed., *Collections des Manuscrits du Marechal de Levis* (Quebec: L'Imprimerie de L.-J. Demers et Frere, 1895), 408; Edward P. Hamilton, ed., *Adventure in the Wilderness: The American Journals of Louis Antoine de Bougainville, 1756–1760* (Norman: University of Oklahoma Press, 1990), 264.

3. Technically the expedition was going "upstream" since Lake George drains north down the La Chute River into Lake Champlain. Most readers do not think of lakes as flowing in a particular direction but tend to look at maps and think of south as "down" and north as "up."

4. The Montcalm Cross, BFTM 2, no. 8, July 1930, 54–56; Reverend C. Irving Cummings, "On the Last Argument of Kings," delivered May 15, 1998, BFTM 16, no. 1, 1998, 13–15. Coincidently, Reverend John Ingersoll, the chaplain of the Connecticut regiment which joined the battle, had also used the 83rd Psalm to invigorate those dispirited troops three weeks earlier.

5. Tragically, there are those generals who fail to heed history's most basic lessons. Abercromby was hardly the last British general in North America to squander his troops and suffer a humiliating defeat by hurling his army against a well-entrenched enemy. Thomas Gage lost nearly a thousand

men to American rebels during the battle of Bunker Hill in 1775, and Edward Pakenham over twenty-five hundred troops during the battle of New Orleans in 1815. Criminal ineptness in North America was not confined to British generals. These numbers would be far surpassed by casualties during the Civil War as generals ordered numerous frontal assaults against massed troops armed with rifles in fortified positions. Most notorious among these was Ambroise Burnside's bloodbath at Fredericksburg, Ulysses Grant's at Cold Harbor, and John Hood's first at Franklin then at Nashville.

6. For example, see Brian Leigh Dunnigan, *Seige 1759: The Campaign against Niagara* (Youngstown, N.Y.: Old Fort Niagara Association, 1996); Ian Steele, *Betrayals: Fort William Henry and the "Massacre"* (New York: Oxford University Press, 1990); Paul Kopperman, *Braddock at the Monongahela* (Pittsburgh: University of Pittsburgh Press, 1977); Gilbert Hagerty, *Massacre at Fort Bull: The De Lery Expedition against Oneida Carry, 1756* (Providence, R.I.: Mowbray, 1971); C. P. Stacey, *Quebec, 1759: The Siege and Battle* (Toronto: Macmillan, 1959).

As for the 1758 campaign, Ian M. McCulloch offers an excellent chapter-length scholarly study entitled, " 'Like Roaring Lions Breaking from Their Chains': The Battle of Ticonderoga, 8 July 1758," in Donald E. Graves, ed., *Fighting for Canada: Seven Battles, 1758–1945* (Toronto: Robin Brass, 2000), 23–80. There is also the beautifully produced introductory work with its clear text, maps, and illustrations by Rene Chartrand, *Ticonderoga, 1758: Montcalm's Victory against All Odds* (London: Osprey Publishing, 2000).

The only book-length work on the subject is John Shy, "James Abercromby and the Campaign of 1758," M.A. thesis, University of Vermont, 1957. Shy takes a very interesting approach in his fine study. As he explains, he permits "the reader to know neither more nor less, at any point in the narrative, than the commander himself knew at that time. The dividends are an increased realization of the difficulty of military command, and a more accurate perception of the significant elements in a particular military situation." Shy admirably achieves these goals. But as he admits, "definitive military history cannot be written in this way, because the approach is intentionally subjective"(i). It was a pleasure to see that Shy's clarity of style and thought was present even while he was a master of arts student.

1. OPENING SHOTS

1. Howard H. Peckham, ed., *The Journals of Major Robert Rogers* (New York: Corinth Books, 1961), 61.
2. Robert Rogers, The Action near Ticonderoga, March 13, 1758, BFMT 6, no. 31, January 1941, 25–26, 25–31.

3. Malartic Journal of Occurrences, 1757 and 1758, in E. B O'Callaghan and Berthold Fernow, eds., *NYCD*, 15 vols. (Albany, N.Y.: Weed, Parsons, and Co., 1856–87), 837.

4. Montcalm to Levis, January 26, 1758, in H. R. Casgrain, ed., *Guerre du Canada, 1756–1760: Montcalm et Levis* (Quebec: L'Imprimerie de L.-J. Demers et Frere, 1891), 6:122; H.-R. Casgrain, ed., *Montcalm Journal*, 7:329–30; Andre Doreil to Belle Isle, April 30, 1758, *NYCD*, 10:703.

5. Malartic Journal of Occurrences, *NYCD*, 10:837.

6. H. R. Casgrain, ed., *Levis Journal* (Montreal: C.O. Beaumachin et Fils, 1889), 1:124–25.

7. D'Huges to Belle Isle, June 1, 1758, *NYCD*, 10:703; Casgrain, ed., *Montcalm Journal*, Levis Papers, 7:332–33.

8. Malartic Journal of Occurrences, *NYCD*, 10:837–38.

9 Brian Leigh Dunnigan, ed., *Pouchot Memoirs* (Youngstown, N.Y.: Old Fort Niagara Association, 1994), 130.

10. Dunnigan, ed., *Pouchot Memoirs*, 130, 466. For another reference to divination, see Montcalm to Bourlamaque, March 19, 1758, in H.-R. Casgrain, ed., *Bourlamaque et Levis* (Quebec: L.-J. Demers et Frere, 1891), 5:212–13. For the Abenaki scouts see Casgrain, *Montcalm Journal*, 7:339–40; Edward P. Hamilton, ed., *Bourgainville Journal* (Norman: University of Oklahoma Press, 1990), 98.

Like nearly all the war's accounts, those for the Battle on Snowshoes are confusing and contradictory. I've reconstructed the battle from the most logically fitting pieces of the various documents and tried to mesh them with the actual ground, which I've explored several times.

My account differs from the traditional version, which asserts the battle took place on the present ground of the Ticonderoga Country Club with the crescent of rangers pointing northwest at an enemy that had marched south up the Bernetz valley. The documents simply do not support that tradition. Instead they talk of the French forces moving along Lake George before cutting inland. That could only mean they took the trail that led northwest between Bald Mountain and Bear Mountain. The battle would have taken place about a mile southeast of the legendary location. For the traditional account see Bob Bearor, *The Battle on Snowshoes* (Bowie, Md.: Heritage Books, 1997).

11. Rogers, Action near Ticonderoga, 29.

12. Malartic Journal of Occurrences, *NYCD*, 10:838. For other accounts, see Montcalm to Paulmy, April 10, 1758, *NYCD*, 10:693; Winter Operations, 1757–58, April 18, 1758, *NYCD*, 10:697; Doreil to Belle Isle, April 30, 1758, *NYCD*, 10:701–10.04. See also, Rogers, Action Near Ticonderoga, 25–31; A Letter from Carillon, *BFTM* 6, no. 31, 32–37.

13. Montcalm to Bourlamaque, March 19, 1758, in Casgrain, ed., *Bourlamaque et Levis*, 5:214; Casgrain, ed., *Montcalm Journal*, 7:339–40; List of Persons Killed and Captured in Major Rogers' Fight Near Ticonderoga, *BFTM* 6, no. 31, January 1941, 31; Peckham, ed., *Rogers Journal*, 62.

As usual the casualty accounts differ. The Indians may have brought back as many as 146 scalps and a few prisoners. For French accounts see, Bulletin of Most Important Operations of Winter of 1757–58, *NYCD*, 10:697; Doreil to Belle Isle, April 30, 1758, *NYCD*, 10:703. Doreil reports 144 scalps and "some prisoners" at a cost of 2 cadets wounded, and 4 Indians killed and 16 wounded. Levis reported 12 dead and 18 wounded Indians (Casgrain, ed., *Levis Journal* 126).

14. Rogers, Action near Ticonderoga, 30.

15. To the colonel of the 27th regiment of foot from a prisoner at Fort Carillon, one of the survivors of the Battle fought on Snowshoes. A volunteer with the rangers, *BFTM* 6, no. 31, January 1941, 32–37.

16. Vaudreuil to Massiac, November 28, 1758, *NYCD*, 10:924.

17. Peckham, *Rogers Journal*, 96.

18. John R. Cuneo, *Robert Rogers of the Rangers* (Ticonderoga, N.Y.: Fort Ticonderoga Museum, 1988).

19. John Ogilvie to William Johnson, March 28, 1758, *Johnson Papers*, 2:801, 800–1.

20. Casgrain, ed., *Montcalm Journal*, 7:340–41.

21. Casgrain, ed., *Montcalm Journal*, 7:341; Montcalm to Bourlamaque, March 28, 30, 1758, in Casgrain, ed., *Bourlamaque et Levis*, 5:217–18, 218–21.

22. Loudoun to William Pitt, February 14, 1758, in Gertrude Selwyn Kimball, ed., *Pitt Correspondence* (New York: Macmillan, 1906), 1:194, 183–96.

23. James Abercrombie to Loudoun, November 29, 1757, January 21, 1758, LO 4915, 5437, Huntington Library (hereafter cited as HL); Clerk, artillery for the Intended expedition, December 18, 1757, LO 2731, HL; James Abercromby to Loudoun, December 30, 1757, February 14, 1758, LO 5162, 5595, HL.

24. For other firsthand accounts of the frontier war that year, see Vaudreuil to Minister, February 13, 1758, in Sylvester K. Stevens and Donald H. Kent, eds., *Wilderness Chronicles of Northwestern Pennsylvania* (Harrisburg: Pennsylvania Historical Commission, 1941), 108–10; Vaudreuil to Minister, June 10, 1758, *Wilderness Chronicles*, 111; Vaudreuil to Minister, July 28, 1758, *Wilderness Chronicles*, 112–15; Examination of Michael la Chauvignerie, *Wilderness Chronicles*, 115–19; Examination of John Hocktattler, *Wilderness Chronicles*, 119–21.

For secondary accounts, see James Titus, *The Old Dominion at War: Society, Politics, and Warfare in Late Colonial Virginia* (Columbia: University of South Carolina Press, 1991), 94–95, 100–1; D. Peter Macleod, *The Canadian Iroquois and the Seven Years War* (Toronto: Dundern Press, 1996), 115–28.

25. Montcalm to Levis, January 19, 1758, in Casgrain, ed., *Bourlamaque et Levis*, 6:119.

26. Bulletin of the Most Important Operations of the Winter of 1757–58, *NYCD*, 10:697.

27. Doreil to Belle Isle, April 30, 1758, *NYCD*, 10:703.

28. D'Huges to Belle Isle, June 1, 1758, NYCD, 10:707; Montcalm to Bourla-maque, May 18, 1758, in Casgrain, ed., Bourlamaque et Levis, 5:254.

29. Casgrain, ed., Montcalm Journal, 7:347, 351,356–57, 361–62, 372.

30. D'Huges to Belle Isle, June 1, 1758, NYCD, 10:707.

31. Malartic Journal of Occurrences, 1757 and 1758, NYCD, 10:840; Lotbinière's Condition of New France, 1758, NYCD, 10:890.

32. Montcalm to Bourlamaque, May 15, 1758, in Casgrain, ed., Bourlamaque et Levis, 5:247.

2. THE STRUGGLE FOR NORTH AMERICA

1. For some good overviews of the imperial struggle between France and Britain for North America, from which I have taken much of the general in-formation that follows, see: Douglas Edward Leach, Roots of Conflict: British Armed Forces and Colonial Americans, 1677–1763 (Chapel Hill: University of North Carolina Press, 1986; Ian K. Steele, Warpaths: Invasions of North Amer-ica (New York: Oxford University Press, 1994); William R. Nester, The Great Frontier War: Britain, France, and the Imperial Struggle for North America, 1607–1755 (Westport, Conn.: Praeger, 2000); William R. Nester, The First Global War: Britain, France, and the Fate of North America, 1756–1775 (West-port, Conn.: Praeger, 2000); William R. Nester, "Haughty Conquerors": Am-herst and the Great Indian Uprising of 1763 (Westport, Conn.: Praeger, 2000).

2. For the statistics on population in this and the following paragraph see, Russell R. Menard, "Growth and Welfare," 1:470, 475, 477,82, 467–82; James Horn, "The British and Dutch Colonies," 2:302, 301–17; and Dale Miquelon, "The French Colonies," 2:317–20, in Jacob Ernest Cooke, ed., Encyclopedia of the North American Colonies, 3 vols. (New York: Scribner's Sons, 1993).

3. Rene Chartrand, French Fortresses in North America, 1535–1763 (New York: Osprey, 2005).

4. Information on strategy and military organization in this chapter has been culled from the following sources: Rene Chartrand, Canadian Military Heri-tage, 1000–1754, vol. 1 (Montreal: Art Global, 1993); Rene Chartrand, Cana-dian Military Heritage, 1755–1871, vol. 2 (Montreal: Art Global, 1995); Ian K. Steele, Guerillas and Grenadiers: The Struggle for Canada, 1698–1760 (Toronto: McClelland Stewart, 1969); Ian K. Steele, Warpaths: Invasions of North America, 189–90; E. Wayne Carp, "Early American Military History: A Review of Re-cent Work," Virginia Magazine of History and Biography 94 (1986), 259–84; Don Higginbotham, "Early American Way of War: Reconnaissance and Apprai-sal," William and Mary Quarterly 44 (1987), 226–41; Peter E. Russell, "Redcoats in the Wilderness: British Officers and Irregular Warfare in Europe and America, 1740–1760," William and Mary Quarterly 35 (1978), 629–52; Daniel J.

Beattie, "The Adaptation of the British Army to Wilderness Warfare, 1755–1763," in Maarten Ultee, ed., *Adapting to Conditions: War and Society in the Eighteenth Century* (Tuscaloosa: University of Alabama Press, 1986), 56–83; H. C. B. Rogers, *The British Army of the Eighteenth Century* (London: Allen and Unwin, 1977); Christopher Duffy, *The Fortress in the Age of Vauban and Frederick the Great* (London: Routledge and Keegan Paul, 1985); William Pencak, "Warfare and Political Change in Mid-Eighteenth Century Massachusetts," *Journal of Imperial and Commonwealth History* 8 (1980), 51–73; Robin May and G. A. Embleton, *Wolfe's Army* (London: Osprey, 1974); Stuart Reid and Paul Chappell, *King George's Army, 1740–93*, 2 vols. (London: Osprey, 1995); Lee Kennett, *The French Armies in the Seven Years' War: A Study in Military Organization and Administration* (Durham, N.C.: Duke University Press, 1967); Rene Chartrand, *The French Soldier in Colonial America* (Bloomfield, Ont.: Museum Restoration Service, 1984); Anthony D. Darling, *Red Coat and Brown Bess* (Bloomfield, Ont.: Museum Restoration Service, 1971); Edward P. Hamilton, *The French Army in America* (Ottawa: Museum Restoration Service, 1967); Christopher Duffy, *The Military Experience in the Age of Reason, 1715–1789* (New York: Barnes and Noble, 1997); Brent Nosworthy, *The Anatomy of Victory: Battle Tactics, 1689–1763* (New York: Hippocrene, 1992).

5. Montcalm to Le Normand, April 12, 1759, in Edmund O'Callaghan and Berthold Fernow, eds., *NYCD*, 15 vols. (Albany: Weed, Parsons, and Co., 1856–1887), 10:962–65.

6. Edward Hamilton, ed., *Bougainville Journal* (Norman: University of Oklahoma, 1964), 252–53.

7. Nester, *The Great Frontier War*, 123.

8. Quoted in Lawrence Henry Gipson, *The Great War for the Empire: The Years of Defeat, 1754–1757* (New York: Alfred A. Knopf, 1959), 7:175n28.

9. Brian Connell, ed., *Knox Journal* (Mississauga, Ont.: Pendragon, 1980), 53.

10. Darling, *Red Coat and Brown Bess*, 15.

11. Ian M. McCulloch, "'Like roaring lions breaking from their chains': The Battle of Ticonderoga, 8 July 1758," in Donald E. Graves, ed., *Fighting for Canada: Seven Battles, 1758–1945* (Toronto: Robin Brass, 2000), 75.

12. Connell, ed., *Knox Journal*, 38.

13. Both currencies lacked the easy decimal systems of today. The British currency included: 1 guinea (21 shillings and 6 pence); 1 pound (20 shillings); 1 crown (5 shillings); 1 shilling (12 pence); and 1 pence (4 farthings). The French currency included: 1 Louis d'Or (8 ecu); 1 ecu/livre/franc (60 sols); 1 sol/turnois (12 deniers).

14. Connell, ed., *Knox Journal*, 7.

15. Hamilton, ed., *French Army*, 13.

16. Connell, ed., *Knox Journal*, 110.

17. Connell, ed., *Knox Journal*, 189–90.

18. Alfred P. James, ed., *The Writings of General John Forbes Relating to His Service in North America* (Menasha, Wis.: Collegiate Press, 1938), 224–25.

19. Francis Jennings, *Empire of Fortune: Crowns, Colonies, and Tribes in the Seven Years' War* (New York: W.W. Norton, 1988), 286.

20. Nathan G. Goodman, ed., *A Benjamin Franklin Reader* (New York: Thomas Y. Crowell, 1945), 175.

21. Julian Gywn, "British Government Spending and the North American Colonies," *Journal of Imperial and Commonwealth History* 8 (1980), 74–84; William Pencak, *War, Politics, and Revolution in Provincial Massachusetts* (Boston: Northwestern University Press, 1981), 135, 154.

22. Gipson, *Great War for the Empire*, 193.

23. Franklin to Fawkener, July 27, 1756, Stanley Pargellis, ed., *Cumberland Papers* (Hamden, Conn.: Anchon Books, 1969), 185.

24. Douglas Leach, *Roots of Conflict: A Military History of the British Colonies in North America, 1607–1763* (New York: Macmillan, 1973); William A. Foote, "The Pennsylvania Men of the American Regiment," *Pennsylvania Magazine of History and Biography* 87 (1963), 31–38; William A. Foote, "The South Carolina Independents," *South Carolina Historical Magazine* 62 (1961), 195–99.

25. Frederick B. Richards, *The Black Watch at Ticonderoga and Major Duncan Campbell of Inverawe* (Ticonderoga, N.Y: Fort Ticonderoga Museum, 1926).

26. John R. Cuneo, *Robert Rogers of the Rangers* (Ticonderoga, N.Y.: Fort Ticonderoga Museum, 1988).

27. Cumberland to Loudoun, 1757, quoted in Cuneo, *Rogers*, 54–55.

28. Loudoun to William Pitt, February 14, 1758, Kimball, Pitt Correspondence, 1:191, 183–96. See also, Ian McCulloch, "'Within Ourselves': The Development of British Light Infantry in North America during the Seven Years' War," *Canadian Military History* 7, no. 2 (Spring 1998), 41–55; Steven Brumwell, "'A Service Truly Critical': The British Army and Warfare with the North American Indians, 1755–1764," *War in History* 5, no. 2 (April 1998), 146–75; John R. Cuneo, "Factors Behind the Raising of the 80th Foot in America," *Military Collector and Historian* 11, no. 4 (Winter 1959), 85–103.

29. James Abercromby to Loudoun, December 18, 1757, LO 5039, HL; James Abercromby to Gordon and Duncan, June 6, 1758, AB 327, Box 7, HL.

30. William Pencak, *War, Politics, and Revolution in Provincial Massachusetts* (Boston: Northeastern University Press, 1981); Harold E. Selesky, *War and Society in Colonial Connecticut* (New Haven: Yale University Press, 1990); Fred Anderson, *A People's Army: Massachusetts' Soldiers and Society in the Seven Years' War* (New York: W. W. Norton, 1984).

31. John C. Fitzpatrick, ed. *The Writings of George Washington*, 39 vols. (Washington, D.C.: Government Printing Office, 1931–44), 2:26.

32. Lawrence Henry Gipson, *Zones of International Friction: The Great Lakes, Frontier, Canada, the West Indies, India, 1748–1754* (New York: Alfred A. Knopf, 1952), 24–26, 56.

33. Montcalm to Argenson, August 28, 1756, *NYCD*, 10:463.

34. Brian Leigh Dunnigan, ed., *Pouchot Memoirs* (Youngstown, N.Y.: Old Fort Niagara Association, 1994), 78.

35. Rene Chartrand, "The French Regiments—Some Background," Fort Ticonderoga Conference on the 1758 Campaign, May 16 and 17, 1998. See also, Rene Chartrand, *Canadian Military Heritage*, 2 vols. (Montreal: Art Global, volume 1, 1993, volume 2, 1995).

36. Montcalm to Paulmy, September 18, 1757, *NYCD*, 10:635–36; Francis Back and Rene Chartrand, "Canadian Militia, 1750–1760," *Military Collector and Historian* 34, no. 1 (Spring 1984), 18–21.

37. Gustave Lanctot, *A History of Canada, from the Treaty of Utrecht to the Treaty of Paris, 1713–1763* (Cambridge, Mass.: Harvard University Press, 1965); W. J. Eccles, *The Canadian Frontier 1534–1760* (New York: Holt, Rinehart, and Winston, 1969).

38. Guy Fregault, *François Bigot: Administrateur Francais*, 2 vols. (Montreal: Universite de Montreal Institute d'Histoire de l'Amerique Française, 1948).

39. Doreil to Belle Isle, July 31, 1758, *NYCD*, 10:769.

40. Montcalm to Belle Isle, April 12, 1759, *NYCD*, 10:960–62.

41. Dunnigan, ed., *Pouchot Memoirs*, 78.

42. Secret Conference with Indians at Montreal, October 23, 1754, *NYCD*, 10:269.

43. Hamilton, ed., *Bougainville Journal*, 37.

44. Dunnigan, ed., *Pouchot Memoirs*, 476–77; Leroy V. Eid, " 'A Kind of Running Fight': Indian Battlefield Tactics in the Late Eighteenth Century," *Western Pennsylvania Historical Magazine* 71 (1988), 147–71; Leroy V. Eid, " 'National' War among Indians of Northeastern North America," *Canadian Review of North American Studies* 16, no. 2 (Summer 1985), 125–54.

45. Hamilton, ed., *Bougainville Journal* 41, 191. For other accounts, see Cornelius J. Jaenen, *The French Relationship with the Native Peoples of New France and Acadia* (Ottawa: Research Branch, Indian and Northern Affairs, 1984); Stephen H. Cutcliffe, "Colonial Indian Policy as a Measure of Rising Imperialism: New York and Pennsylvania, 1700–1755," *Western Pennsylvania Historical Magazine* 64 (1981), 237–68; James Axtell, *The European and the Indian: Essays in the Ethnohistory of Colonial North America* (New York: Oxford University Press, 1981); James Axtell, *The Invasion Within: The Contest of Cultures in Colonial North America* (New York: Oxford University Press, 1985); Robert Berkhofer, The French and Indians at Carillon, *BFTM* 9, no. 6, 1956, 134–69; Wilbur R. Jacobs, *Diplomacy and Indian Gifts: Anglo-French Rivalry along the Ohio and Northwest Frontiers, 1748–1763* (Stanford, Calif.: Stanford University Press, 1950).

3. GRAND STRATEGIES AND COMMANDERS

1. William R. Nester, *The Great Frontier War: Britain, France, and the Imperial Struggle for North America, 1607–1755* (Westport, Conn.: Praeger, 2000), 110.
2. Sir Julian S. Corbett, *England in the Seven Years' War: A Study in Combined Strategy*, 2d ed., 2 vols. (London: Longmans, Green, 1918); Richard Middleton, *The Bells of Victory: The Pitt-Newcastle Ministry and the Conduct of the Seven Years' War, 1757–1762* (Cambridge: Cambridge University Press, 1985).
3. For that year's strategy, see Pitt to American Governors, December 30, 1757, in Gertrude Selwyn Kimball, ed., *Pitt Correspondence* (New York: Macmillan, 1906), 1:135–36; Pitt to Northern Governors, December 30, 1757, *Pitt Correspondence*, 136–40; Pitt to Southern Governors, December 30, 1757, *Pitt Correspondence*, 43; Pitt to Abercromby, December 30, 1757, *Pitt Correspondence*, 143–51; Pitt to Lawrence, December 30, 1757, *Pitt Correspondence*, 151; Pitt to DeLancey, December 30, 1757, *Pitt Correspondence*, 151–53; Pitt to Abercromby, January 11, 1758, *Pitt Correspondence*, 159–60. All the above sources were used to determine the various numbers.

   For the change in commanders, see Pitt to Loudoun, December 30, 1757, Kimball, ed., *Pitt Correspondence*, 1:133–34; Pitt to Abercromby, December 30, 1757, *Pitt Correspondence*, 134–35.
4. M. John Cardwell makes this arguments in his "Mismanagement: The 1758 Expedition against Carillon," *BFTM* 15, no. 4, 1992, 236–91. Unfortunately, Cardwell overstates an otherwise sound analysis by trying to argue that the delays caused by Pitt's demands for too many provincial troops caused the Carillon disaster. As will be seen, that at best is debatable. Regardless, Abercromby was solely responsible for the disastrous attacks he ordered on the breastworks before Fort Carillon.
5. Francis Parkman, *Montcalm and Wolfe* (New York: Da Capo Press, 1995), 331–32.
6. Stanley McCrory Pargellis, *Lord Loudoun in America* (New Haven: Yale University Press, 1933), 42, 151.
7. L. B. Namier, *The Structure of Politics at the Ascension of George III* (London: Macmillan, 1929), 1:37; 2:314.
8. See the discussion in John Shy, "James Abercromby and the Campaign of 1758" (M.A. thesis, University of Vermont, 1957), 21–27.
9. Lawrence Henry Gipson, *The British Empire before the American Revolution: The Victorious Years, 1758–1760* (New York: Alfred A. Knopf, 1949), 7:221.
10. Edward Hamilton, ed., *Bougainville Journal* (Norman: University of Oklahoma Press, 1964), 227.
11. James Abercromby to Thomas Pownall, May 1, 1758, AB 223, Box 5, HL.

12. Loudoun to Cumberland, October 2, 1756, Stanley Pargellis, ed., *Military Affairs in North America, 1748–1763: Selected Documents from the Cumberland Collection in Windsor Castle* (hereafter cited as *Cumberland Papers* (1936; Hamden, Conn.: Archon Books, 1969), 235.

13. Cumberland to Loudoun, December 2, 1756, Pargellis, ed., *Cumberland Papers*, 253.

14. Stanley Pargellis, "Abercromby," *Dictionary of American Biography*, Allen Johnson and Dumas Malone, eds. (New York: Charles Scribner's Sons, 1928–1935), 1:29.

15. Shy, "Abercromby and the Campaign of 1758," 1.

16. James Abercromby to Lord Barrington, March 17, 1758, AB 51, Box 2, HL.

17. George II to James Abercromby, December 30, 1757, AB 7, Box 1, HL.

18. George II to James Abercromby, December 30, 1757, AB 8, Box 1, HL.

19. William Pitt to James Abercromby, December 30, 1757, AB 9, Box 1, HL.

20. William Pitt to James DeLancey, December 30, 1758, in E. B. O'Callaghan and Berthold Fernow, eds., *NYCD*, 15 vols. (Albany, N.Y.: Weed, Parsons, and Co., 1856–87), 7:339, 339–41.

21. William Pitt to James Abercromby, January 11, 1758, AB 13, Box 1, HL; William Pitt to James Abercromby, January 9, 11, 27, 1758, Kimball, ed., *Pitt Correspondence*, 1:157–59, 159–60, 167–69.

22. William Pitt to James Abercromby, December 30, 1757, Kimball, ed., *Pitt Correspondence*, 1:144.

23. James Abercromby to William Pitt, March 16, 1758, AB 47, Box 2, HL; James Abercromby to William Pitt, March 16, 1758, AB 48, Box 2, HL.

24. James Abercromby to Thomas Pownall, March 15, 1758, AB 40, Box 1, HL; James Abercromby to Thomas Pownall, March 20, 1758, AB 56, Box 2, HL.

25. William Pitt to Loudoun, December 30, 1758, LP 5151 A & B, HL.

26. James Campbell to James Abercromby, March 10, 1758, AB 33, Box 1, HL.

27. *Pennsylvania Gazette,* July 6, 1758, quoted in Milton Hamilton, *Sir William Johnson: Colonial American, 1715–1763* (Port Washington, N.Y.: Kennikat Press, 1976), 233–34.

28. James Thomas Flexner, *Mohawk Baronet: A Biography of Sir William Johnson* (Syracuse, N.Y.: Syracuse University Press, 1959).

29. William Johnson to Loudoun, December 10, 1757, in James Sullivan and A. C. Flick, eds., *Johnson Papers*, 14 vols. (Albany: State University of New York, 1921–1965), 2:761–62.

30. William Johnson to James DeLancey, March 1758, Sullivan and Flick, eds., *Johnson Papers*, 2:808–9.

31. William Johnson to James Abercromby, December 29, 1757, Sullivan and Flick, eds., *Johnson Papers*, 2:771–73.

32. William Johnson to James Abercromby, April 13, 1758, Sullivan and Flick, eds., *Johnson Papers*, 2:817–18; William Johnson Report to James Abercromby, May 24, 1758, *Johnson Papers*, 2:921–22.

33. Invitation to Onondaga Congress, April 26, 1758, Sullivan and Flick, eds., *Johnson Papers*, 2:822–24; William Johnson to James Abercromby, April 28, 1758, *Johnson Papers*, 2:830–34.

34. James Abercromby to William Pitt, May 24, 1758, Sullivan and Flick, eds., *Johnson Papers*, 2:838–41; William Johnson to James Abercromby, June 18, 1758, *Johnson Papers*, 2:843–45; John Appy to Robert Wood, July 2, 1758, *Johnson Papers*, 2:866–70; James Abercromby to William Pitt, May 24, 1758, AB 284, Box 6, HL.

35. Memoir on the Position of the French and English in North America, January 1758, *NYCD*, 10:930–35.

36. Memoir on the Position of the French and English in North America, War Ministry, January 1758, *NYCD*, 10:925–30.

37. Memoir on the Position of the French and English in North America, January 1758, *NYCD*, 10:934.

38. Memoir on the Position of the French and English in North America, January 1758, *NYCD*, 10:935.

39. Bougainville to Mme. Herault, June 30, 1757, Hamilton, ed., *Bougainville Journal*, 331.

40. Doreil to Belle Isle, July 31, 1758, *NYCD*, 10:770.

41. W. J. Eccles, "Montcalm, Louis-Joseph de, Marquis de Montcalm," *Dictionary of Canadian Biography*, 3:458–69.

42. Montcalm Commission, March 1, 1756, *NYCD*, 10:395.

43. Journal of Quebec, *NYCD*, 10:1043–44.

44. Montcalm to Vaudreuil, August 2, 1758, *NYCD*, 10:779.

45. Doreil to Moras, July 28, 1758, *NYCD*, 10:746.

46. Doreil to Belle Isle, July 28, 1758, *NYCD*, 10:754.

47. Montcalm to Massiac, August 3, 1758, *NYCD*, 10:778.

48. Moras to Montcalm, March 3, 1758, H.-R. Casgrain, ed., *Collections des Manuscrits* (Quebec: A. Cote, 1884), 3:101–92.

4. PREPARING FOR CAMPAIGN

1. James Abercromby to William Pitt, May 22, 1758, Gertrude Selwyn Kimball, ed., *Pitt Correspondence* (New York: Macmillan, 1906), 1:255, 248–56. For other staff issues, see James Abercromby, list of staff, June 25, 1758, AB 381, Box 8, HL. See also James Abercromby to James Furnis, April 8, 20, 27, 1758, AB 134, 178, 203, Box 4, HL; May 4, 1758, AB 233, Box 5, HL; June 20, 1758, AB 924, Box 8, HL; Agreement with carpenters, shipwrights, and boat builders sent to Albany by Lord Loudoun, March 10, 1758, AB 34, Box 1, HL; Account of money paid by Benjamin Hallowell for carpenters, shipwrights, and boat builders sent to Albany, March 10, 1758, AB 35, Box 1, HL; Benjamin Hallowell to James Abercromby, March 14, 1758, AB 38, Box

1, HL; Benjamin Hallowell to James Abercromby, March 17, 1758, AB 53, Box 2, HL; James Abercromby circular letter to governors, March 22, 1758, AB 63, HL; James Abercromby to Thomas Pownall, March 25, 1758, AB 72, Box 2, HL; Minutes of Private Conference, John Stanwix, March 25, 1758, AB 75, Box 2, HL; Thomas Pownall to James Abercromby, March 28, 1758, AB 84, Box 2, HL; James Abercromby to Thomas Pownall, April 3, 1758, AB 107, Box 3, HL; Joshua Loring to James Abercromby, April 3, 1758, AB 108, Box 3, HL; Thomas Fitch to Ebenezer Silliman, Johnathan Trumball, and William Wolcotte, April 5, 1758, AB 116, Box 3, HL; James Abercromby to Fitch, May 14, 1758, AB 252, Box 6, HL.

2. William Pitt Disposition of His Majesty's Forces in North America for 1758, AB 851, Box 1, HL; William Pitt to James Abercromby, January 9, 1758, AB 12, Box 1, HL; List of Ordnance for Pennsylvania, January 9, 1758, AB 858, Box 1, HL; List of Ordnance for Halifax, January 9, 1758, AB 859, Box 1, HL.

3. William Pitt to James Abercromby, January 9, 1758, AB 12, Box 1, HL; List of Ordnance for New York, January 9, 1758, AB 860, Box 1, HL; James Montresor, Abstract of Ordnance, December 1757, LO 1581 A & B, Box 114, HL; James Montresor, Ordnance and stores for expeditions A, B, and C, December 1757, LO 2112 A & B, 2091 A & B, LO 1735, Box 114, HL. William Pitt to James Abercromby, June 10, 1758, in E. B O'Callaghan and Berthold Fernow, eds., Documents Relative to the Colonial History of the State of New York (NYCD), 15 vols. (Albany, N.Y.: Weed, Parsons, and Co., 1856–1887), 7:344–45; Daniel Weir, Account of stores aboard transports, April 25, 1758, AB 892, Box 4, HL.

4. James Abercromby to William Pitt, May 22, 1758, AB 280, Box 6, HL.

5. James Abercromby to William Pitt, May 22, 1758, AB 280, Box 6, HL.

6. James Abercromby to Governors, circular letter, March 15, 1758, AB 44, 45, Box 1, HL; James Abercromby to Governors Lyttleton and Dobbs, March 16, 1758, AB 49, Box 2, HL; James Abercromby Circular letter to Governors, March 29, 1758, AB 87, Box 2, HL.

7. James DeLancey to William Pitt, March 17, 1758, NYCD, 7:343, 343–44.

8. Thomas Pownall to James Abercromby, March 12, 1758, AB 37, Box 1, HL.

9. Official documents sometimes are inaccurate or give figures that don't add up. My sharp-eyed editor noted a discrepancy and provided an accurate account. James Abercromby, provincial returns, 1758, AB 865, Box 16, HL; James Abercromby to Thomas Fitch, March 20, 1758, AB 58, Box 2, HL; Stephen Hopkins to James Abercromby, March 20, 1758, AB 57, Box 2, HL; William Denny to James Abercromby, March 24, 1758, AB 66, Box 2, HL; Pennsylvania General Assembly Resolution on Troops, March 24, 1758, AB 68, Box 2, HL; Benning Wentworth to James Abercromby, March 24, 1758, AB 69, Box 2, HL; Thomas Pownall, arming provincial problems, April 10, 1758, AB 138, Box 3, HL; John Reading to James Abercromby, April 13, 1758, AB 154, Box 3, HL; James Abercromby to Horatio Sharpe, April 14,

1758, AB 161, Box 3, HL; William Lyttleton to James Abercromby, April 15, 1758, AB 163, Box 3, HL. No figures are available for North Carolina.

10. John Reading to James Abercromby, March 30, 1758, AB 87, Box 2, HL; James Abercromby to John Reading, April 3, 1758, AB 100, Box 3, HL.

11. Benning Wentworth to James Abercromby, April 13, 1758, AB 152, Box 3, HL.

12. Thomas Pownall to James Abercromby, May 7, 1758, AB 238, Box 5, HL; James Abercromby to Thomas Pownall, March 25, 1758, AB 72, Box 2, HL.

13. Thomas Pownall Orders to Colonels and Troops of Massachusetts, May 6, 1758, AB 235, Box 5, HL.

14. Loudoun to Cumberland, March 8, 1757, Stanley Pargellis, ed., *Cumberland Papers* (1936; Hamden, Conn.: Archon Books, 1969), 324, 317–25; James De-Lancey, Provision estimates, September 7, 1758, AB 867, Box 12, HL.

15. Stephen Hopkins to James Abercromby, March 27, 1758, AB 83, Box 2, HL.

16. Ebenezer Silliman and Jonathan Trumball to James Abercromby, April 11, 1758, AB 145, Box 3, HL.

17. James Abercromby to John Reading, May 2, 1758, AB 224, Box 5, HL. See also James Abercromby to John Reading, April 3, 1758, AB 100, Box 3, HL; James Abercromby to James Furnis, April 4, 1758, AB 884, Box 3, HL; James Abercromby to DeLancey, April 6, 1758, AB 121, Box 3, HL; James De-Lancey to James Abercromby, May 22, 1758, AB 279, Box 6, HL.

18. James Abercromby to William Pitt, May 22, 1758, AB 280, Box 6, HL.

19. James Abercromby to William Pitt, May 22, 1758, AB 280, Box 6, HL.

20. James Abercromby to James Abercrombie, August 19, 1758, Chatham Papers, Bundle 98, 30, quoted in John M. Cardwell, "Mismanagement: The 1758 British Expedition against Carillon," *BFTM* 15, no. 4, 1992, 271.

21. James Abercromby to Loudoun, December 30, 1758, LP 5159, Box 114, HL.

22. James Abercromby to Loudoun, January 2, 1758, quoted in Burt Garfield Losescher, *The History of Rogers Rangers* (Burlingame, Calif.: privately published, 1957), 217–18.

23. James Abercromby to Thomas Pownall, March 15, 1758, AB 40, Box 1, HL; James Abercromby to recruiting officer of 43rd, April 24, 1758, AB 190, Box 4, HL; James Abercromby to John Calcraft, April 8, 1758, AB 131, Box 3, HL; James Abercromby to James Napier, April 5, 1758, AB 119, Box 3, HL. List of Commissions to rangers by Robert Rogers to James Abercromby, April 7, 1758, AB 124, Box 3, HL.

24. James Abercromby to John Bradstreet, April 4, 1758, AB 114, Box 3, HL.

25. James Abercromby warrant for transports, April 14, 1758, AB 159, Box 3, HL; Joshua Loring, Bond of transport owners, April l14, 1758, AB 157, Box 3, HL; William Denny to James Abercromby, March 17, 28, 1758, AB 52, 85, Box 2, HL.

26. James Abercromby to principal naval officers, May 22, 1758, AB 281, Box 6, HL; Edward Lloyd petition to Horatio Sharpe, April 1758, AB 220, Box 5,

HL; Simon Fraser to Fitch, May 20, 1758, AB 273, Box 6, HL; James Abercromby circular to governors, May 8, 1758, AB 239, Box 5, HL.

27. James Abercromby to William Pitt, April 28, 1758, AB 215, Box 5, HL.
28. Malartic Journal of Occurrences in Canada, 1757 and 1758, NYCD, 10:836.
29. Daine to Belle Isle, May 19, 1758, NYCD, 10:704.
30. H.-R. Casgrain, ed., Journal du Marquis de Montcalm durant ses campagnes au Canada de 1756 a 1760 (hereafter cited as Montcalm Journal) (Quebec: L.-J. Demers er Freres, 1895), 7:342.
31. Casgrain, ed., Montcalm Journal, 7:351, 363–64, 330, 336.
32. Vaudreuil to Massiac, November 1, 1758, NYCD, 10:863.
33. Montcalm to Palmy, April 18, 1758, NYCD, 10:699, 698–700.
34. Doreil to Belle Isle, April 30, 1758, NYCD, 10:702.
35. Levis to Paulmy, April 22, 1758, in H.-R. Casgrain, ed., Levis Lettres (Quebec: C.O. Beaumachin et Fils, 1889), 2:181.
36. Montcalm to Paulmy, April 18, 1758, NYCD, 10:699.
37. Louis Antoine Bougainville to Mme. Heault, February 20, 1758, in Edward P. Hamilton, ed., Bougainville Journal (Norman: University of Oklahoma Press, 1964), 333.
38. Hamilton, ed., Bougainville Journal, 112.
39. Montreuil to [], June 12, 1756, NYCD, 10:419.
40. Montcalm to Paulmy, April 18, 1758, NYCD, 10:699.
41. Montcalm to Paulmy, April 18, 1758, NYCD, 10:699.
42. Montcalm to Bourlamaque, March 30, 3, November 9, 1758, in H.-R. Casgrain, ed., Bourlamaque et Levis (Quebec: L.-J. Demers et Frere, 1891), 5:220, 201–06, 274; Montcalm to Levis, February 3, 12, 1758, in H.-R. Casgrain, ed., Montcalm et Levis (Quebec: L.-J. Demers et Frere, 1891), 6:124–27, 128–29.
43. Montcalm to Bourlamaque, April 5, May 4, 1758, in Casgrain, ed., Bourlamaque et Levis, 5:221–22, 236.
44. Vaudreuil to Montcalm, January 1758, in H.-R Casgrain, ed., Lettres et Pieces Militaires: Instructions, Ordres, Memoires, Plans de Campagne et de Defense (hereafter cited as Lettres Militaires) (Quebec: L.-J. Demers et Frere, 1891), 4:25–28.
45. Montcalm to Bourlamaque, March 11, 1758, in Casgrain, ed., Bourlamaque et Levis, 5:211.
46. Montcalm to Vaudreuil, January 25, 1758, in Casgrain, Lettres Militaires, 4:29–32.
47. Levis to Belle Isle, June 17, 1758, NYCD, 10:719.
48. Levis to Paulmy, May 6, 1758, in Casgrain, ed., Levis Lettres, 2:183; Levis to Belle Isle, June 26, 1758, in H.-R. Casgrain, ed., Levis Journal (Montreal: C.O. Beaumachin et Fils, 1889), 1:129–30, 186.
49. Montcalm to Bourlamaque, March 14, 1758, in Casgrain, Bourlamaque et Levis, 5:211.

50. Montcalm to Le Mercier, March 17, 1758, in Casgrain, ed., *Lettres Militaires,* 4:37–39; Le Mercier to Montcalm, March 1758, March 18, 1758, in Casgrain, ed., *Lettres Militaire,* 4:32–37, 40–43.

51. Montcalm to Bourlamaque, March 30, 1758, in Casgrain, ed., *Bourlamaque et Levis,* April 6, 1758, 5:221.

52. Montcalm to Bourlamaque, May 4, 1758, in Casgrain, ed., *Bourlamaque et Levis,* 5:233–34.

53. Casgrain, ed., *Montcalm Journal,* 7:393.

54. Montcalm to Bourlamaque, May 7, 12, 1758, in Casgrain, ed., *Bourlamaque et Levis,* 5:239–43, 245–46.

55. Daine to Belle Isle, May 20, 1758, *NYCD,* 10:706; Casgrain, ed., *Montcalm Journal,* 7:353–54.

56. Casgrain, ed., *Levis Journal,* 1:128–29.

57. Casgrain, ed., *Montcalm Journal,* 7:372.

58. Lotbinière Operation of 1758, *NYCD,* 10:891.

59. Quote from Doreil to Belle Isle, June 16, 1758, *NYCD,* 10:718; Casgrain, ed., *Montcalm Journal,* 7:370.

60. Marlartic Journal of Occurrences, 1757 and 1758, *NYCD,* 10:840.

61. Malartic Journal of Occurrences, 1757 and 1758, *NYCD,* 10:837.

62. Memoir on the Position of the French and English in America, January 1759, *NYCD,* 10:926.

63. Malartic Journal of Occurrences, 1757 and 1758, *NYCD,* 10:840.

64. Daine to Belle Isle, July 31, 1758, *NYCD,* 10:813.

65. Doreil to Belle Isle, June 16, 1758, *NYCD,* 10:717.

66. Casgrain, ed., *Montcalm Journal,* 7:371, 373.

67. Memoir of Instructions to Montcalm, June 23, 1758, *NYCD,* 10:783–86.

68. Montcalm to Vaudreuil, June 23, 1758, *NYCD,* 10:786.

69. Montcalm Memoir, July 23, 1758, *NYCD,* 10:786–87.

70. Montcalm Memoir, July 23, 1758, *NYCD,* 10:786–87.

5. WILDERNESS WAR

1. James Abercromby to James DeLancey, May 13, 15, 1758, AB 244, 253, Box 5, HL; James Abercromby to William Pitt, May 22, 1758, AB 280, Box 6, HL; George Howe to James Abercromby, May 28, 1758, AB 293, Box 6, HL; George Howe to James Abercromby, May 30, 1758, AB 299, Box 7, HL.

2. James Abercromby to James Furnis, May 15, 1758, AB 255, Box 6, HL; Thomas Hancock to James Abercromby, May 19, 1758, AB 269, Box 6, HL; James Abercromby to DeLancey, May 22, 1758, AB 278, Box 6, HL; James Abercromby to William Pitt, May 27, 1758, AB 289, Box 6, HL; James Abercromby to DeLancey, June 13, 1758, AB 352, Box 8, HL; Francis Bernard to James Abercromby, June 17, 1758, AB 358, Box 8, 1758, HL.

3. John Appy to James DeLancey, June 22, 1758, AB 373, Box 8, HL.

4. Thomas Pownall to James Abercromby, April 24, 1758, AB 192, Box 4, HL; James Abercromby to Thomas Pownall, April 26, 1758, AB 201, Box 4, HL.

5. Thomas Pownall to James Abercromby, June 12, 1758, AB 350, Box 8, HL; James Abercromby to Thomas Pownall, May 21, 1758, AB 275, Box 6, HL.

6. John Appy to Thomas Pownall, June 17, 1758, AB 359, Box 8, HL.

7. James Abercromby to William Pitt, May 22, 1758, in Gertrude Selywyn Kimball, ed., *Pitt Correspondence* (New York: Macmillan, 1906), 1:251, 248–56.

8. Horatio Gage to John Stanwix, June 23, 1758, AB 378, Box 8, HL; William Johnson to John Stanwix, June 25, 1758, AB 383, Box 8, HL; William Johnson to John Appy, June 25, 1758, AB 384, Box 8, HL; James Abercromby to William Pitt, June 29, 1758, AB 397, Box 8, HL.

9. Hugh Arnot journal, June 17 to July 9, 1758, in Nicolas Westbrook, ed., "'Like Roaring Lions Breaking from Their Chains': The Highland Regiment at Ticonderoga," *BFTM* 16, no. 1, 1998, 30–31.

10. Hugh Arnot journal, June 17 to July 9, 1758, in Westbrook, "'Like Roaring Lions," 31–32.

11. James Abercromby to William Pitt, June 29, 1758, AB 397, Box 8, HL; Return of Provincial Troops at Lake George, June 29, 1758, AB 400, Box 8, HL; James Abercromby to William Pitt, June 29, 1758, AB 397, Box 8, HL; Return of Provincial Forces, John Appy to Robert Wood, July 2, 1758, C.O. (Colonial Office) 5:50.

12. Hugh Arnot journal, June 17 to July 9, 1758, in Westbrook, "'Like Roaring Lions," 31–33.

13. Monypenny Orderly Book, March 23 to June 29, 1758, *BFTM* 12, no. 5, December 1969, 339.

14. Monypenny Orderly Book, *BFTM,* 345.

15. James Abercromby to William Johnson, June 21, 24, 1758, in James Sullivan and A. C. Flick, eds., *Johnson Papers,* 14 vols. (Albany: State University of New York, 1921–1965), 2:849–50, 852–53; William Johnson to James Abercromby, June 22, 1758, *Johnson Papers,* 2:851–52; John Appy to Robert Wood, July 2, 1758, *Johnson Papers,* 2:866–70; William Johnson to James Abercromby, June 27, 1758, *Johnson Papers,* 2:854, 854–55.

16. James Campbell's examination, March 24, 1758, in Sullivan and Flick, eds., *Johnson Papers,* 2:786–87; William Johnson to James Abercromby, December 19, 1757, *Johnson Papers,* 2:763; Loudoun to William Johnson, December 25, 1757, *Johnson Papers,* 2:764–67.

17. George Howe to William Johnson, March 28, 1758, in Sullivan and Flick, eds., *Johnson Papers,* 2:800, 799–800.

18. Timothy J. Todish, ed., *Rogers Journal* (Fleischmanns, N.Y.: Purple Mountain Press, 2002), 115, 117; James Abercromby to William Pitt, June 29, 1758, AB 397, Box 8, HL; John Appy to James DeLancey, June 21, 1758, AB 370, Box 8, HL.

19. Indian intelligence, June 18, 1758, in Sullivan and Flick, eds., *Johnson Papers*, 2:845–46; James Abercromby to William Johnson, June 21, 1758, *Johnson Papers*, 2:849–50.

20. James Abercromby to Vaudreuil (two letters), April 24, 1758, AB 194, 195, Box 4, HL; James Abercromby to Montcalm, April 24, 1758, AB 191, Box 4, HL.

21. Vaudreuil to Abercromby, June 4, 10, 1758, AB 317, 341, Box 7, HL; Vaudreuil to Abercromby, June 5, 1758, in E. B. O'Callaghan and Berthold Fernow, eds., *NYCD*, 15 vols. (Albany, N.Y.: Weed, Parsons, and Co., 1856–1887), 10:716.

22. Abercromby to Vaudreuil, June 26, 1758, *NYCD*, 10:772–74; John Appy to Peter Schuyler, June 21, 1758, AB 369, Box 8, HL; James Abercromby to Vaudreuil, June 26, 1758, AB 387, Box 8, HL; John Appy circular letter to governors, June 30, 1758, AB 401, Box 8, HL; William Pitt to James Abercromby, June 10, 1758, AB 343 A & B, Box 7, HL.

23. "Malartic Journal of Occurrences, 1757 and 1758," *NYCD*, 10:847; "Lotbinière's Condition of New France in 1758," *NYCD*, 10:892.

24. H.-R. Casgrain, ed., *Montcalm Journal* (Quebec: L'Imprimerie de L.-J. Demers et Frere, 1895), 7:382.

25. Casgrain, ed., *Montcalm Journal*, 7:383, 385.

26. Montcalm to Belle Isle, July 12, 1758, *NYCD*, 10:732; Casgrain, ed., *Montcalm Journal*, 7:150.

27. Casgrain, ed., *Montcalm Journal*, 7:382, 373–74.

28. Levis to Montcalm, June 30, 1758, H.-R. Casgrain, ed., *Levis Letters* (Montreal: C.O. Beaumachin et Fils, 1889), 2:189–90; Levis to Belle Isle, June 26, July 10, 1758, in Casgrain, ed., *Levis Letters*, 2:185, 196; H.-R. Casgrain, ed., *Levis Journal* (Montreal: C.O. Beaumachin et Fils, 1889), 1:135.

29. Brian Leigh Dunnigan, ed., *Pouchot Memoir* (Youngstown, N.Y.: Old Fort Niagara Association, 1994), 134–36; Montcalm to Belle Isle, July 12, 1758, *NYCD*, 10:732; Casgrain, ed., *Levis Journal*, 1:129–31.

30. Vaudreuil's commentary on Montcalm's memoir of the campaign, *NYCD*, 10:789; Montcalm report, 1758, H.-R. Casgrain, ed., *Guerre du Canada* (Quebec: L.-J. Demers, 1895), 11:152; Casgrain, ed., *Montcalm Journal*, 7:385, 386.

31. Vaudreuil to Lotbinière, September 20, 1758, BFTM 1, no. 3, January 1758, 2–3; Edward Hamilton, *Fort Ticonderoga: Key to a Continent* (Ticondergoga, N.Y.: Fort Ticonderoga Press, 1995; originally published in 1961), 42.

32. Remarks on the Situation of Fort Carillon and its Approaches, d'Hugues to Belle Isle, June 1, 1758, *NYCD*, 10:708.

33. Remarks on the Situation of Fort Carillon, d'Hugues to Belle Isle, June 1, 1758, *NYCD*, 10:708; Memoir on Fort Carillon by M. de Pont le Roy, Engineer in Chief, *NYCD*, 10:720.

34. Remarks on the Situation of Fort Carillon, d'Hugues to Belle Isle, June 1, 1758, *NYCD*, 10:709.

35. Doreil to Cremilles, July 15, 1758, *NYCD*, 10:763.
36. Doreil to Belle Isle, July 31, 1758, *NYCD*, 10:769.
37. Lotbinière to Belle Isle, November 11, 1758, *NYCD*, 10:890.
38. Belle Isle's notes in the margin of a letter to him from Lotbinière, November 11, 1758, *NYCD*, 10:889–90.
39. I have culled details of French operations for the rest of this chapter from the following sources: Montcalm to Belle Isle, July 12, 1758, *NYCD*, 10:733; Account of the Operations at Ticonderoga, July 14, 1758, *NYCD*, 10:735; Adjutant Malartic Journal of Military Operations before Fort Carillon, July 1 to July 10, 1758, *NYCD*, 10:721–25; Anonymous English Account, July 14, 1758, *NYCD*, 10:734–36; Montcalm Report on Carillon Battle, July 8, 1758, *NYCD*, 10:737–41; French Official Account of Carillon Battle, *NYCD*, 10:741–44; Doreil to Moras, July 28, 1758, *NYCD*, 10:744–47; Montcalm to Vaudreuil, July 9, 1758, *NYCD*, 10:738–51; Doreil to Cremille, July 28, 1758, *NYCD*, 10:762–64; Doreil to Paulmy, July 30, 1758, *NYCD*, 10:765–67; Doreil to Belle Isle, July 31, 1758, *NYCD*, 10:767–71; Daine to Belle Isle, July 31, 1758, *NYCD*, 10:813–17; Vaudreuil to Noailles, August 6, 1758, *NYCD*, 10:808–10; Doreil to Belle Isle, August 31, 1758, *NYCD*, 10:818–21; Malartic Journal, July 1 to July 25, 1758, *NYCD*, 10:844–49; Parole of French officers taken July 6, 1758, AB 424, Box 9, HL.
40. Casgrain, ed., *Levis Journal*, 1:132.
41. "Monypenny Orderly Book, June 30th to August 7, 1758," *BFTM* 2, no. 8, 1970, 56–60; John Forbes monthly return, January 24, 1758, LP 2480 Box 6, HL.
42. Edward P. Hamilton, ed., *Bougainville Journal* (Norman: University of Oklahoma Press, 1964), 141.
43. James Abercromby orders, July 3, 1758, AB 407, Box 9, HL; Abercrombie to Pitt, July 12, 1758, *NYCD*, 10:725–26.
44. Account of the Operations at Ticonderoga, July 14, 1758, *NYCD*, 10:734. Though the account is anonymous, the writer is most likely an officer of the 46th regiment since that is the only unit whose casualties he records of the Battle of Fort Carillon.
45. Lotbinière's Condition of New France in 1758, *NYCD*, 10:894.
46. Montcalm Report, 1758, in H. R. Casgrain, ed., *Guerre du Canada, Relations et Journaux de Differentes Expeditions Faites Durant les annees 1755, 1756, 1757, 1758, 1759, 1760* (Quebec: L.-J. Demers, 1895), 11:152.
47. Montcalm to Belle Isle, July 12, 1758, 10:732–33.
48. William Grant letter extract, August 17, 1758, in Westbrook, "Like Roaring Lions," 55.
49. Brian Connell, ed., *Knox Journal* (Mississauga, Ont.: Pendragon, 1980), 79.
50. Account of the Operations at Ticonderoga, July 14, 1758, *NYCD*, 10:735.
51. William Eyre to Robert Napier, July 10, 1758, Stanley Pargellis, ed., *Cumberland Papers*, reprinted (Hamden, Conn.: Archon Books, 1969), 419.
52. David Perry, "Life of David Perry," *BFTM* 14, no. 1, Summer 1981, 5–6.

53. Montcalm to Belle Isle, July 12, 1758, *NYCD*, 10:733; Account of the Operations at Ticonderoga, July 14, 1758, *NYCD*, 10:735. See also, Malartic Journal of Military Operations before Fort Carillon, July 1 to July 10, 1758, *NYCD*, 10:721–25; Anonymous English Account, July 14, 1758, *NYCD*, 10:734–36; Montcalm Report on Carillon Battle, July 8, 1758, *NYCD*, 10:737–41. See Vaudreuil's point-by-point rebuttal of Montcalm's battle report; Vaudreuil's Observations on Montcalm's Account of the July 8, 1758 battle, *NYCD*, 10:788–98; French Official Account of Carillon Battle, *NYCD*, 10:741–44; Doreil to Moras, July 28, 1758, *NYCD*, 10:744–47; Montcalm to Vaudreuil, July 9, 1758, *NYCD*, 10:738–51; Doreil to Cremille, July 28, 1758, *NYCD*, 10:762–64; Doreil to Paulmy, July 30, 1758, *NYCD*, 10:765–67; Doreil to Belle Isle, July 31, 1758, *NYCD*, 10:767–71; Daine to Belle Isle, July 31, 1758, *NYCD*, 10:813–17; Vaudreuil to Noailles, August 6, 1758, *NYCD*, 10:808–10; Doreil to Belle Isle, August 31, 1758, *NYCD*, 10:818–21; Malartic Journal, July 1 to July 25, 1758 *NYCD*, 10:844–49; Parole of French officers taken July 6, 1758, AB 424, Box 9, HL.

54. Account of the Operations at Ticonderoga, July 14, 1758, *NYCD*, 10:734.

55. Monypenny to Calcraft, July 11, 1758, *BFTM* 2, no. 8, July 1930, 52.

56. Abercromby to Pitt, July 12, 1758, *NYCD*, 10:726.

57. Thomas Mante, *The History of the Late War in North America, and the Islands of the Late War in North America, and the Islands of the West Indies, Including the Campaigns of 1763 and 1764 against His Majesty's Indian Enemies* (1772; New York: Research Reprints, 1970), 147.

58. Hamilton, ed., *Bougainville Journal*, 229.

59. Wolfe to Father, July 27, 1758, in Beckles Willson, *The Life and Letters of James Wolfe* (hereafter cited as *Life and Letters*) (London: Heineman, 1909), 384.

60. Francis Parkman, *Montcalm and Wolfe: The French and Indian War* (1886; New York: Da Capo Press, 1995), 360.

61. James Abercromby to William Pitt, July 12, 1758, *NYCD*, 10:726.

62. Montcalm to Belle Isle, July 12 1758, *NYCD*, 10:733; Account of Operations at Ticonderoga, July 14 1758, *NYCD*, 10:735.

63. Robert Pell, "The Strategy of Montcalm, 1758," *BFTM* 9, no. 3, Summer 1953, 175–201.

6. THE BATTLE OF FORT CARILLON

1. Abercromby to Pitt, July 12, 1758, E. B. O'Callaghan and Berthold Fernow, eds., *NYCD*, 15 vols. (Albany, N.Y.: Weed, Parsons, and Co., 1856–1887), 10:726.

2. William G. Godfrey, *The Pursuit of Profit and Preferment in Colonial North America: John Bradstreet's Quest* (Waterloo, Ont.: Wilfred Laurier University Press, 1982).

3. Hugh Arnot journal, June 17 to July 9, 1758; James Abercrombie letter, July 10, 1758, in Nicholas Westbrook, ed., "Like Roaring Lions Breaking from Their Chains: The Highland Regiment at Ticonderoga," *BFTM* 16, no. 1, 1998, 39, 66.

4. John Brainard to P. V. B. Livingston, July 11, 1758, Fort Ticonderoga Library.

5. Anonymous to John Knox, July 29, 1758, in Brian Connell, ed., *The Siege of Quebec and the Campaigns in North America, 1757–1760,* by Captain John Knox (Mississauga, Ont.: Pendragon, 1980), 79.

6. French Account of the Battle of Ticonderoga, *NYCD*, 10:742.

7. William Hervey, July 8, 1758, journals, 50, in Westbrook, ed., "Like Roaring Lions," 63.

8. William Grant letter extract, August 17, 1758, in Westbrook, ed., "Like Roaring Lions," 56.

9. "Lotbinière's Condition of New France in 1758," *NYCD*, 10:895.

10. Abstract of Despatches Complaining of Vaudreuil, 1758, *NYCD*, 10:857. For slightly different statistics, see H.-R. Casgrain, ed., *Montcalm Journal* (Quebec: Imprimerie de L.-J. Demers et Frere, 1895), 7:397–98.

11. Montcalm's Order of Battle, July 7, 1758, *BFTM* 2, no. 8, July 1930, 68.

12. Montcalm to Vaudreuil, July 16, 1758, *NYCD*, 10:802; Vaudreuil to Montcalm, July 21, 1758, *NYCD*, 10:804.

13. Brian Leigh Dunnigan, *Pouchot Memoir* (Youngstown, N.Y.: Old Fort Niagara Association, 1994), 145.

14. William Grant letter extract, August 17, 1758, in Westbrook, ed., "Like Roaring Lions," 56.

15. See the discussion in Westbrook, ed., "Like Roaring Lions," n56.

16. Abercromby to Pitt, July 12, 1758, *NYCD*, 10:726.

17. James Abercromby to James Abercrombie, August 19, 1758, Chatham Papers, Buddle 98, 28, quoted in John M. Cardwell, "Mismanagement: The 1758 British Expedition against Carillon," *BFTM* 15, no. 4, 1992, 279–80.

18. Charles Lee, "Narrative," accompanying letter to Miss Sydney Lee, September 16, 1759, Fort Ticonderoga Collection, FTA #M-6008, #M-6009, quoted in Cardwell, "Mismanagement," 279–81.

19. Rev. Cleaveland, July 27, 1758, Journal, *BFTM* 10, no. 3, 1959, 204–5.

20. Anonymous letter, July 1758, *BFTM* 7, no. 1, January 1945, 16.

21. J. B. to Clerk family, August 25, 1758, in Westbrook, ed., "Like Roaring Lions," 84–86. Westbrook identifies J. B. as Jacob Bryant, the secretary for the board of ordnance.

22. Charles Lee's "Narrative," September 16, 1758, the Lee Papers, New York Historical Society, Collections, 1871, 1:13.

23. Hugh Arnot journal, June 17 to July 9, 1758; J. B. [Jacob Bryant] to Clerk family, August 25, 1758, in Westbrook, ed., "Like Roaring Lions," 41, 84–85.

24. William Johnson to James Abercromby, July 5, 1758 (two letters), in James Sullivan and A. C. Flick, eds., *Johnson Papers,* 14 vols. (Albany: State University of New York, 1921–1965), 2:872, 871.

25. Summary of Indian transactions, August 3, 1758, in Sullivan and Flick, eds., *Johnson Papers*, 2:884–87; John Appy to Robert Wood, July 2, 1758, *Johnson Papers*, 2:866–70.

26. Montcalm's Report of the Battle of Fort Carillon, *NYCD*, 10:740.

27. Hugh Arnot journal, in Westbrook, ed., "Like Roaring Lions," 40.

28. Doreil to Moras, July 28, 1758, *NYCD*, 10:746.

29. Anonymous letter, July 1758, *BFTM* 7, no. 1, January 1945, 17.

30. Abercromby to Pitt, July 12, 1758, *NYCD*, 10:727.

31. William Eyre to Robert Napier, July 10, 1758, in Stanley Pargellis, ed., *Cumberland Papers* (1936; New York: Archon Books, 1969), 420.

32. John Shy, "James Abercromby and the Campaign of 1758" (M.A. thesis, University of Vermont, 1957), 163.

33. See for example, Montcalm report, H.-R. Casgrain, ed., *Guerre du Canada* (Quebec: L.-J. Demers, 1895), 11:156–60.

34. General Orders for the Attack on Ticonderoga, AB 407, HL.

35. James Abercrombie to Harry Erskine, July 10, 1758, in Westbrook, ed., "Like Roaring Lions," 69.

36. For various accounts of the battle—before and the aftermath—see Relation de l'affaire du 8 Juillet, 1758, AB 423, Box 9, HL; Adjutant Malartic Journal of Military Operations before Fort Carillon, July 1 to July 10, 1758, *NYCD*, 10:721–25; Anonymous English Account, July 14, 1758, *NYCD*, 10:734–36; French Official Account of Carillon Battle, *NYCD*, 10:741–44; Doreil to Moras, July 28, 1758, *NYCD*, 10:744–47; Montcalm to Vaudreuil, July 9, 1758, *NYCD*, 10:738–51; Doreil to Cremille, July 28, 1758, *NYCD*, 10:762–64; Doreil to Paulmy, July 30, 1758, *NYCD*, 10:765–67; Doreil to Belle Isle, July 31, 1758, *NYCD*, 10:767–771; Daine to Belle Isle, July 31, 1758, *NYCD*, 10:813–17; Vaudreuil to Noailles, August 6, 1758, *NYCD*, 10:808–10; Doreil to Belle Isle, August 31, 1758, *NYCD*, 10:818–21; Malartic Journal, July 1 to July 25, 1758, *NYCD*, 10:844–49; John Appy to Thomas Pownall, July 10, 1758, AB 431, Box 9, HL; Montcalm Report on Carillon Battle, July 8, 1758, *NYCD*, 10:737–41. See Vaudreuil's point-by-point rebuttal of Montcalm's battle report in Vaudreuil's Observations on Montcalm's Account of the July 8, 1758 battle, *NYCD*, 10:788–98.

    There are conflicts between Montcalm's official reports and Vaudreuil's commentary over what happened at Fort Carillon between June 30 and July 8. Since the general was there and the governor was not, I have relied on the former.

37. Hugh Arnot journal, June 17 to July 9, 1758, in Westbrook, ed., "Like Roaring Lions," 41.

38. James Abercrombie to Harry Erskine, July 10, 1758, in Westbrook, ed., "Like Roaring Lions," 68–69.

39. J. B. [Jacob Bryant] to Clerk family friend, August 25, 1758, in Westbrook, ed., "Like Roaring Lions," 85.

40. Montreuil Account of Campaigns in North America from 1755 to 1758, *NYCD*, 10:922.

41. Account of the Operations at Ticonderoga, July 14, 1757, *NYCD*, 10:736.

42. Anonymous letter, *BFTM* 7, no. 1 (January 1945), 17.

43. Parsons, July 8, 1758, Journal, in Westbrook, ed., "Like Roaring Lions," 83.

44. James Abercromby to Captain James Abercrombie, August 19, 1758, in Westbrook, ed., "Like Roaring Lions," 74–75.

45. William Grant letter extract, August 17, 1758, in Westbrook, ed., "Like Roaring Lions," 56–57.

46. Frederick Richards, *The Black Watch at Ticonderoga and Major Duncan Campbell of Inverawe* (Ticonderoga, N.Y.: Fort Ticonderoga Museum, 1926), 52.

47. "Life of David Perry," *BFTM* 14, no. 1, Summer 1981, 6, 4–8.

48. Dunnigan, ed., *Pouchot Memoir*, 149.

49. Dunnigan, ed., *Pouchot Memoir*, 147.

50. Anonymous, *BFTM*, 17.

51. Thomas Mante, *The History of the Late War in North America, and the Islands of the Late War in North America, and the Islands of the West Indes, Including the Campaigns of 1763 and 1764 against His Majesty's Indian Enemies* (1772; New York: Research Reprints, 1970), 151.

52. James Abercrombie to Harry Erskine, July 10, 1758, in Westbrook, ed., "Like Roaring Lions," 69, 66.

53. "Life of David Perry," *BFTM* 14, no. 1 (Summer 1981), 7.

54. Abercromby to Pitt, July 12, 1758, *NYCD*, 10:727; Montcalm to Belle Isle, July 12, 1758, *NYCD*, 10:733; James Abercromby, return of officers killed or wounded, July 8, 1758, AB 425, Box 9, HL. For slightly different statistics, see French Casualities at Carillon, *BFTM* 1, no. 3, January 1928, 12; British Casualty List at Carillon, *BFTM* 2, no. 8, July 1930, 76–78; Brian Connell, ed., *The Siege of Quebec and the Campaigns in North America, 1757–1760*, by Captain John Knox (Mississauga, Ont.: Pendragon, 1980), 81; Abercromby to Pitt, July 12, 1758, *NYCD*, 10:727; Levis to Moras, July 10, 1758, H.-R. Casgrain, ed., *Levis Lettres* (Montreal: C.O. Beaumachin et Fils, 1889), 2:197.

55. Montcalm report, in Casgrain, ed., *Relations et Journaux, Guerre de Canada*, 11:173.

56. Abercromby to Pitt, July 12, 1758, *NYCD*, 10:727.

57. Gen. James Abercromby to Captain James Abercrombie, August 19, 1758, in Westbrook, ed., "Like Roaring Lions," 77.

58. Gen. James Abercromby to Captain James Abercrombie, August 19, 1758, in Westbrook, ed., "Like Roaring Lions," 75.

59. Gen. James Abercromby to Captain James Abercrombie, August 19, 1758, in Westbrook, ed., "Like Roaring Lions," 76.

60. Anonymous, *BFTM* 7, no. 1 (January 1945), 18.

61. Account of the Operations at Ticonderoga, July 14, 1758, *NYCD*, 10:736.

62. Quoted in Godfrey, *Pursuit of Profit and Preferment*, 130–31.

63. Montcalm to Abercromby, July 24, 1758, *NYCD*, 10:775.

64. Doreil to Moras, July 28, 1758, *NYCD*, 10:746.

65. Malartic Journal of Occurrences, 1757 and 1758, *NYCD*, 10:848; H.-R. Casgrain, ed., *Montcalm Journal*, 7:408.

66. Casgrain, ed., *Montcalm Journal*, 7:406; Montcalm to Belle Isle, July 20, 1758, *NYCD*, 10:737.

67. John Entick, *The General History of the Late War Containing Its Rise, Progress, and Events in Europe, Asia, Africa, and America.* 5 vols. (London: Edward Dilly and John Millan, 1763–1764), 3:257–58.

68. Mante, *History of the Late War in North America*, 159–61.

69. Francis Parkman, *Montcalm and Wolfe* (New York: Da Capo Press, 1995), 371.

70. Lawrence Gipson, *The British Empire before the American Revolution.* Vol. 8, *The Great War for the Empire: The Victorious Years, 1758–1760* (New York: Alfred A. Knopf, 1946), 7:232.

71. John M. Cardwell, "Mismanagement: The 1758 Expedition against Carillon," *BFTM* 15, no. 4, 1992, 236–91.

72. Leslie Buell, "In Defense of the General," *BFTM* 12, no. 3, October 1967, 223–32.

73. John Shy, "James Abercromby and the Campaign of 1758" (M.A. thesis, University of Vermont, 1957), 167.

74. Shy, "Abercromby," 166.

75. James Abercromby to DeLancey, July 18, 1758, AB 445, Box 9, HL.

76. James Abercromby to Lord Barrington, July 12, 1758, AB 437, Box 9, HL. See also James Abercromby to William Pitt, July 12, 1758, AB 436, Box 9, HL.

7. PURSUITS

1. Minutes of council of war, July 13, 1758, AB 438, Box 9, HL; James Abercromby to John Bradstreet, July 13, 1758, AB 439, Box 9, HL; Malartic Journal of Occurances, 1757 and 1758, in E. B. O'Callaghan and Berthold Fernow, eds., *NYCD*, 15 vols. (Albany, N.Y.: Weed, Parsons, and Co., 1856–87), 10:850–51.

2. James Abercromby to Jeffrey Amherst, July 18, 1758, AB 450, Box 9, HL.

3. Abercromby to Montcalm, July 21, 1758, *NYCD*, 10:774. See also, James Abercromby to John Small, July 21, 1758, AB 461, Box 10, HL; Jacques Coriveau to James Abercromby, July 21, 1758, AB 462, Box 10, HL; James Abercromby, certificate of Schuyler's delay, July 21, 1758, AB 935, Box 10, HL; James Abercromby to Peter Schuyler, July 21, 1758, AB 936, Box 10, HL; James Abercromby to DeLancey, July 25, 1758, AB 476, Box 10, HL.

4. Montcalm to Abercromby, July 24, 1758, *NYCD*, 10:744.

5. Vaudreuil to Abercromby, August 1, 1758, *NYCD*, 10:776–77.

6. James Abercromby to Montcalm, August 12, 1758, AB 530, Box 11, HL; James Abercromby to Vaudreuil, August 12, 1758, AB 529, Box 11, HL.

7. James Abercromby to Montcalm, August 14, 1758, AB 534, Box 11, HL; Vaudreuil to Abercromby, August 27, 1758, AB 567, Box 12, HL; James Abercromby to Vaudreuil, October 1, 1758, AB 712, Box 14, HL; James Abercromby to Peter Schuyler, October 1, 1758, AB 713, Box 14, HL; James Abercromby to Montcalm, October 1, 1758, AB 714, Box 14, HL; Montcalm to James Abercromby, October 2, 1758, AB 718, Box 14, HL; Vaudreuil to James Abercromby, November 1, 1758, AB 804, Box 15, HL; Vaudreuil, rolle of prisoniers, November 1, 1758, AB 805, Box 15, HL; Vaudreuil to Massiac, November 3, 1758, *NYCD*, 10:877; Abercromby to Vaudreuil, October 1, 1758, *NYCD*, 10:878–79.

8. Prevost to Becourt, November 13, 1758, *NYCD*, 10:897; Abercromby to Schuyler, October 1, 1758, *NYCD*, 10:879; Vaudreuil to Abercromby, October 19, 1758, *NYCD*, 10:879–80; List of English Prisoners Delivered to Colonel Schulyer, November 1, 1758, *NYCD*, 10:881–84.

9. James Abercromby, list of extra staff, December 24, 1758, AB 843, Box 16, HL; list of staff, December 25, 1758, AB 844, Box 16, HL.

10. James Robertson to Earl of Morton, December 19, 1758, in Stanley Pargellis, ed., *Cumberland Papers* (1936; Hamden, Conn.: Archon Books, 1969), 432.

11. James Wolfe to Father, August 7, 1758, in Beckles Willson, ed., *The Life and Letters of James Wolfe* (London: Heineman, 1909), 391.

12. Thomas Gage and James Prevost to James Abercromby, July 20, 1758, and James Prevost to James Abercromby, July 29, 1758, in Pargellis, *Cumberland Papers*, 422–23, 423–25.

13. James Prevost and Thomas Gage to James Abercromby, July 20, 1758, Ian McCulloch, "'Believe Us, Sir, This Will Impress Few People!': Spin Doctoring, 18th Century Style," *BFTM* 16, no. 1, 1998, 101.

14. James Prevost to James Abercromby, August 20, 1758, AB 548. See also James Prevost to Cumberland, August 21, 1758, in Pargellis, ed., *Cumberland Papers*, 427–28.

15. James Abercromby to James Prevost, August 21, 1758, AB 553; James Prevost to Cumberland, August 21, 1758, in McCulloch, "'Believe Us, Sir,'" 100.

16. James Prevost to Cumberland, August 21, 1758, in McCulloch, "'Believe Us, Sir,'" 99–100.

17. David Perry, "Life of David Perry," *BFTM* 14, no. 1, Summer 1981, 7.

18. Thomas Hutchinson to James Abercromby, July 29, 1758, AB 483, Box 10, HL; Thomas Hutchinson list of deserters, July 29, 1758, AB 498, Box 10, HL; Joseph Cotis examination of three deserters, August 2, 1758, AB 497, Box 10, HL; Jame Abercromby to Thomas Pownall, August 3, 1758, AB 503, Box

10, HL; Thomas Hutchinson to James Abercromby, August 8, 1758, AB 517, Box 10, HL; James Abercromby to Thomas Hutchinson, August 22, 1758, AB 556, Box 11, HL.

19. James Abercromby to John Stanwix, July 23, 1758, AB 468, Box 10, HL. See also, James Abercromby to DeLancey, August 14, 1758, AB 536, Box 11, HL; and Charles Cruickshank to Captain Christie, July 19, 1758, AB 455, 456, Box 10, HL. For other good examples, see James Abercromby to Simon Fraser, July 19, 1758, AB 457, Box 10, HL; James Abercromby to Captains Hugh Arnot and Quinton Kennedy, July 23, 1758, AB 939, Box 10, HL; James Abercromby to William Martin, July 24, 1758, AB 471, Box 10, HL; James Abercromby to Captain Wrighton, July 24, 1758, AB 941, Box 10, HL; James Abercromby to James Prevost, August 4, 1758 (two letters), AB 504, 947, Box 11, HL; James Abercromby to William Martin, August 25, 26, 1758, AB 560, 562, Box 11, HL.

20. James Abercromby to DeLancey, August 10, 1758, AB 522, Box 11, HL.

21. Montcalm to Belle Isle, July 12, 1758, NYCD, 10:733.

22. Montcalm to Vaudreuil, July 9, 1758, NYCD, 10:750.

23. Doreil quoting Montcalm in a letter to Moras, July 28, 1758, NYCD, 10:746. For a classic letter in which Vaudreuil takes credit for all successes and heaps on Montcalm and others blame for all failures, see Vaudreuil to Noailles, August 6, 1758, NYCD, 10:808–810.

24. Vaudreuil to Massiac, August 4, 1758, NYCD, 10:719–20.

25. In H. R. Casgrain, ed., Montcalm Journal (Quebec: L.-J. Demers et Frere, 1895), 7:410.

26. In Casgrain, ed., Montcalm Journal, 7:418; Vaudreuil to Massiac, August 4, 1758, NYCD, 10:720.

27. In Casgrain, ed., Montcalm Journal, 7:408, 423.

28. Montcalm to Belle Isle, July 12, 1758, NYCD, 10:733.

29. Vaudreuil to Massiac, August 4,1 758, NYCD, 10:783.

30. Vaudreuil to Montcalm, July 12, 1758, Montcalm's Commentary, July 16, 1758, NYCD, 10:801; Vaudreuil to Montcalm, July 12, July 16, July 17, 1758, NYCD, 10:757, 759, 760.

31. Montcalm's Commentary, July 16, 1758, NYCD, 10:801.

32. Montcalm to Vaudreuil, July 16, 1758, NYCD, 10:801, 800–1, 800–3.

33. Montcalm to Massiac, July 28, 1758, NYCD, 10:756.

34. Vaudreuil to Montcalm, July 17, 1758, NYCD, 10:760.

35. Observations of Montcalm to Vaudreuil's July 12 Letter, July 16, 1758, NYCD, 10:757, 758; Montcalm to Vaudreuil, July 18, 1758, NYCD, 10:759–60; Vaudreuil to Montcalm, July 17, 1758, NYCD, 10:760; Montcalm to Vaudreuil, 10:760–61; Vaudreuil to Montcalm, July 21, 1758, NYCD, 10:803–5; Vaudreuil to James Abercromby, August 1, 1758, AB 493, Box 10, HL; Montcalm to Vaudreuil, August 2, 1758, NYCD, 10:778; Vaudreuil letter to Montcalm and the latter's observations, July 16, 1758, NYCD, 10:800–3.

36. Vaudreuil to Levis, July 11, 1758, in H.-R. Casgrain, ed., *Vaudreuil et Levis Letters* (Quebec: L.-J. Demers, 1895), 8:49.

37. Vaudreuil to Levis, July 12, 1758, in Casgrain, ed., *Vaudreuil et Levis*, 8:51.

38. Vaudreuil to Levis, July 22, 1758, in Casgrain, ed., *Vaudreuil et Levis*, 8:52.

39. Levis to Mirepoix, October 28, 1758, in H.-R. Casgrain, ed., *Levis Lettres* (Montreal: C.O. Beaumachin et Fils, 1889), 2:213–14.

40. Levis to king, October 30, 1758, in Casgrain, ed., *Levis Lettres*, 2:216–17.

41. Pean to Levis, July 23, 1758, in H.-R. Casgrain, ed., *Lettres Divers* (Quebec: L.-J. Demers et Frere, 1895), 10:89.

42. In Casgrain, ed., *Montcalm Journal*, 7:409, 406–7.

43. In Casgrain, ed., *Montcalm Journal*, 7:412, 406; Council Speeches, July 29, 1758, *NYCD*, 10:805.

44. Brian Leigh Dunnigan, ed., *Pouchot Memoir* (Youngstown, N.Y.: Old Fort Niagara Association, 1994), 151–52.

45. In Casgrain, ed., *Montcalm Journal*, 7:423.

46. Malartic Journal, July 22 to 25, 1758, *NYCD*, 10:849–50.

47. Indian Council with Montcalm, July 30, 1758, *NYCD*, 10:805.

48. Indian Council with Vaudreuil, July 30, 1758, *NYCD*, 10:806.

49. Vaudreuil to Montcalm, August 1, 1758, *NYCD*, 10:811.

50. Montcalm to Vaudreuil, August 6, 1758, *NYCD*, 10:811–12.

51. Montcalm to Massiac, August [n.d.] 1758, *NYCD*, 10:810.

52. Bigot to Massiac, August 13, 1758, *NYCD*, 10:812.

53. Doreil to Belle Isle, July 31, 1758, *NYCD*, 10:768.

54. Doreil to Belle Isle, August 31, 1758, *NYCD*, 10:820.

55. Vaudreuil to Massiac, November 20, 1758, *NYCD*, 10:903–04.

56. Observations of Montcalm to Vaudreuil's July 12 Letter, July 16, 1758, *NYCD*, 10:758.

57. Vaudreuil to Montcalm, July 21, 1758, *NYCD*, 10:804.

58. Malartic correctly attributes this attack to Courtmache and maintains that St. Luc and la Corne were near Fort Carillon during this time (Malartic Journal of Occurrences, 1757 and 1758, *NYCD*, 10:848). Pouchot said that Courtemache led 200 Canadians and 400 Indians from Fort Carillon on July 10. Ten days later, his force attacked a British detachment, taking 20 scalps and 8 prisoners (Dunnigan, *Pouchot Memoir*, 152; see also Edward P. Hamilton, ed., *Bougainville Journal* [Norman: University of Oklahoma Press, 1964], 245).

59. James Abercromby to John Stanwix, July 25, 1758, AB 475, Box 10, HL; James Abercromby to William Pitt, August 19, 1758, in Gertrude Selwyn Kimball, ed., *Pitt Correspondence* (New York: Macmillan, 1906), 1:317, 316–27.

60. Doreil to Belle Isle, August 31, 1758, *NYCD*, 10:818.

61. In Casgrain, ed., *Montcalm Journal*, 7:414.

62. Doreil to Belle Isle, August 31, 1758, *NYCD*, 10:818; Malartic's journal appears to offer the most accurate account, Malartic Journal of Occurrences,

1757 and 1758, *NYCD*, 10:849–50; see also, News from Carillon, *NYCD*, 10:750; Daine to Belle Isle, July 31, 1758, *NYCD*, 10:817; Dunnigan, ed., *Pouchot Memoir*, 151–52.

63. James Abercromby to John Forbes, August 2, 1758, AB 493, Box 10, HL. James Abercromby to John Stanwix, July 29, 1758, AB 484, Box 10, HL; James Abercromby to Colonel Massey, July 30, AB 490, Box 10, HL; William Haviland to James Abercromby, July 30, 1758, AB 486, Box 10, HL; John Wrighton to James Abercromby, July 30, 1758, AB 489, Box 10, HL.

64. James Abercromby to DeLancey, August 10, 1758, AB 522, Box 11, HL.

65. Albert Spicer, Journal for 1758, in Russell P. Bellico, ed., *Chronicles of Lake George: Journeys in War and Peace* (Fleischmanns, N.Y.: Purple Mountain Press, 1995), 109; Doreil to Belle Isle, August 31, 1758, *NYCD*, 10:818–19. Marin himself reported leaving 17 on the field (Malartic Journal of Occurrences, 1757 and 1758, *NYCD*, 10:851).

66. Malartic Journal of Occurrences, 1757 and 1758, *NYCD*, 10: 851; James Abercromby to John Stanwix, August 12, 1758, AB 531, Box 11, HL; James Abercromby to John Forbes, August 20, 1758, AB 551, Box 11, HL; Doreil to Belle Isle, August 31, 1758, *NYCD*, 10:818–19; Hamilton, *Bougainville Journal*, 249, 253, 259, 261.

67. James Abercromby to William Pitt, August 19, 1758, in Kimball, *Pitt Correspondence*, 1:322, 316–27.

68. Malartic Journal of Occurrences, 1757 and 1758, *NYCD*, 10:851.

69. In Casgrain, ed., *Montcalm Journal*, 7:445.

70. In Casgrain, ed., *Montcalm Journal*, 7:435–37, 452, 465–66, 468.

71. In Casgrain, ed., *Montcalm Journal*, 7:427. For three accounts, see the appropriate chapters in J. S. MacLennan, *Louisbourg: From Its Foundation to Its Fall, 1713–1758* (1918) (Halifax: Book Room Limited, 1979); Hugh Downey, *Louisbourg: Key to a Continent* (Englewood Cliffs, N.J.: Prentice Hall, 1965); Bruce W. Fry, *An Appearance of Strength: The Fortifications of Louisbourg*, 2 vols. (Ottawa: Parks Commission, 1984).

72. Montcalm to Cremille, September 21, 1758, *NYCD*, 10:856; Malartic Journal of Occurrences, 1757 and 1758, *NYCD*, 10:850, 851.

73. In Casgrain, ed., *Montcalm Journal*, 7:433, 435.

74. H.-R. Casgrain, ed., *Levis Journal* (Montreal: C.O. Beaumachin et Fils, 1889), 1:148–53; Levis to Belle Isle, September 8, 1758, in Casgrain, ed., *Levis Lettres*, 2:201–3; Vaudreuil to Levis, September 12, 1758, H.-R. Casgrain, ed., *Lettres de Vaudreuil au Chevalier de Levis* (Quebec: L.-J. Demers, 1895), 8:5556; Vaudreuil to Massaic, September 2, 1758, *NYCD*, 10:822–26; William Godfrey, *The Pursuit of Profit and Preferment in Colonial North America: John Bradstreet's Quest* (Waterloo, Ont.: Wilfred Laurier University Press, 1982), 106–10, 123–25; Richard A. Preston and Leopold LaMontagne, *Royal Fort Frontenac* (Toronto: Champlain Society, 1958); Frederick A. Rahmer, *Dash to Frontenac: An Account of Lt. Col.*

John Bradstreet's Expedition to and Capture of Fort Frontenac (Rome, N.Y.: Frederick A. Rahmer, 1973).

75. James Abercromby to Amherst, August 29, 1758, AB 582, Box 12, HL. See also James Abercromby to William Pitt, September 8, 1758, in Kimball, ed., *Pitt Correspondence*, 1:343–46.

76. James Abercromby to James DeLancey, August 28, 1758, AB 574, Box 12, HL.

77. James Abercromby to William Pitt, September 8, 1758, AB 629, Box 12, HL.

78. Alexander Monypenny, return of men fit for duty at Lake George and down to Albany, October 6, 1758, AB 724, Box 14, HL; Alexander Monypenny, return of troops from Lake George to Albany, October 6, 1758, AB 724, Box 14, HL. By September 2, there were 464 troops laid up in Albany hospitals and hundreds more sick soldiers elsewhere (James Napier, account of sick in Albany, September 2, 1758, AB 599, HL).

79. Jeffrey Amherst to James Abercromby, July 27, 1758, AB 478, Box 10, HL.

80. Jeffrey Amherst to James Abercromby, August 10, 1758, AB 523, Box 11, HL.

81. Jeffrey Amherst to William Pitt, August 10, 1758, in Kimball, ed., *Pitt Correspondence*, 1:313, 312–14.

82. Jeffrey Amherst to James Abercromby, September 3, 1758, AB 606, Box 12, HL.

83. James DeLancey to James Abercromby, September 3, 1758, AB 604, Box 12, HL.

84. James Abercromby to Thomas Pownall, September 4, 1758, AB 611, Box 12, HL; Thomas Pownall to James Abercromby, September 12, 1758, AB 648, HL.

85. James DeLancey to James Abercromby, September 14, 1758, AB 657, Box 13, HL; James Abercromby to DeLancey, September 9, 1758, AB 632, Box 12, HL; James Abercromby to William Pitt, September 8, 1758, AB 629, Box 12, HL.

86. Jeffrey Amherst to James Abercromby, September 15, 1758, AB 663, Box 13, HL; Thomas Pownall to James Abercromby, September 20, 1758, AB 681, Box 13, HL; James DeLancey to James Abercromby, October 26, 1758, AB 789, Box 15, HL.

87. James Abercromby to Thomas Pownall, September 22, 1758, AB 687, Box 13, HL.

88. James Abercromby to Jeffrey Amherst, September 30, 1758, AB 704, Box 13, HL; Jeffrey Amherst to William Pitt, June 11, July 6, 27, August 10, September 18, October 13, 1758, in Kimball, ed., *Pitt Correspondence*, 1:271–75, 291–93, 305–7, 312–14, 352–53, 364–65; Thomas Pownall to William Pitt, September 12, 25, 1758, in *Pitt Correspondence*, 1:348–50, 355.

89. James Abercromby to John Stanwix, October 7, 1758, AB 731, Box 14, HL; Jeffrey Amherst, route from Boston to Albany, September 25, 1758, AB 847,

Box 13, HL; Jeffrey Amherst to James Abercromby, September 25, 1758, AB 697, Box 13, HL.

90. James Abercromby to John Stanwix, October 7, 1758, AB 731, Box 14, HL.

91. James Abercromby to Jeffrey Amherst, November 2, 1758, AB 810, Box 15, HL; James Abercromby to Thomas Pownall, November 6, 1758, AB 815, Box 16, HL.

92. Thomas Pownall to James Abercromby, November 14, 1758, AB 822, Box 16, HL.

93. James Abercromby to John Forbes, November 1, 1758, AB 807, Box 15, HL.

94. James Abercromby to Thomas Pownall, October 19, 1758, AB 775, Box 15, HL.

95. James Abercromby to Thomas Pownall, October 19, 1758, AB 775, Box 15, HL; James Abercromby to James DeLancey, October 24, 1758, AB 786, Box 15, HL; James DeLancey to James Abercromby, October 26, 1758, AB 789, Box 15, HL; James Abercromby to Jeffrey Amherst, October 30, 1758, AB 795, Box 15, HL.

96. James Abercromby, list of winter quarters, 1758, AB 849, Box 16, HL; James Abercromby to William Pitt, November 25, 1758, AB 828, Box 16, HL.

97. In Casgrain, ed., *Levis Journal*, 1:157–58.

98. Bougainville to Cremille, November 8, 1758, *NYCD*, 10:889; Casgrain, ed., *Montcalm Journal*, 7:470, 479, 481; Casgrain, ed., *Levis Journal*, 1:157–60.

8. PARTING SHOTS

1. Montcalm's Reflection on Defense, September 12, 1758, in E. B. O'Callaghan and Berthold Fernow, eds., *NYCD*, 15 vols. (Albany, N.Y.: Weed, Parsons, and Co., 1856–1887) 10:874. See also Daine to Belle Isle, November 3, 1758, *NYCD*, 10:885; and Bougainville to Cremille, November 8, 1758, *NYCD*, 10:887–89.

2. Vaudreuil to Massiac, November 1, 1758, *NYCD*, 10:863; Requisition request to France, November 1, 1758, *NYCD*, 10:864–65.

3. Pean on Canada's Condition, November 15, 1758, *NYCD*, 10:897–900.

4. Doreil to Belle Isle, July 31, 1758, *NYCD*, 10:821.

5. Montcalm to Belle Isle, October 27, 1758, *NYCD*, 10:861.

6. In Edward P. Hamilton, ed., *Bougainville Journal* (Norman: University of Oklahoma Press, 1964), 257–58.

7. Montcalm to Belle Isle, November 15, 1758, *NYCD*, 10:900.

8. Montcalm's Reflections on Defense, September 12, 1758, *NYCD*, 10:874–77; Montcalm's Memoir on Lake Sacrament, September 12, 1758, *NYCD*, 10:873.

9. Vaudreuil to Massiac, November 1, 1758, *NYCD*, 10:868.

10. Vaudreuil's Observations on Montcalm's Memoir, September 12, 1758, *NYCD*, 10:872.

11. Vaudreuil to Massiac, November 1, 1758, *NYCD*, 10:866–68; Vaudreuil's Plan for Lake Ontario submitted to Montcalm, November 1, 1758, *NYCD*, 10:868–70.

12. Vaudreuil's Response to Montcalm's Memoir on Lake Sacrament, September 12, 1758, *NYCD*, 10:874; see also Vaudreuil to Massiac, November 1, 1758, *NYCD*, 10:867.

13. Montcalm Memoir on Lake Ontario's Defense, November 1, 1758, *NYCD*, 10:870, 870–72.

14. Montcalm's Observations on Defense, September 12, 1758, *NYCD*, 10:876.

15. Memoir on the Position of the French and English in America, January 1759, *NYCD*, 10:926, 925–30. See also the discussion of French strategy in Canada in chapter 3, above.

16. Memoir of the Position of the French and English in America, January 1759, *NYCD*, 10:927. See also Abstract of Dispatches from Canada, December 28, 1758, *NYCD*, 10:906–7.

17. William Pitt to James Abercromby, September 18, 1758, AB 675, Box 13, HL.

18. William Pitt to James Abercromby, September 18, 1758, AB 675, Box 13, HL.

19. James Abercromby to Thomas Pownall, November 16, 1758, AB 823, Box 16, HL.

20. James Abercromby to William Pitt, November 25, 1758, AB 829, HL: James Abercromby to Barrington, December 17, 1758, AB 836, Box 16, HL; James Abercromby to William Pitt, December 17, 1758, AB 837, Box 16, HL.

In 1759, Amherst successfully besieged and took Fort Carillon, although nearly all of the French forces escaped before he could cut them off. Amherst renamed the captured fort Ticonderoga.

BIBLIOGRAPHY

MANUSCRIPT COLLECTIONS

Henry E. Huntington Library, San Marino, California: Loudoun Papers; Abercromby Papers.
Public Archives, Ottawa: Indian Records and Claus Papers,
Public Records Office: Sir Jeffrey Amherst Papers; William Pitt, Earl of Chatham papers, King George III papers.
William L. Clement Library, Ann Arbor, Michigan: Thomas Gage Papers.
Huntington Library, San Marino, California: Abercromby Papers, Loudoun Papers.

PRIMARY

Arnot, Hugh. "A Journal or Proceedings of the Army Under the Command of Maj. Gen. Abercromby from June the 17th Until July the 9th Campaign 1758." *Bulletin of the Fort Ticonderoga Museum* 16, no. 1, November 1, 1998, 16–91.
"Attack and Repulse at Ticonderoga, July 1758." *Bulletin of the Fort Ticonderoga Museum* 7, no. 1, January 1945, 15–18.
The Battle of Carillon. *Bulletin of the Fort Ticonderoga Museum* 2, no. 8, July 1930, 69–78.
Bellico, Russell P., ed. *Chronicles of Lake George: Journeys in War and Peace.* Fleischmanns, N.Y.: Purple Mountain Press, 1995.
———. *Chronicles of Lake Champlain: Journeys in War and Peace.* Fleischmanns, N.Y.: Purple Mountain Press, 1998.
Blanchette, Paul O., ed. "Captain William Sweat's Personal Diary of the Expedition against Ticonderoga, May 2–September 7, 1758." *Essex Institute Historical Collections* 93, January 1957, 40–46.
Bory, Gabriel de. *Memoires sur l'Administration de la Marine et Colonies.* Paris: P. D. Pierres, 1789–1790.

Brigham, Clarence S., ed. *British Royal Proclamations Relating to America, 1603–1783.* Vol. 12. Worcester, Mass.: Transactions and Collection of the American Antiquarian Society, 1911.

British Casuality List at Carillon. *Bulletin of the Fort Ticonderoga Museum* 2, no. 8, July 1930, 76–78.

Calloway, Colin G., ed. *North Country Captives: Selected Narratives of Indians from Vermont and New Hampshire.* Hanover: University Press of New England, 1992.

Casgrain, H.-R., ed. *Collections des Manuscrits Contenant Lettres, Memoires, et autres Documents Historiques Relatifs a l'Histoire de la Nouvelle-France.* Quebec: A. Cote, 1884.

———, ed. *Journal des Campagnes du Chevalier de Levis en Canada, de 1756 a 1760.* Montreal: C.O. Beaumachin et Fils, 1889.

———, ed. *Lettres du Chevalier de Levis concernant la guerre du Canada, 1756–1760.* Montreal: C.O. Beaumachin et Fils, 1889.

———, ed. *Extraits des Archives des Ministeres de la Marine et de la Guerres a Paris.* Quebec: L.-J. Demers et Frere, 1890.

———, ed. *Guerre du Canada, 1756–1760: Montcalm et Levis.* Quebec: L'Imprimerie de L.-J. Demers et Frere, 1891.

———, ed. *Lettres de M. de Bourlamaque au marechal de Levis.* Quebec: L.-J. Demers et Frere, 1891.

———. *Montcalm et Levis.* 2 vols. Quebec: Imprimeries de L.J. Demers et Freres, 1891.

———, ed. *Journal du Marquis de Montcalm durant ses campagnes au Canada de 1756 a 1760.* Quebec: L'Imprimerie de L.-J. Demers et Frere, 1895.

———, ed. *Guerre du Canada: Relations et Journaux de Differentes Expeditions faites durant les annees 1755, 1756, 1757, 1758, 1759, 1760.* Quebec: L.-J. Demers, 1895.

———, ed. *Lettres de Divers particuliers au Chevalier de Levis.* Quebec: L.-J. Demers et Frere, 1895.

———, ed. *Lettres du marquis de Vaudreuil au Chevalier de Levis.* Quebec: L.-J. Demers, 1895.

———, ed. *Collection des Manuscrits des Marechal de Levis,* 12 vols. Montreal: Public Archives of Canada, 1889–1895.

Clark, David Saunders, ed. "Journals and Orderly Books Kept by Massachusetts Soldiers During the French and Indian War." *New England Historical and Genealogical Register* 95, April 1941, 118–21.

Colden, Cadwallader. *The Letters and Papers of Cadwallader Colden.* New York: New York Historical Society Collections, 1921.

Colonel Charles Clinton's Journal, July to October 1758. *Bulletin of the Fort Ticonderoga Museum* 15, no. 4, 1992, 310, 292–315.

Connell, Brian, ed. *Siege of Quebec and the Campaigns in North America, 1757–1760, by Captain John Knox.* Mississauga, Ont.: Pendragon, 1980.

Cour, Charles-Joseph Mathon de la. *Etats et Tableaux Concernant les Financiers de la France Depuis 1758 jusqu'au 1787*. Paris: Cuchet et Gattey, 1788.

De Forest, Louis E., ed. *The Journals and Papers of Seth Pomeroy, Sometime General in the Colonial Service*. New Haven, Conn.: Society of Colonial Wars, 1926.

Dorr, Moses. "A Journal of an Expedition against Canady." *New York History* 16, October 1935, 452–64.

Dunnigan, Brian Leigh, ed. *Memoirs on the Late War in North America between France and England*, by Pierre Pouchot. Youngstown, N.Y.: Old Fort Niagara Association, 1994.

Duverger, de Saint-Blin. *Memoire Pour le Sieur Duverger de Saint-Blin, Lieutenant d'Infanterie dans les Troupes Etant Ci-Devant en Canada*. Paris: Moreau, 1763.

Extracts from Captain Monypenny's Orderly Book, June 30 to July 7, 1758. *Bulletin of the Fort Ticonderoga Museum* 2, no. 8, July 1930, 56–67.

Fitzpatrick, John C., ed. *The Writings of George Washington*. 39 vols. Washington, D.C.: Government Printing Office, 1931–44.

Gaffarel, Dufy, ed. *Adjuntant Malartic Journal des campagnes de 1755 . . . 1760*. Dijon: Libraire Plon, 1890.

Glasier, Benjamin, "French and Indian War Diary of Benjamin Glasier of Ipswich, 1758–1760." *Essex Institute Historical Collections* 86, January 1930, 67–77.

Goodman, Nathan G., ed. *A Benjamin Franklin Reader*. New York: Thomas Y. Crowell, 1945.

Hamilton, Charles, ed. *Braddock's Defeat*. Norman: University of Oklahoma Press, 1959.

Hamilton, Edward P., ed. *Adventure in the Wilderness: The American Journals of Louis Antoine de Bougainville, 1756–1760*. (1964) Norman: University of Oklahoma Press, 1990.

James, Alfred Procter, ed. *Writings of General John Forbes Relating to His Service in North America*. Menasha, Wis.: Collegiate Press, 1938.

Jennings, Francis, William N. Fenton, Mary A. Druke, and David R. Miller, eds. *Iroqouis Indians: A Documentary History of the Six Nations and Their League*. Woodbridge, Conn.: Research Publications, 1985.

Jennings, Francis, et al. *The History and Culture of Iroquois Diplomacy: An Interdisciplinary Guide to the Treaties of the Six Nations and Their League*. Syracuse, N.Y.: Syracuse University Press, 1985.

Jordan, John W., ed. "James Kenny Journals, 1758–59." *Pennsylvania Magazine of History and Biography* 32, 1913, 1–47, 152–201, 395–449.

Josiah Goodrich Orderbook. *Bulletin of the Fort Ticonderoga Museum* 14, no. 1, summer 1981, 39–61.

"A Journal of an Expedition against Canaday by Moses Dorr Ensin of Capt Parker's Company Roxbury May 25, 1758." *New York History* 16, 1935, 452–64.

Journal of Captain Samuel Cobb. *Bulletin of the Fort Ticonderoga Museum* 14, no. 1, summer 1981, 12–31.

Kent, Donald H., ed. *The Papers of Henry Bouquet*. 6 vols. Harrisburg: Pennsylvania Historical and Museum Commissions, 1951–94.

Kimball, Gertrude Selwyn, ed. *Correspondence of William Pitt, when Secretary of State with Colonial Governors and Military and Naval Commissioners in America*. New York: Macmillan, 1906.

Lincoln, Charles Henry, ed. "Manuscript Records of the French and Indian War in the Library of the Society." *Transactions and Collections of the American Antiquarian Society*, vol. 11. Worcester, Ma.: American Antiquarian Society, 1909.

List of French Killed and Wounded, July 8, 1758. *Bulletin of the Fort Ticonderoga Museum* 1, no. 3, January 1928, 12.

List of Persons killed and captured in Major Rogers' Fight Near Ticonderoga. *Bulletin of the Fort Ticonderoga Museum* 6, no. 31, January 1941, 31.

Memoir on the Defense of the Fort of Carillon. *Bulletin of the Fort Ticonderoga Museum* 8, no 3, 1972, 196–226.

Montcalm at Carillon. *Bulletin of the Fort Ticonderoga Museum* 1, no. 3, January 1928, 4–11.

Montcalm's Order of Battle. *Bulletin of the Fort Ticonderoga Museum* 2, no. 8, July 1930, 67–69.

Montcalm-Gozon, Louis Joseph de. "Montcalm's Correspondence." Pages 31–108. *Report of the Public Archives of Canada for the Year 1929*. Ottawa: Public Archives, 1930.

Montresor, Col. James. "Journals of Col. James Montresor, 1757–1759." New York Historical Society, Collections 14, 1881.

Monypenny, Alexander. "Diary of Alexander Moneypenny." *Journal of Cherokee Studies* 2, Summer 1877, 302–31.

Monypenny's Orderly Book, July 15 to August 3, 1759. *Bulletin of the Fort Ticonderoga Museum* 2, no. 10, July 1932, 219–53.

Monypenny Orderly Book, June 30 to August 7, 1758. *Bulletin of the Fort Ticonderoga Musuem* 12, no. 6, October 1970, 434–61.

Monypenny Orderly Book, March 23 to June 29, 1758. *Bulletin of the Fort Ticonderoga Museum* 12, no. 5, December 1969, 328–57.

Mulligan, Robert E., ed. Colonel Charles Clinton's Journal of the Campaign in New York July to October, 1758, during the French War. *Bulletin of the Fort Ticonderoga Museum* 15, no. 4, 1992, 293–315.

Nevis, Allan, ed. *Ponteach, or the Savages of America: A Tragedy by Robert Rogers*. New York: Lenox Hill Publishers, 1971.

O'Callaghan, Edmund, and Berthold Fernow, eds., *Documentary History of the State of New York*, 4 vols., New York: Weed, Parsons, and Co, 1850–51.

———. *Documents Relative to the Colonial History of the State of New York*. 15 vols., Albany: Weed, Parsons, and Co., 1856–1887.

Pargellis, Stanley, ed. *Military Affairs in North America, 1748–1763: Selected Documents from the Cumberland Papers in Windsor Castle*. Hamden, Conn.: Archon Books, 1969. First published in 1936.

Peckham, Howard H., ed. *The Journals of Major Robert Rogers*. New York: Corinth Books, 1961.

Pell, Robert. The Strategy of Montcalm, 1758. *Bulletin of the Fort Ticonderoga Museum* 9, no. 3, summer 1953.

Perry, David. Life of David Perry. *Bulletin of the Fort Ticonderoga Museum* 14, no. 1, summer 1981. 4–11.

Rogers, Robert. The Action Near Ticonderoga, March 13, 1758. *Bulletin of the Fort Ticonderoga Museum* 6, no. 31, January 1941, 25–31.

Rogers, Robert. A Letter from Carillon. *Bulletin of the Fort Ticonderoga Museum* 6, no. 31, January 1941, 32–37.

Rogers, Robert. Regulations for the Rangers Drawn Up by Robert Rogers. *Bulletin of the Fort Ticonderoga Museum* 4, no. 31, January 1941, 1–19.

Roy, Pierre-George, ed. *Inventaries des Papiers de Lery.* 3 vols. Quebec: Archives de la Province de Quebec, 1939–1940.

Shortt, A., ed. *Documents Relating to Canadian Currency, Exchange, and Finance during the French Period.* 2 vols. Ottawa: King's Printer, 1925.

Simmons, R. C. and P. D. G. Thomas, eds. *Proceedings and Debates of the British Parliaments Respecting North America, 1754–1783.* Vol. 1; 1754–1764. Millwood, N.Y.: Kraus International Publications, 1982.

Stevens, Syvester K., and Donald H. Kent, eds. *Wilderness Chronicles of Northwestern Pennslyvania.* Harrisburg: Pennsylvania Historical Commission, 1941.

Sullivan, James, and A. C. Flick, eds. *The Papers of William Johnson.* 14 vols. Albany: State University of New York, 1921–1965.

Thwaites, Reuben Gold, ed. *The Jesuit Relations and Allied Documents: Travels and Explorations of the Jesuits Missionaries in New France, 1610–1791.* 73 vols. New York: Pageant Book Co., 1959. Originally published 1896–1901.

Todish, Timothy J., ed. *The Annotated and Illustrated Journals of Major Robert Rogers.* Fleischmanns, N.Y.: Purple Mountain Press, 2002.

Vanderbeets, Richard, ed. *Held Captive by the Indians: Selected Narratives, 1642–1836.* Knoxville: University of Tennessee Press, 1973.

Walpole, Horatio, Lord. *Memoirs of King George II.* Edited by John Brooke. 3 vols. New Haven, Ct.: Yale University Press, 1985.

Webster, J. Clarence, ed. *The Journal of Jeffrey Amherst: Recording the Military Career of General Amherst in America from 1758 to 1763.* Toronto: Ryerson Press, 1931.

Welles, Lemuel Aiken. "Letters of Col. Nathan Whiting, Written from Camp During the French and Indian War." *Papers of the New Haven Colony Historical Society,* vol. 6. New Haven: New Haven Colony Society, 1900.

Westbrook, Nicholas, ed. "Like Roaring Lions Breaking from Their Chains: The Highland Regiment at Ticonderoga." *Bulletin of the Fort Ticonderoga Museum* 16, no. 1, 1998.

Willson, Beckles, ed. *The Life and Letters of James Wolfe.* London: Heineman, 1909.

Wood, William, ed. *The Logs of the Conquest of Canada.* Toronto: Champlain Society Publications, 4, 1909.

SECONDARY

Alden, John. *General Gage in America*. Baton Rouge: University of Louisiana Press, 1948.

Anderson, Fred W., "Why Did Colonial New Englanders Make Bad Soldiers? Contractual Principles and Military Conduct during the Seven Years' War." *William and Mary Quarterly* 38, 1981: 395–417.

Anderson, Fred. *A People's Army: Massachusetts' Soldiers and Society in the Seven Years' War*. New York: W. W. Norton, 1984.

———. *Crucible of War: The Seven Years' War and the Fate of Empire in British North America, 1754–1766*. New York: Alfred A. Knopf, 2000.

Axtell, James. *The European and the Indian: Essays in the Ethnohistory of Colonial North America*. New York: Oxford University Press, 1981.

———. *The Invasion Within: The Contest of Cultures in Colonial North America*. New York: Oxford University Press, 1985.

Ayling, Stanley. *The Elder Pitt, Earl of Chatham*. London: Collins, 1976.

Back, Francis, and Rene Chartrand. "Canadian Militia, 1750–1760." *Military Collector and Historian* 34, no. 1, Spring 1984, 18–21.

———. "French Engineers, New France, 1750–1763." *Military Collector and Historian* 38, no. 1 (Spring 1986), 26–27.

Bean, Walton E. "War and the British Colonial Farmer: A Reevaluation in the Light of New Statistical Records." *Pacific Historical Review* 11, 1942, 439–47.

Bearor, Bob. *The Battle on Snowshoes*. Bowie, Md.: Heritage Books, 1997.

Beattie, Daniel J. "The Adaptation of the British Army to Wilderness Warfare, 1755–1763." In Maarten Ultee, ed., *Adapting to Conditions: War and Society in the Eighteenth Century*. Tuscaloosa: University of Alabama Press, 1986, 56–83.

Berkhofer, Robert. The French and Indians at Carillon. *Bulletin of Fort Ticonderoga Museum* 9, no. 6, 1956, 134–69.

Bird, Harrison. The Uniforms of Robert Rogers' Rangers. *Bulletin of the Fort Ticonderoga Museum* 8, no. 2, July 1948, 65–71.

Black, Jeremy. *Pitt the Elder*. New York: Cambridge University Press, 1992.

Bosse, David. "The Maps of Robert Rogers and Jonathan Carver." *American Magazine and Historical Chronicle* 2, no. 1, Spring-Summer 1986, 45–61.

Brown, George, et al., eds. *Dictionary of Canadian Biography*. Toronto: University of Toronto Press, 1966.

Brown, M. L. *Firearms in Colonial America: The Impact of History and Technology, 1492–1792*. Washington, D.C.: Smithsonian Institute, 1980.

Brown, Peter Douglas. *William Pitt, Earl of Chatham: The Great Commoner*. London: George Allen and Unwin, 1978.

Brumwell, Steven. "'A Service Truly Critical': The British Army and Warfare with the North American Indians, 1755–1764." *War in History* 5, no. 2, April 1998, 146–75.

Buell, Leslie. In Defense of the General. *Bulletin of the Fort Ticonderoga Museum* 12, no. 3, October 1967, 223–32.

Cardy, Michael. "The Memoirs of Pierre Pouchot: A Soldier's View of a Doomed Campaign." *War, Literature and the Arts* 4, Spring 1992, 1–23.

Cardwell, John M. Mismanagement: The 1758 Expedition against Carillon. *Bulletin of the Fort Ticonderoga Museum* 15, no. 4, 1992, 236–91.

Carp, E. Wayne. "Early American Military History: A Review of Recent Work," *Virginia Magazine of History and Biography* 94, 1986, 259–84.

Chapais, Thomas. *Le Marquis de Montcalm.* Quebec: J.P. Garneau, 1911.

Chartrand, Rene. "The Troops of French Louisiana, 1699–1769." *Military Collector and Historian* 25, no. 2, Summer 1973, 58–65.

———. "Les Drapeaux en Nouvelle-France," *Conservation Canada* 1, no. 1, 1974, 24–26.

———. *The French Soldier in Colonial America.* Bloomfield, Ont.: Museum Restoration Service, 1984.

———. *Canadian Military Heritage, 1000–1754.* Vol. 1. Montreal: Art Global, 1993.

———. *Canadian Military Heritage, 1755–1871.* Vol. 2. Montreal: Art Global, 1995.

———. "The French Regiments—Some Background." Fort Ticonderoga Conference on the 1758 Campaign, May 16 and 17, 1998.

———. *Ticonderoga, 1758: Montcalm's Victory against All Odds.* London: Osprey Military, 2000.

———. *French Fortresses in North America, 1535–1763.* London: Osprey, 2005.

Chevalier, Captaine de Vaisseau E. *Histoire de la Marine Francaise depuis le Debut de la Monarchie jusqu'au Traite de Paix de 1763.* Paris: Hachette, 1902.

Cole, W. A. "Trends in Eighteenth Century Smuggling." *Economic History Review,* 2nd series, 10, 1957–1958, 394–410.

Colley, Linda. *Britons: Forging the Nation, 1707–1837.* New Haven, Conn.: Yale University Press, 1992.

Cooke, Jacob Ernest, ed. *Encyclopedia of the North American Colonies.* Vols. 1–3. New York: Scribner's Sons, 1993.

Coolidge, Guy Omeron. *The French Occupation of the Champlain Valley from 1609 to 1759.* Harrison, N.Y.: Harbor Hill Books, 1979. Originally published 1838.

Corbett, Sir Julian S. *England in the Seven Years' War: A Study in Combined Strategy.* 2d ed., 2 vols. London: Longmans, Green, 1907.

Corvisier, Andre. "La societe militaire francaise au temps de la Nouvelle France." *Histoire Sociale/Social History* 10, no. 20, 1977.

———. "Clientales et fidelites dans l'armee francaise aux XVIIe et XVIIIe siecles." In Yves Durand, ed., *Homage a Roland Mousnier, Clienteles et Fidelities en Europe a l'Epoque Moderne.* Paris: Presses Universitaires de France, 1981, 217–18.

Cummings, Reverend C. Irving. "On the Last Argument of Kings," delivered May 15, 1998. *Bulletin of the Fort Ticonderoga Museum* 16, no. 1, 1998, 13–15.

Cuneo, John R. "Factors Behind the Raising of the 80th Foot in America." *Military Collector and Historian* 11, no. 4, Winter 1959, 85–103.

————. *Rangers Life on Rogers Island*. Fort Edward, N.Y.: Rogers Island Historical Society, 1969.

————. *Robert Rogers of the Rangers*. Ticonderoga, N.Y.: Fort Ticonderoga Museum, 1988.

Cutcliffe, Stephen H. "Colonial Indian Policy as a Measure of Rising Imperialism: New York and Pennsylvania, 1700–1755," *Western Pennsylvania Historical Magazine* 64, 1981, 237–68.

Darling, Anthony D. *Red Coat and Brown Bess*. Bloomfield, Ont.: Museum Restoration Service, 1971.

Day, Gordon M. "Rogers' Raid in Indian Tradition." *Historical New Hampshire* 17, 1962, 3–17.

Downey, Hugh. *Louisbourg: Key to a Continent*. Englewood Cliffs, N.J.: Prentice Hall, 1965.

Duffy, Christopher. *The Fortress in the Age of Vauban and Frederick the Great, 1660–1789*. London: Routledge & Kegan Paul, 1985.

————. *The Military Experience in the Age of Reason, 1715–1789*. New York: Barnes and Noble, 1997.

Dunnigan, Brian Leigh. *Siege 1759: The Campaign Against Niagara*. Youngstown, N.Y.: Old Fort Niagara Association, 1996.

Eccles, W. J. "The History of New France According to Francis Parkman." *William and Mary Quarterly* 18, 3rd ser. (1961), 163–75.

————. "The French Forces in North America during the Seven Years' War." In G. Brown et al., eds., *Dictionary of Canadian Biography*. Toronto: University of Toronto Press, 1966, 3:xv–xxii.

————. "Montcalm, Louis-Joseph de, Marquis de Montcalm." In G. Brown et al., eds., *Dictionary of Canadian Biography*. Toronto, University of Toronto Press, 1966, 3:458–69.

————. *The Canadian Frontier 1534–1760*. New York: Holt, Rinehart, and Winston, 1969.

Eid, Leroy V. "'National' War among Indians of Northeastern North America." *Canadian Review of North American Studies* 16, no. 2 (Summer 1985), 125–54.

————. "'A Kind of Running Fight': Indian Battlefield Tactics in the Late Eighteenth Century." *Western Pennsylvania Historical Magazine* 71, 1988, 147–71.

Entick, John. *The General History of the Late War: Containing Its Rise, Progress, and Events in Europe, Asia, Africa, and America*. 5 vols. London: Edward Dilly and John Millan, 1763–1764.

Fautaux, Aegidius. *Les Chevaliers de Saint-Louis en Canada*. Montreal: Les Edition Dix, 1940.

————. "Officier e Montcalm." *Revue d'Historique de l'Amerique Francaise* 3 no. 3, December 1949, 367–82.

————. "Quelques officiers de Montcalm." *Revue d'Historique de l'Amerique Francaise* 5 no. 3, December 1951, 404–15.

Ferling, John F. *A Wilderness of Miseries: War and Warriors in Early America.* Westport, Conn.: Greenwood Press, 1980.

Flexner, James Thomas. *Mohawk Baronet: A Biography of Sir William Johnson.* Syracuse, N.Y.: Syracuse University Press, 1959.

Foote, William A. "The American Units of the British Regular Army, 1664–1772." M.A. thesis, Texas Western College, 1959.

——. "The South Carolina Independents." *South Carolina Historical Magazine* 62, 1961, 195–99.

——. "The Pennsylvania Men of the American Regiment. *Pennsylvania Magazine of History and Biography* 87, 1963, 31–38.

Fortescue, Sir John W. *A History of the British Army.* New York: AMS Press, 1976.

Frazier, Patrick. *The Mohegans of Stockbridge.* Lincoln: University of Nebraska Press, 1992.

Fregault, Guy. *Francois Bigot: Administrateur Francais.* 2 vols. Montreal: Universite de Montreal Institute d'Histoire de l'Amerique Francaise, 1948.

——. *Canada: The War of the Conquest, 1754–1760.* (1955). Translated by Margaret M. Cameron. Toronto: Oxford University Press, 1969.

Frey, Sylvia R. "Courts and Cats: British Military Justice in the Eighteenth Century." *Military Affairs* 43, 1979, 5–9.

——. *The British Soldier in America: A Social History of Military Life in the Revolutionary Period.* Austin, Tex.: University of Texas Press, 1981.

Fry, Bruce W. *An Appearance of Strength: The Fortifications of Louisbourg.* 2 vols. Ottawa: Parks Commission, 1984.

Furcron, Thomas B., and Elizabeth Ann Boyle. The Building of Fort Carillon, 1755–1758. *Bulletin of the Fort Ticonderoga Museum* 10, 1955, 13–67.

Gelinas, Cyrille. *The Role of Fort Chambly in the Development of New France, 1665–1760.* Ottawa: Parks Canada, 1983.

Gilbert, Arthur N. "The Changing Face of British Military Justice, 1757–1783." *Military Affairs* 49, 1979, 80–84.

Gipson, Lawrence Henry. *The Great War for the Empire: The Victorious Years, 1758–60.* New York: Alfred A. Knopf, 1949.

——. *Zones of International Friction: The Great Lakes Frontier, Canada, the West Indies, India, 1748–1754.* New York: Alfred A. Knopf, 1952.

——. *The British Empire before the American Revolution.* 12 vols. New York: Alfred A. Knopf, 1958–1970.

——. *The Great War for the Empire: The Years of Defeat, 1754–1757.* New York: Alfred A. Knopf, 1959.

——. *A Biographical Guide to the History of the British Empire, 1748–1776.* New York: Alfred A. Knopf, 1968.

Godfrey, William G. "Bradstreet, John (baptised Jean-Baptiste)." In G. Brown et al., eds., *Dictionary of Canadian Biography.* Toronto: University of Toronto Press, 1966, 4:83–87.

Godfrey, William G., *The Pursuit of Profit and Preferment in Colonial North America: John Bradstreet's Quest.* Waterloo, Ont.: Wilfred Laurier University Press, 1982.

Graham, Gerald S. "The Naval Defense of British North America, 1739–1763." *Royal Historical Society Transactions,* 4th ser., 30, 1948, 95 –110.

Graves, Donald E. *French Military Terminology, 1670–1815.* Saint John, N.B.: New Brunswick Museum, 1979.

——, ed. *Fighting for Canada: Seven Battles, 1758–1945.* Toronto: Robin Brass Studio, 2000.

Gwyn, Julian. "British Government Spending and the North American Colonies, 1740–1775." In Peter Marshall and Glyn Williams, eds., *The British Atlantic Empire before the American Revolution.* London: Frank Cass, 1980.

Haan, Richard L. "Covenant and Consensus: Iroquois and English, 1676–1760." In Daniel K. Richter and James H. Merrell, eds., *Beyond the Covenant Chain: The Iroquois and Their Neighbors in Indian North America, 1600–1800.* Syracuse, N.Y.: Syracuse University Press, 1987, 41–57.

Hackman, W. K. "William Pitt and the Generals: Three Case Studies in the Seven Years' War." *Albion: Proceedings of the Conference on British Studies* 3, no. 3, 1971, 128 –37.

Hadlock, Wendell Stanwood. "War Among the Northeastern Woodland Indians." *American Anthropologist* 59, April–June 1947, 204 –21.

Hagerty, Gilbert. *Massacre at Fort Bull: The De Lery Expedition against the Oneida Carry, 1756.* Providence, R.I.: Mowbray, 1971.

Hamilton, Edward. *Fort Ticonderoga: Key to a Continent.* Ticonderoga, N.Y.: Fort Ticonderoga Press, 1995. Originally published in 1969.

——. *The French Army in America.* Ottawa: Museum Restoration Service, 1998. Originally published in 1964.

——. "Colonial Warfare in North America." *Massachusetts Historical Society Proceedings* 80, 1968, 3 –15.

Hamilton, Milton. *Sir William Johnson: Colonial America, 1715–1763.* Port Washington, N.Y.: Kennikat Press, 1976.

Hammang, Francis H. *The Marquis de Vaudreuil: New France at the Beginning of the Eighteenth Century.* Louvain, Belgium: Universite de Louvain, Recueil de travaux, 2d Ser., 1938.

Hayes, James. "Scottish Officers in the British Army, 1714 –63." *Scottish Historical Review* 26, 1958, 23 –33.

Higginbotham, Don. "Early American Way of War: Reconnaissance and Appraisal." *William and Mary Quarterly* 44, 1987, 226 –41.

Higham, Robin, ed. *A Guide to Sources of British Military History.* Berkeley: University of California Press, 1971.

Houlding, J. A. *Fit for Service: The Training of the British Army, 1715–1795.* Oxford: Oxford University Press, 1980.

——. *French Arms Drill of the 18th Century.* Bloomfield, Ont.: Museum Restoration, 1988.

Hunter, William A. "Provincial Negotiations with the Western Indians, 1754– 58." *Pennsylvania History* 18, July 1951, 213–19.

———. *Forts on the Pennsylvania Frontier, 1753–1758.* Harrisburg: Pennsylvania Historical and Museum Commission, 1960.

Jacobs, Wilber R. *Diplomacy and Indian Gifts: Anglo-French Rivalry along the Ohio and Northwest Frontiers, 1748–1763.* Stanford, Calif.: Stanford University Press, 1950.

Jaenen, Cornelius J. *The French Relationship with the Native Peoples of New France and Acadia.* Ottawa: Research Branch, Indian and Northern Affairs Canada, 1984.

Jaenen, Randolph C. Cornelius. "The Role of Presents in French-Amerindian Trade." In *Explorations in Canadian Economic History: Essays in Honor of Irene M. Spry.* Ottawa: University of Ottawa Press, 1985, 231–50.

Johnson, Allen, and Dumas Malone, eds. *Dictionary of American Biography.* New York: Charles Scribner's Sons, 1928–1944.

Kennett, Lee. *The French Armies in the Seven Years' War: A Study in Military Organization and Administration.* Durham, N.C.: Duke University Press, 1967.

Kopperman, Paul. *Braddock at the Monongahela.* Pittsburgh: University of Pittsburgh Press, 1977.

Lacour-Gayet, G. *La Marine Militaire de la France sous la Regne de Louis XV.* Paris: Librarie Ancienne, 1910.

Lanctot, Gustave. *A History of Canada, from the Treaty of Utrecht to the Treaty of Paris, 1713–1763.* Cambridge, Mass.: Harvard University Press, 1965.

Leach, Douglas. *Roots of Conflict: British Armed Forces and Colonial Americans, 1677–1763.* Chapel Hill: University of North Carolina Press, 1986.

Leliepvre, Eugene, and Rene Chartrand. "Bearn Regiment, New France, 1755– 1757." *Military Collector and Historian* 39, no. 3, Fall 1987, 126–27.

Losescher, Burt Garfield. *The History of Rogers Rangers.* Burlingame, Calif.: privately printed, 1957.

Long, John C. *Lord Jeffrey Amherst, A Soldier of the King.* New York: Macmillan, 1933.

Lunn, Jean Elizabeth. "Agriculture and War in Canada, 1740–1760." *Canadian Historical Review* 16, June 1935, 123–36.

MacLennan, Alastair. "Highland Regiments in North America." *Bulletin of the Fort Ticonderoga Museum* 12, no. 2, September 1966, 118–25.

MacLennan, J. S. *Louisbourg: From Its Foundation to Its Fall, 1713–1758* (1918), Halifax: Book Room Limited, 1979.

Macleod, D. Peter. *The Canadian Iroquois and the Seven Years War.* Toronto: Dundern Press, 1996.

Mante, Thomas. *The History of the Late War in North America, and the Islands of the Late War in North America, and the Islands of the West Indes, Including the Campaigns of 1763 and 1764 against His Majesty's Indian Enemies.* New York: Research Reprints, 1970. Originally published 1772.

Martin, Felix. *Le Marquis de Montcalm et les Dernieres Anness de la Colonie Fran-caise au Canada*. Paris: P. M. Laroche, 1879.

Mauders, Eric, Brian Leigh Dunningan, and John Elting. "80th Regiment of Foot, 1757–1764." *Military Collector and Historian* 36, no. 4, Winter 1987, 172–73.

May, Robin, and G. A. Embleton. *Wolfe's Army*. London: Osprey, Military Men at Arms Series, 1974.

McCulloch, Ian. "Buckskin Soldier: The Rise and Fall of Major Robert Rogers." *The Beaver*, April/May 1993, 17–26.

———. "Believe Us, Sir, This Will Impress Few People!": Spin Doctoring, 18th Century Style. *Bulletin of the Fort Ticonderoga Museum* 16, no. 1, 1998, 101.

———. "'Within Ourselves': The Development of British Light Infantry in North America during the Seven Years' War." *Canadian Military History* 7, no. 2, Spring 1998, 41–55.

———. "'Like Roaring Lions Breaking from Their Chains': The Battle of Ticonderoga, 8 July 1758." In Donald E. Graves, ed., *Fighting for Canada: Seven Battles, 1758–1945*. Toronto: Robin Brass, 2000.

Michalon, Roger. "Vaudreuil et Montcalm, les hommes, leurs relations, influence de ces relations sur la conduite de la guerre, 1756–1759. In Jean Delmas, ed., *Conflits des Societes au Canada Francais Pendant la Guerre de Sept Ans et Leurs Influence sur les Operations*. Vincennes, France, 1978.

Middleton, Richard. *The Bells of Victory: The Pitt-Newcastle Ministry and the Conduct of the Seven Years' War, 1757–1762*. Cambridge: Cambridge University Press, 1985.

Mouillard, Lucien. *Les Regiments sous Louis XV*. Paris: Librarie Militaire de J. Dumaine, 1882.

Mullet, Charles F. "James Abercromby and the French Encroachments in America." *Canadian Historical Review* 26, 1945, 48–59.

Namier, L. B. *The Structure of Politics at the Ascension of George III*. London: Macmillan, 1929.

Nester, William R., *The First Global War: Britain, France, and the Fate of North America, 1756–1775*. Westport, Conn.: Praeger, 2000.

———. *The Great Frontier War: Britain, France, and the Imperial Struggle for North America, 1607–1755*. Westport, Conn.: Praeger, 2000.

———. "Haughty Conquerors": *Amherst and the Great Indian Uprising of 1763*. Westport, Conn.: Praeger, 2000.

———. *The Frontier War for American Independence*. Mechanisburg, Penn.: Stackpole Books, 2004.

Nosworthy, Brent. *The Anatomy of Victory: Battle Tactics, 1689–1763*. New York: Hippocrene, 1992.

Padeni, Scott A. Forgotten Soldiers: The Role of Blacks in New York's Northern Campaigns of the Seven Years' War, *Bulletin of the Fort Ticonderoga Museum* 16, no. 2, 1999, 152–69.

Pares, Richard. "American versus Continental Warfare, 1739–1763," *English Historical Review* 51, 1963, 429–65.

Pargellis, Stanley McCrory. *Lord Loudoun in America*. New Haven: Yale University Press, 1933.

Parkman, Francis. *Montcalm and Wolfe: The French and Indian War*. New York: Da Capo Press, 1995. Originally published in 1886.

Pell, Robert. The Strategy of Montcalm, 1758. *Bulletin of the Fort Ticonderoga Museum* 9, no. 3, Summer 1953, 175–201.

Pencak, William. "Warfare and Political Change in Mid-Eighteenth Century Massachusetts." In *The British Atlantic Empire before the American Revolution*. *Journal of Imperial and Commonwealth History* 8, 1980, 51–73.

———. *War, Politics, and Revolution in Provincial Massachusetts*. Boston: Northeastern University Press, 1981.

Peters, Marie. "The Myth of William Pitt, Earl of Chatham, Great Imperialist, Part I: Pitt and Imperial Expansion, 1738–1763." *Journal of Imperial and Commonwealth History* 21, 1993, 31–74.

Preston, Richard A., and Leopold LaMontagne. *Royal Fort Frontenac*. Toronto: Champlain Society, 1958.

Pritchard, James. *Louis XV's Navy, 1748–1762: A Study of Organization and Administration*. Kingston, Ont.: McGill-Queen's University Press, 1982.

Proulx, Gilles. "Le Dernier Effort de la France au Canada—secours au fraude?" *Revue de l'Amerique Francaise* 36, 1982, 413–26.

Rahmer, Frederick A. *Dash to Frontenac: An Account of Lt. Col. John Bradstreet's Expedition to and Capture of Fort Frontenac*. Rome, N.Y.: Frederick A. Rahmer, 1973.

Reid, Stuart, and Paul Chappell. *King George's Army, 1740–93*. 2 vols. London: Osprey, 1995.

Richards, Frederick B. *The Black Watch at Ticonderoga and Major Duncan Campbell of Iverawe*. Bowie, Md.: Heritage Books, 1999.

Richter, Daniel K. *The Ordeal of the Longhouse: The Peoples of the Iroquois League in the Era of European Colonization*. Chapel Hill: University of North Carolina Press, 1992.

———. "War and Culture: The Iroquois Experience." *William and Mary Quarterly* 3d Ser., 60, 1983, 528–59.

Richter, Daniel K., and James H. Merrell, eds. *Beyond the Covenant Chain: The Iroquois and Their Neighbors in Indian North America, 1600–1800*. Syracuse, N.Y.: Syracuse University Press, 1987.

Robitaille, Georges. *Montcalm et ses Historiens: Etude Critique*. Montreal: Levis, 1936.

Robson, Eric. "British Light Infantry in the Mid-Eighteenth Century: The Effect of American Conditions." *Army Quarterly* 62, 1952, 209–22.

Rodgers, N. A. M., *The Wooden World: An Anatomy of the Georgian Navy*. Annapolis, Md.: Naval Institute Press, 1982.

Rogers, Alan. *Empire and Liberty: American Resistance to British Authority, 1755–1763*. Berkeley: University of California Press, 1974.

Rogers, H. C. B. *The British Army of the Eighteenth Century*. London: Allen and Unwin, 1977.

Rogers, J. Alan. "Impressment in Western Pennsylvania, 1755–1759." *Western Pennsylvania Historical Magazine* 52, 1969, 255–62.

———. "Colonial Opposition to the Quartering of Troops During the French and Indian War." *Military Affairs* 34, 1970, 7–11.

Roy, Pierre-George. "Les Commandants du Saint Frederic." *Le Bulletin des Recherches Historique* 51, no. 3, September 1945, 317–32.

———. *Homme et Choses du Fort Saint Frederic*. Montreal: Les Editions Dix, 1946.

———. *Bigot et sa Bannde et L'Affaires du Canada*. Toronto: 1959.

Russell, Peter E. "Redcoats in the Wilderness: British Officers and Irregular Warfare in Europe and America, 1740–1760. *William and Mary Quarterly* 35, 1978, 629–52.

Sautai, Maurice. *Montcalm au combat du Carillon*. Translated by John S. Watts. Fort Ticonderoga, N.Y.: Fort Ticonderoga Museum, 1909.

———. *Montcalm at the Battle of Carillon*. Ticonderoga, N.Y.: Fort Ticonderoga Museum, 1941.

Schutz, John A. "The Disaster of Fort Ticonderoga: The Shortage of Muskets During the Mobilization of 1758." *Huntington Library Quarterly* 14, May 1951, 307–15.

Selesky, Harold E. *War and Society in Colonial Connecticut*. New Haven: Yale University Press, 1990.

Shy, John. "James Abercromby and the Campaign of 1758." M.A. thesis. University of Vermont, 1957.

———. "Quartering His Majesty's Forces in New Jersey." *New Jersey Historical Society Proceedings* 78, 1960, 82–94.

———. "A New Look at Colonial Militia." *William and Mary Quarterly* 3d ser., 20, 1963, 175–85.

———. *Toward Lexington: The Role of the British Army in the Coming of the American Revolution*. Princeton, N.J.: Princeton University Press, 1965.

———, ed. *A People Numerous and Armed*. New York: Oxford University Press, 1976.

Stacey, C. P. *Quebec, 1759: The Siege and Battle*. Toronto: Macmillan, 1959.

Steele, Ian K. *Guerrillas and Grenadiers: The Struggle for Canada, 1689–1760*. Toronto: McClelland Stewart, 1969.

———. *Betrayals: Fort William Henry and the "Massacre"*. New York: Oxford University Press, 1990.

———. *Warpaths: Invasions of North America, 1513–1765*. New York: Oxford University Press, 1994.

Stotz, Charles Morse. *Outposts of the War for Empire: The French and English in Western Pennsylvania: Their Armies, Their Forts, Their People, 1749–1764*. Pittsburgh, Pa.: Historical Society of Western Pennsylvania, 1985.

Summers, Jack L., and Rene Chartrand. *Military Uniforms in Canada, 1665–1970*. Ottawa: Canadian War Museum, 1981.

Thorpe, F. J. "Chaussegros de Lery, Gaspard-Joseph." In G. Brown et al., eds., *Dictionary of Canadian Biography*. Toronto: University of Toronto Press, 1966, 4:145–47.

Titus, James. *The Old Dominion at War: Society, Politics, and Warfare in Late Colonial Virginia*. Columbia: University of South Carolina Press, 1991.

Turnbull, J. R. "Jean-Armand Dieskau." In G. Brown et al., eds., *Dictionary of Canadian Biography*. Toronto: University of Toronto Press, 1966, 3:185–86.

Ultree, Maarten, ed. *Adapting to Conditions: War and Society in the Eighteenth Century*. Tuscaloosa: University of Alabama, 1986.

Verge-Franceshi, Michel. *La Marine Francaise au XVIIIe Siecle*. Paris: Sedes, 1996.

Waddington, Richard. *La Guerre de Sept Ans: Histoire Diplomatique et Militaire*. 5 vols. Paris: Firmin-Didot et Cie, 1888–1910.

Waddington, Richard. *Louis XV et le Renversements des Alliancs*. 5 vols. Paris: Firmin-Didot, 1888–1910.

Wells, Robert V. *The Population of the British Colonies in North America before 1776: A Survey of Census Data*. Princeton: Princeton University Press, 1975.

White, Richard. *The Middle Ground: Indians, Empires, and Republics in the Great Lakes Regions, 1650–1815*. Cambridge: Cambridge University Press, 1991.

Index

The spelling of eighteenth century names can differ widely in the original documents. French names can be especially tricky. In both French and British sources, a Frenchmen's "last" name might be written as some portion of his title or family name. For the benefit of the history buffs who are familiar with this period, I generally used the most commonly cited name for that person, even when the official spelling or name order may have differed. For instance, English speakers are more familiar with a certain intrepid French leader with his name spelled Langy, rather than by the correct Langis, so I used the former. At the same time I can understand the protests of the purists.

Mohawk, 21, 32, 54, 66, 88, 89, 95,
100, 104, 105, 107, 195, 202
Monogahela, 60
Ohio, 7, 25, 28, 29
Onondaga, 32, 44
Richelieu, 4, 107, 109
Saint Lawrence, 4, 28, 29, 30, 32, 33,
59, 89, 94, 191, 203
Shenandoah, 32
Susquehanna, 32
Wabash, 30
Rivez, Charles, 143, 170
Robertson, James, 171
Rogers, Robert, 9–12, 13–19, 20, 44,
46, 47, 66, 82, 101, 104, 105, 117,
118, 120, 124, 128, 129–30, 136,
137, 172, 187–89, 197
Rogers Island, 21
Rochebeaucourt, Colonel, 142
Roguemanure, Colonel de, 115
Ross, Andrew, 13
Ruggles, Timothy, 99, 102, 148
Rutherford, John, 120

Sabbath Day Point, 13, 122, 172
Sabrevoix de Bleury, Jean Clement,
189
Saint Clair, John, 76
Saint Jean, 107
Saint John's River, 21
Saratoga, 101
Sault Saint Louis Mission Indians, 15
Savannah, 32
Saxe, Maurice de, 49, 65
Schenectady, 99, 168
Schuyler, Philip, 106, 169–70
Scohary Indians, 146
Scotland, 60
Seneca Indians, 146
Senezergues de La Rodde, Etienne
Guillaume, 115, 155
Shawnee Indians, 65
Shirley, William, 60
Six Nation Indians, 28, 67, 146
South America, 26
South Bay, 82, 187–88
South Carolina, 79

Stanwix, John, 62, 99, 100, 105, 173
Stark, John, 136
Stewart, Bonnie Prince Charles, 65
Stillwater, 101
Stockbridge Indians, 101

Ticonderoga, 1, 4, 6, 7, 8, 25, 26, 110,
112, 113, 138, 145, 163, 173, 174,
192, 196, 198, 207
Treaties
Aix-la-Chapelle, 30
Utrecht, 29–30, 58
Trecesson, Colonel de, 115, 139
Trepezec, Captain, 119, 126–28, 132
Trivio, Colonel de, 133
Tulliken, John, 120
Tuscarora Indians, 146
Two Mountain Mission Indians, 15

Vaudreuil de Cavagnal, Pierre-
Francois de Rigaud, 6, 11, 19–20,
22, 23, 34, 49, 69–70, 72, 73, 84–96,
104, 106, 107, 108, 109, 110, 114,
141, 169, 170, 174–86, 190, 199–204
Virginia, 30, 31, 38, 42, 65, 79
Voltaire, Francois-Marie Arouet de, 25

Warren, Peter, 66
Wars
French and Indian/Seven Years, 3,
27, 34, 44, 49, 136
Huguenot, 27
King George's/Austrian Succes-
sion, 27, 28, 29, 30, 60
King William's/League of Augs-
burg, 27
Queen Anne's/Spanish Succession,
27
Washington, George, 3, 31, 44
Webb, Daniel, 44
Webster, Robert, 76
Wellington, Arthur Wellesley, 44
Wentworth, Benning, 79
West Africa, 7, 25
White, James, 13, 15
Whitemore, Edward, 63
Whiting, Nathan, 120